D0511464

cool britannia? british political drama in the 1990s

cool britannia? british political drama in the 1990s

edited by
rebecca d'monté and graham saunders

Selection and editorial matter © Rebecca D'Monté and Graham Saunders 2008
Introduction © Graham Saunders 2007. Individual chapters (in order) © Aleks Sierz; Ken Urban; Mary Luckhurst; Rebecca D'Monté; Lynette Goddard; Elaine Aston; David Pattie; Roger Owen; Nadine Holdsworth; Wallace McDowell; Dan Rebellato; David Greig 2007.

First published 2008 by
PALGRAVE MACMILLAN
Houndmills, Basingstoke, Hampshire RG21 6XS and
175 Fifth Avenue, New York, N.Y. 10010
Companies and representatives throughout the world

PALGRAVE MACMILLAN is the global academic imprint of the Palgrave Macmillan division of St. Martin's Press, LLC and of Palgrave Macmillan Ltd. Macmillan® is a registered trademark in the United States, United Kingdom and other countries. Palgrave is a registered trademark in the European Union and other countries.

ISBN-13: 978–1–4039–8812–6 hardback
ISBN-10: 1–4039–8812–9   hardback
ISBN-13: 978–1–4039–8813–3 paperback
ISBN-10: 1–4039–8813–7   paperback

This book is printed on paper suitable for recycling and made from fully managed and sustained forest sources. Logging, pulping and manufacturing processes are expected to conform to the environmental regulations of the country of origin.

A catalogue record for this book is available from the British Library.

A catalog record for this book is available from the Library of Congress.

10   9   8   7   6   5   4   3   2   1
17   16   15   14   13   12   11   10   09   08

Printed and bound in China

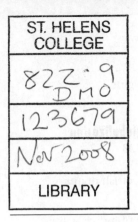

contents

acknowledgements

This book sprang from the 'In-Yer-Face? British Drama in the 1990s' Conference, held at the University of the West of England, Bristol, in 2002. We would like to thank the University, the English and Drama Department (particularly Dr William Greenslade), and the contributors. We would also like to acknowledge the support given to us by Paula Kennedy and Kate Wallis at Palgrave, and the helpful comments made by the various readers of this project.

The authors and publishers are grateful to Methuen Publishing Ltd, Faber and Faber Ltd and Grove/Atlantic Inc. for permission to reproduce material. Every effort has been made to contact all the copyright-holders, but if any have been inadvertently omitted the publishers will be pleased to make the necessary arrangement at the earliest opportunity.

contributors

Elaine Aston is Professor of Contemporary Performance at Lancaster University. She has published extensively on feminist theatre and performance. Her major works include *An Introduction to Feminism and Theatre* (Routledge, 1995) and *Feminist Views on the English Stage* (Cambridge, 2003). With Gerry Harris she has recently completed a three-year AHRC-funded research project on 'Women's Writing for Performance' and co-edited *Feminist Futures?: Theatre, Performance, Theory* (Palgrave, 2006).

Rebecca D'Monté is Senior Lecturer in Drama at the University of the West of England, Bristol. With Nicole Pohl she has edited a volume on female utopias, *Female Communities 1600–1800: Literary Visions and Cultural Realities* (Macmillan, 1999). She has written on British drama 1900–1950 for the *Year's Work in English Studies* (Oxford University Press, 2007), and female monologues in *Monologues: Theatre, Performance, Subjectivity*, ed. Clare Wallace (Litteraria Pragensia, 2006). At present, she is preparing a monograph, *Images of England: Popular Women Dramatists 1930–1960*.

Lynette Goddard is a lecturer in Drama and Theatre at Royal Holloway, London. Her publications on black British women's theatre include pieces in *Alternatives Within the Mainstream II: British Postwar Queer Theatres* (Cambridge Scholars Press, 2006), *Companion to Black British Culture* (Routledge, 2002) and *Contemporary Theatre Review*. She is currently completing her monograph, *Staging Black Feminisms: Identity, Politics, Performance* (Palgrave, 2007).

David Greig is a playwright and director. He has been commissioned by the Royal Court, National Theatre and Royal Shakespeare Company, and was Dramaturg of the National Theatre of Scotland. His plays include *Europe* (Methuen, 1994), *The Cosmonaut's Last Message to the Woman He Loved in the Former Soviet Union* (Methuen, 1999), *Outlying Islands* (Faber, 2002), and *The American Pilot* (Faber, 2005).

Nadine Holdsworth is Senior Lecturer in Theatre and Performance Studies at the University of Warwick. She has written essays on 7:84, Theatre Workshop, Glasgow Unity and contemporary Scottish theatre. She edited John McGrath's collected writings on theatre, *Naked Thoughts That Roam About* (Nick Hern, 2002) and his *Plays for England* (Exeter University Press, 2005). Most recently, she has written a book on Joan Littlewood for Routledge's Performance Practitioners series.

Mary Luckhurst is Co-Director of Drama at the University of York. Her recent publications include: *Theatre and Celebrity in Britain, 1660–2000* (Palgrave, 2005); *Dramaturgy: A Revolution in Theatre* (Cambridge, 2006); and *A Companion to Modern British and Irish Drama* (Blackwell, 2006). She is a playwright and director and runs the Comedy Laboratory in York.

Wallace McDowell worked as a professional theatre practitioner for over 20 years. He is now undertaking doctoral research at the University of Warwick, where his research centres on contemporary attitudes to theatre, performance and performativity in working-class Protestant/ Unionist/Loyalist communities.

Roger Owen is a lecturer in Theatre and Performance Studies at the Department of Theatre, Film and Television Studies, University of Wales, Aberystwyth. He has published in English and Welsh on theatre and performance in Wales, and has also worked as a performer with Brith Gof, Eddie Ladd and Lurking Truth/Gwir sy'n Llechu.

David Pattie is Reader in Drama and Theatre Studies at the University of Chester. He is the author of *The Complete Critical Guide to Samuel Beckett* (Routledge, 2001) and has published widely on contemporary British theatre, Beckett, and popular performance. He has recently completed a book entitled *Rock Music in Performance* (Palgrave, 2008).

Dan Rebellato is Professor of Contemporary Theatre at Royal Holloway, University of London. His book *1956 and All That* was published in 1999 and he has published on Mark Ravenhill, David Greig, Sarah Kane, Simon Stephens, Suspect Culture, and a variety of topics related to contemporary theatre. He is currently completing a new book, *British Drama and Globalization: Ethics and Aesthetics in Contemporary Playwriting*. He is also a playwright; his recent plays include *Outright*

Terror Bold and Brilliant, Here's What I Did With My Body One Day, A Modest Adjustment and *Chekhov in Hell*.

Graham Saunders lectures in Theatre Studies at the University of Reading. He is author of *'Love Me or Kill Me': Sarah Kane and the Theatre of Extremes* (Manchester University Press, 2002) and a series editor for Continuum's *Modern Theatre Guides*. He has contributed articles on contemporary British and Irish drama to journals including *Modern Drama, Journal of Beckett Studies, Contemporary Theatre Review, Theatre Research International, New Theatre Quarterly* and *Studies in Theatre and Performance*. He is currently completing a volume on Sarah Kane for Faber's *The Playwright and the Work* series and a short monograph study of Patrick Marber's play *Closer* for Continuum Press.

Aleks Sierz is Visiting Research Fellow at Rose Bruford College, and author of *In-Yer-Face Theatre: British Drama Today* (Faber, 2001) and *The Theatre of Martin Crimp* (Methuen, 2006). He also works as a journalist, broadcaster, lecturer and theatre critic.

Ken Urban is a playwright and director. His plays have been produced or developed by Moving Arts, Lincoln Center, Soho Rep, Rude Guerrilla, Annex Theatre, Luna Stage, kef productions, Son of Semele Ensemble and others. His plays have been anthologized in *Plays and Playwrights 2002* (ed. Martin Denton) and *New York Theatre Review* (edited by Brook Stowe). He is currently completing a book-length study called *Cruel Britannia: British Theatre in the 1990s*. He teaches at Harvard University.

introduction

graham saunders

When attempting to assess a decade in British culture or politics, critics often grasp towards a received or truncated view: so, the 1960s were 'swinging' to Harold Wilson's vision that the 'white heat of technology' would replace Britain's declining heavy industries; the 1970s were a long series of strikes, a three-day week and power cuts, set to a sound-track of Pink Floyd's *Dark Side of the Moon* and Mike Oldfield's *Tubular Bells*; and the 1980s was the decade of avaricious Thatcherism, where yuppies and former Essex barrow boys turned bond dealers supped champagne in London wine bars, while New Romantics out-posed each other until dawn at the Blitz Club.

So what of the 1990s? To date, at least in terms of theatre history, any assessment of British drama in this period has been dominated by the term 'In-Yer-Face Theatre'. Based on Aleks Sierz's influential book of the same name, the period is defined by a group of young writers whose names included Sarah Kane, Mark Ravenhill, Jez Butterworth and Joe Penhall. Below, Sierz briefly classifies its key features:

> Characterised by a rawness of tone . . . [it] uses explicit scenes of sex and violence to explore the depths of human emotion . . . it is aggressive, confrontational and provocative . . . it can be so intense audiences may feel they have lived through the events shown on stage.[1]

Commentators such as Sierz and Dominic Dromgoole claimed that the new writing produced during this period constituted a new golden age in British theatre – one that recalled the impact of John Osborne's *Look Back in Anger* in 1956; more than this, Sierz even maintained that in-yer-face theatre saved British playwriting from a slow decline that had been taking place ever since the 1980s.[2] To date this view has

1

remained largely unchallenged, to the extent of becoming something almost like a received orthodoxy.

The need for at least some attempt at reappraisal came after a conference in September 2002 at the University of the West of England, Bristol, entitled 'In-Yer-Face? British Drama in the 1990s'.[3] Phrasing the title with a question mark was deliberate, and arose from a need to interrogate both the validity and influence of in-yer-face theatre with regard to other forms of playwriting that had marked the decade. When the call for papers was put out, it was envisaged that the majority of delegates would be eager to challenge the received history and broaden the criteria as to what constituted British playwriting in the 1990s. However, many of the proposals received were only too ready to work within the framework already established by Sierz, and seemed to validate his claim that in-yer-face theatre was indeed the dominant theatrical style of the 1990s.

Perhaps not surprisingly, the writer who most dominated proceedings was Sarah Kane. Sierz maintains that she is 'central to the story of new writing' in the 1990s, and it is this very dominance that has prompted our decision not to commission for this volume any specific chapters relating to her work.[4] It is hoped that this decision to exclude Kane will allow other voices to be heard, although many of the contributors do discuss her work freely within a wider context of 1990s British theatre.

Despite at first appearing to be a straightforward advocacy of Sierz's ideas, the conference itself was far from narrow or parochial in its outlook. Papers by the playwright David Greig and academics such as Nadine Holdsworth, Dan Rebellato and David Pattie (which are included in this volume) all attempted to widen definitions of the events that shaped theatre's relationship with politics in the 1990s. Aleks Sierz in his keynote address also did much to provide a self-critique and develop further his original ideas. These papers not only suggested that a far greater degree of variety and complexity exisited within the various forms of playwriting in the 1990s, but also exposed crucial gaps which had not been met by the conference itself. In response to these, other chapters in the volume have been specially commissioned to highlight these underrepresented areas that challenge certain tenets of in-yer-face theatre.

political drama in the 1990s

Writing in 2003, the playwright David Edgar observes that talk of a crisis in British political theatre has been a constant feature in his career

– even during such high-water marks as 1968 and the early 1970s: yet he also maintains that in spite of such Cassandras, 'the great project of British theatre writing since 1956', namely 'the anatomising of contemporary society', has continued unabated via a series of new writing 'waves' that continue to break against the theatrical landscape; it is simply the size and impact of the waves that fluctuate in any given generation.[5]

However, this sense of a permanent if evolving process seemed to become disrupted – even broken – during the mid-1990s, when there appeared to be a disengagement and dismantlement from recognizable forms of political engagement by the new generation of young dramatists. Plays that had attempted to make sense of the grand sweep of history such as David Hare's *Plenty* (1978) and Edgar's *Maydays* (1983) seemed to have given way to a political sentiment that could best be summed up in an often-quoted speech from Mark Ravenhill's 1996 play *Shopping and Fucking*:

> I think . . . I think we all need stories, we make up stories so that we can get by. And I think a long time ago there were big stories. Stories so big you could live your whole life in them. The Powerful Hands of the Gods and Fate. The Journey to Enlightenment. The March to Socialism. But they all died or the world grew up or grew senile or forgot them, so now we're all making up our own stories. Little stories.[6]

These micro-narratives seemed to dominate much of the new drama produced from the mid-1990s onwards: these manifested themselves in the girl-gang rivalries of Judy Upton's *Ashes and Sand* (1994) and Rebecca Prichard's *Yard Gal* (1998); they seeped into plays about relationships and adultery such as Nick Grosso's *Sweetheart* (1996) and Patrick Marber's *Closer* (1997); and they also preoccupy Conor McPherson's *The Weir* (1997), which as David Edgar observes 'is actually a narrative about a narrative'.[7]

Max Stafford-Clark, who directed the first producions of Ravenhill's *Shopping and Fucking* and *Some Explicit Polaroids*, argues that the emphasis on personal stories in many of the plays from this period comes about through a self-conscious rejection of a model based on political analysis that distinguished earlier writers such as Howard Brenton and David Hare. Stafford-Clark sees the reason for this coming about through major political events – namely the collapse of communism in Eastern Europe after 1989. This state of political indeterminacy becomes reflected in the playwriting culture during the period of 1992–93, which many saw as a period of 'unjustified gloom', to the emergence of the so-called in-yer-face writers in 1994, who with a cocksure, yet politically vague, sense of themselves, heralded in a new era of equally 'unjustified optimism'.[8] It is also worth adding to Stafford-Clark's account that this new generation's supposedly apolitical stance was not only shaped by the seismic shifts taking place in geopolitics throughout Eastern Europe, but through an equally cogent feeling of political inertia at home; despite the overthrow of Mrs Thatcher in 1990 as Prime Minister, the Conservative administration continued under John Major, who remained in power until 1997.

Robbie's speech in *Shopping and Fucking* also provides a neat précis of the old certainties and equilibrium that lay on either side of the Berlin Wall before 1989 – what the French philosopher Jean-François Lyotard calls 'grand narratives' – until their replacement after its collapse with the 'micro-narratives' that define and explain much of the culture associated with the term 'postmodernity'. Writing in 1999, Elizabeth Sakellaridou addresses this position bluntly and without sentiment: to those nostalgic for the earlier recognizable certainties in political theatre, she curtly says, 'I think it is time we accept as final the fall of the "grand narratives" even in the theatre world.'[9]

Arguably, British political theatre has always relied on personal stories: for instance, Caryl Churchill's *Cloud Nine* (1979) and *Top Girls* (1982) are two plays that, while frequently cited as exemplary demonstrations of an epic form, each with a bold first half that engages with history and politics, have second halves taken up with an exploration of personal and domestic relationships in a manner not so far removed from the plays that would follow in the mid-1990s. Yet, as John Bull observes, the 1980s mantra of 'the personal is the political' was to be taken literally by their contemporaries in the 1990s, who would 'push and test the implications of this credo to the limit'.[10] Arguably it was this strategy that produced a politically denatured theatre, retreating into the realms of domestic relationships and personal stories rather than rational analysis.

David Eldridge, one such playwright from this new generation, and who since *Serving it Up* (1996) has gone on to produce notable work in the millennial decade such as *Under the Blue Sky* (2000) and *Incomplete and Random Acts of Kindness* (2005), provides an interesting account of how domestic and world events stifled a sense of political optimism in the new drama produced during the mid-1990s:

Clearly, a generation had grown up in the UK fearing the five-minute warning, watching the Berlin Wall come down, that experimented with E and club culture, was finding a voice. This generation had had its youthful optimism pickled by the new horrors that visited their imaginations in the shape of atrocities in the Balkans and by a sense of outrage at the erosion of the UK's notion of community and society by the mean-spirited Thatcher and Major malaise.We responded to that shifting culture with dismay and anger.[11]

As mentioned, these feelings were often expressed in the plays themselves through individual narratives, based on what Aleks Sierz calls 'personal pain rather than public politics'.[12] However, such responses could also be interpreted as apathetic retreats from engagement with social issues. Ian Rickson, who was Artistic Director of the Royal Court towards the end of the in-yer-face period, finds what he sees as 'privatized dissent' in many of their plays, a consequence Klaus Peter Müller sees as arising out of the 'overpowering structures' associated with postmodernity such as globalization.[13]

The results can be glimpsed in plays such as Nick Grosso's *Peaches* and Che Walker's *Been so Long*, where the characters and subject matter are drawn from the disaffected metropolitan young; and while Eldridge is right to point out that 'writers have to respond however they can, and in the way they can, not in the way that others desire', it perhaps becomes difficult to concur fully with Aleks Sierz's assessment that the in-yer-face writers' 'aim was no less than to help change society'.[14]

Sierz also believes that the use of provocation and taboo in the work of these dramatists renders their work intrinsically political because 'it tells us more about who we really are'; yet at the same time Sierz recognizes that exposing its audiences to a form almost wholly predicated on the intensity of experiences risks producing a theatre that is both trivial and voyeuristic, especially when 'shock [becomes] a marketing tool'.[15] John Bull also points out that because in-yer-face theatre defined itself by a representation of extremes, it was always going rapidly to lose impetus; and by the time of Simon Bennett's *Drummers* in 1999 he concludes that the form had deteriorated into a series of mannerist cliches.[16] John London also observes that claims for an inherent politics based alone on a provocative theatrical style 'automatively implies criticism of a whole power system'.[17]

Other commentators also discerned little or no political impetus whatsoever in the new plays being written during this time. Vera Gottlieb, for example, felt that Sarah Kane's *Blasted* (1995) demonstrated 'the abstraction or absence of a Beckett play' via its reluctance to enage directly with any social and political issues; she argues instead that truly effective political theatre comes out of a situation based 'on how social and political realities happen – on cause and effect'.[18] Even Aleks Sierz, who did much to provide an advocacy of many of these new writers' political commitment, still acnowledges that key plays from the period such as Patrick Marber's *Closer* and Phyllis Nagy's *Neverland* (1998) tended to favour a strategy within solipsistic worlds rather than direct political enagagement with society.[19]

Yet it could also be said that drama from this period was inscribing a new form of politics – reacting directly not only to shifts in British politics but to the impact of globalization, technology, and theories posited by postmodernist thinkers such as Baudrillard and Lyotard, who questioned the nature and veracity of 'reality' – and with it the viability of eliciting social or political change.

However, this is not to say that the new dramatists ever entirely concurred with the positions put forward by these theorists: as David Ian Rabey observes, Ravenhill's *Shopping and Fucking* shows 'the studied observations of resolute superficiality, which rebrands love as dependency . . . [and] the reductivity of 1990s consumerism'.[20] Elizabeth Sakellaridou goes further and argues that the new dramatists also construct new narratives that help explain and resist the changes brought about by late capitalism; moreover, she points out, 'rather than asking the the question "whatever happened to political theatre?", which reveals a nostalgic, regressive attitude, theatre theorists and critics should revise the definitions and prescriptions of politically orientated theatre . . . according to the new cultural ethics of postmodernity regarding the production and reception of the arts'.[21]

By this Sakellaridou seems to be saying that the new generation of dramatists belong entirely to the continuum of playwriting 'waves' that Edgar and Sierz saw as 'anatomizing' society. The only difference with the 1990s dramatists was that the process had become confused by the new conditions and orthodoxies that now prevailed, where older dramatic forms and definitions of what constitutes 'political theatre' seemed to be looking increasingly anachronistic.

Some sense of this shift in playwriting cultures can be glimpsed through observing the overlap that continued some years into the new decade where plays such as David Edgar's *The Shape of the Table* (1990), Sarah Daniels's *Beside Herself* (1990) and Winsome Pinnock's *Talking in Tongues* (1991), despite being produced in the 1990s, exhibited qualities of the previous decade: defined by a committed politics based on careful analysis and a clear ideological position, they slowly gave way to work such as Anthony Neilson's *Penetrator* (1993), David Mamet's *Oleanna* (1993) and Rebecca Prichard's *Essex Girls* (1994); these new plays were stylish, modishly contemporary and morally ambigous, and they *seemed* to render the work of Daniels, Edgar and Pinnock as curiously anachronistic period pieces that had somehow accidently beached themselves on the shores of the voguish new decade.

Patrice Pavis, while making a case for Mark Ravenhill's work, provides a narrative of how this situation may have come about – how the certainties of the 1980s gave way to a more uncertain political terrain where 'we have left behind the time of revolutionary utopias and have embarked on a period of reformism, economic liberalism and of stupefying global consumerism'; and while conceding that a play such as *Some Explicit Polaroids* breaks with the past in that it is a 'a "problem play" rather than a "thesis play"', Pavis believes that 'its chief ambition is to deal simultaneously with the problems of our time'.[22]

Yet it is also discernible that the plays by Ravenhill and his contemporaries sometimes become uncomfortably close to – the actual point of complicity with – the very aspects of globalization and consumer capitalism that they set out to critique. Ravenhill's work in particular is evasive about advocating moral absolutes or a clear ideological position and resists putting forward other possibilities for resistance or change.

Klaus Peter Müller has argued that in the wake of postmodernism's erosive effects throughout the 1990s, it has become increasingly difficult to define with certainty what constitutes a political play.[23] Müller goes even further in that he also detects 'a strong element of pessimism mixed with a strange sense of relish in the destructive and dehumanising worlds depicted' in many of these plays.[24] Whereas an earlier dramatist such as Edward Bond carefully structured violence in works such as *Saved* (1965) and *Lear* (1971), employing a neo-Brechtian methodology, 1990s writers such as Jez Butterworth in *Mojo* (1995) and Martin McDonagh in the *Leenane Trilogy* (1996–97) seemed to fetishize violence, often by referencing it within a framework derived from films such as *The Long Good Friday* (1980) and *Reservoir Dogs* (1992). It is this voyeuristic glamorization of violence, rather than its analysis, that leads Müller to conclude that 'any celebration of violence and viciousness in plays produces serious doubts about their political implications'.[25]

Coupled with this glib treatment of violence, there often co-exisits a naïve sentimentality in many of these plays: in *Shopping and Fucking*, the final image is one of Lulu, Mark and Robbie feeding each other, played out in the original production to the mawkish tune of 'Love is the Sweetest Thing'. While the choice of song should perhaps be treated – like so much else in the play – with a sense of deliberate irony, this seems a long way from Sierz's belief that Ravenhill and others from his generation belong to 'the great tradition of nihilistic, romantic, sentimental and utopian rebels'[26] in the mould of William Blake, Lord Byron and Thomas Paine.

Arguably, the legacy of the in-yer-face dramatists has helped shape both definitions and trends in political theatre up until the latter half of the millennial decade: their effect can be most closely discerned in the generation of new writers who have followed them. David Edgar, writing in 2004, makes the interesting, if somewhat pessimistic, observation that the archetypal cliché of in-yer-face writing, 'about young people shooting up in flats', which becomes political in the hands of writers such as Kane and Ravenhill, loses this trait when treated by their millennial contemporaries: much of the politics has 'burnt off, like alcohol [so] what has been left is the young people in flats'.[27]

Aleks Sierz also identifies a growing trend that he terms 'me and my mates' drama, which he summarizes as 'naturalistic plays set on underclass council estates', although often written by young middle-class writers whose 'visits to the lower depths are pure cultural tourism'.[28] Specific examples are always subjective, but might include Grae Cleugh's *Fucking Games* (2001) and Maggie Neville's *The Shagaround* (2001); yet perhaps the best definition of Sierz's term has been the recent televison series *Skins* (2007–), where it seems more than likely that the writers have read and engaged at university with in-yer-face drama. Not only do we see a replication of themes from the plays (owing money to a drug dealer; the embrace of shallow 'new-age' ideals), but the series explores each week the personal stories and background drawn from its young middle-class characters. However, all the stories are devoid of any frames of reference that a dramatist such as Ravenhill provides regarding either a past age or a critique of the present one. Fortunately, the legacy of the 1990s dramatists does not end with *Skins*, and even the long-standing accusation that dramatists from this period evaded political enagagment has been seen in some quarters as paradoxically giving rise to popular strands of political theatre writing in the early years of the new millennium: the best-known example of this was Verbatim Theatre, a form of drama usually constructed around documented evidence such as public inquiries, court records or witness statements.

David Edgar, speaking in 2004, includes this category alongside two other developments in political theatre towards the end of 1990s and which continued well into the latter part of the millennial decade: Faction and Satire. Edgar sees the popularity of Verbatim Theatre in particular (especially in 'tribunal plays' such as Richard Norton-Taylor's *The Colour of Justice* in 1999 and plays based on interviews such as David Hare's 2003 *The Permanent Way*, which examined the state of the British railways since privatization) arising out of the political vacuum that followed in-yer-face theatre; to accentuate this, Edgar draws on the parallel between the establishment of the Theatre of Fact movement in the 1950s being a direct reaction against the playwrights associated with the apolitical Theatre of the Absurd.[29]

Edgar's category 'Faction' has perhaps been the most significant dramatic genre to establish itself within recent years, in film, theatre and television. Ten years ago it would have been difficult to convince anyone that the 1977 television interviews between David Frost and former President Richard Nixon would make promising material for a play, but Peter Morgan's *Frost/Nixon* successfully transferred in 2006 from the Almeida Theatre to a long West End residency. *Frost/Nixon* has followed a successful formula in which established historical events – often based around political figures or activities – are blended with a series of imagined 'what if' scenarios. Morgan has become the most successful writer specializing in this genre and has produced work for television such as *The Deal* (2003) (which looked at the events leading up to the Labour election victory of 1997) and films such as the *The Queen* (2006) (which looked at the relationship between Tony Blair and the royal family immediately after Princess Diana's death), and an adaptation of Giles Fodden's novel *The Last King of Scotland* (2006) (about the Ugandan dictator Idi Amin).

Edgar's last category of Satire is a genre more confined to theatre, and it is worth noting that Andy De La Tour's play *Landslide*, premiered during in the 1997 election, provides an indication that theatre was among the earliest dissenting voices in the arts against New Labour: in contrast, little or no opposition came from other quarters, perhaps owing to the fact that, in the preceding years, New Labour had assiduously courted the arts and media – consequently they gave the government a far more extended period of *laissez-faire* than theatre, which had always been regarded (with the exception of the Musical) as unglamourous and unpopulist by the apparatchiks of New Labour.

Theatre's readiness to satirize New Labour from its very earliest days in power also came about due to its outsider status on the fringes of what has come to be known as 'Cool Britannia'. Lasting from approximately 1994 to 1997, this brief cultural period is of considerable importance when coming to an understanding not only of political theatre, but of politics itself through the 1990s, and into the millennial decade.

cool britannia and political theatre

Thus the early 1990s saw new theatre writing undergoing a crisis: there was widespread talk of a decline in both the quality and number of new plays being produced; theatres were under financial pressure to play safe with revivals of popular classics rather than take risks in commissioning new work; there also seemed to be a perception that British directors were more interested in establishing their repuations by working within the classical repertoire than by tackling new writing. Mark Ravenhill recalls this grim period, where writing plays had given way to a vogue for 'physical theatre, performance work, devised work . . . To get into LeCoq, to learn some circus skills were the things to do . . . The idea of sitting down to write a play seeemed pretty redundant.'[30]

Yet David Edgar, writing at the time, argued that audiences had not suddenly started clamouring for 'Live Art', classical revivals or musicals; rather the decline in new writing had been driven predominantly by economic contingencies.[31] Consequently, the 1994 season at the Royal Court's Theatre Upstairs has been seen as the turning point in the fortunes of new writing, and while David Edgar favours a model of post-war British theatre based around a series of intergenerational 'waves', theatre writing itself got itself caught – and subsequently surfed – on a far larger cultural wave that was about to break that year: Cool Britannia.

Writing in 1996, Robert Hewison gives an enthusiastic account of the newly discovered energy that suddenly seemed to be transforming all branches of the arts in Britain. The extract below, while hyperbolic, gives a strong sense of the mood produced during this short-lived but giddy period in British culture:

> We have the makings of a cultural renaissance, based on a new gener-
> ation of young talent that is being recognized nationally and inter-
> nationally. From Britpop to Bryn Terfel, from Stephen Daldry to
> Damien Hirst, from Jenny Saville to Nicholas Hytner, from Rachel
> Whiteread to Mark Wigglesworth, there is a renewed sense of creative
> vigour and excitement.We are on the threshold of either a decadent
> *fin de siècle* or the breakthrough that characterized Vienna in 1900,
> when artists, playwrights, poets and composers launched twentieth
> century modernism.[32]

Ken Urban reckons the zenith of Cool Britannia was reached the following year, and like Hewison sees this brief cultural period as important to
British self-identity as it approached the new millennium:

> No longer would Britain be the land of bad food and crooked teeth;
> London was now to be the epicentre of a cultural renaissance, its
> inhabitants no longer citizens of a fading imperial power, but the
> vital members of a country blazing into the new millennium high on
> a rush of newness.[33]

Cool Britannia's high point also coincided with New Labour's landslide election victory, and it is also true to say that Cool Britannia had
as many political associations as it did artistic and cultural ones. Shortly
after its defeat in the 1992 election, the Labour Party, keen to rebrand
itself, and later under its new leader Tony Blair, attempted to associate
itself with the embryonic stirrings of youthful creativity taking place in
the arts. Just as Harold Wilson associated himself with The Beatles leading up to the 1964 general election, Cool Britannia became a useful
mechanism by which New Labour could shed its reputation for being
stuck with postwar socialist dogma and be seen instead as a youthful
and forward-thinking alternative to a beleaguered, fractious and increasingly weary-looking Conservative Party.

Yet, as we have seen, the feeling was that Cool Britannia, much like
New Labour, was more interested in surface appearance and presentation rather than a radical engagement with politics. Matthew Collin in
his book *Altered State: The Story of Ecstasy Culture and Acid House*, draws
an analogy between the drug that became most associated with the
period and the corresponding lack of interest in established politics
within the culture of Cool Britannia:

> Ecstasy culture . . . has an open-access formula: rather than a defined
> ideology . . . It is endlessly malleable, pragmatic to new meaning . . .
> The idea of Ecstasy culture has no politics because it has no mani-
> festo or slogans, it *isn't saying anything* or actively opposing the social
> order.[34]

Mark Ravenhill makes a point of critiquing this so-called Ecstasy
culture in both *Shopping and Fucking* and *Some Explicit Polaroids*. In the
former play, after taking Ecstasy, Robbie enters an altered state where he
sees the suffering of the world as if from a great height – 'I see this kid
in Rwanda, crying but he doesn't know why. And this granny in Kiev,

selling everything she's ever owned' – but his conclusion after witness-
ing all this misery is simply to 'Fuck the bitching world and let's be . . .
beautiful. Beautiful. And happy.'[35] In *Some Explicit Polaroids*, Tim points
out to Nick that since his imprisonment in 1984, British society has
irrevocably changed, whereby the society he knew, based on clear ideological demarcations, has given way to the 'happy world' of hedonism
and instant gratification through shopping and sex; yet Nick in his
retort comments, 'Nothing's connected . . . with anything and you're
not fighting anymore'; later, Tim alludes to both the lassitude of this
society and his own imminent death when he observes, 'one day
I might get bored with being in the happy land'.[36]

The fascination that Tim and Victor have in *Some Explicit Polaroids*
with 'trash music, trash food, trash people' also became one of central
criticisms levelled at Cool Britannia itself: its three chief cornerstones of
music, art and theatre lacked political conviction, and were in thrall to
the ethics of consumer capitalism.[37] This seemed most apparent with
Brit art, where despite much of its provocative subject matter, many of
its artists were supported by Charles Saatchi, a patron with strong associations to Tory politics and whose celebrated 1997 'Sensation' exhibition took place at the Royal Academy – an institution right at the very
heart of the British art establishment.

While young in-yer-face dramatists such as Jez Butterworth, Martin
McDonagh and Anthony Neilson faced similar accusations of using
deliberately violent and sexual imagery for shallow effect, new theatre
writing during the period never commanded (with the notable exception of Kane's *Blasted*) the same degree of media attention that Brit art
received – nor was it ever embraced as part of New Labour's vision of a
new Britain. The government treated new theatre writing during this
period with some degree of circumspection, and despite Mark
Ravenhill's *Shopping and Fucking* frequently being cited as theatre's main
contribution to Cool Britannia, the play was publicly condemned in
1998 by Education Secretary David Blunkett, after going on a British
Council-funded European tour. Blunkett's disparaging comments about
the play being a waste of taxpayers' money lost much of its sting when
it was later revealed that he had neither seen the play nor been aware
that it had been endorsed by Culture Secretary Chris Smith. And while
in-yer-face theatre has been accused of evading political engagement, it
was at least never ready to cosy up to New Labour in the same way that
Britpop and Brit art so readily appeared to do.

While it is true to say that Kane and Ravenhill's work (as well as
Harry Gibson's adaptation of Irvine Welsh's novel *Trainspotting*) popu-

larized theatre-going amongst a section of the younger generation, and while on the surface their work seems to capture the 1990s zeitgeist through Kane's brutal imagery and Ravenhill's exploration of consumerism and club culture, the plays themselves enter into a far more profound exploration of these elements than simply displaying them uncritically before an audience. Other writers such as David Eldridge and Che Walker also presented a far bleaker picture of 'New Britain', and while the imagery they employed was just as violent as anything presented by Brit art, it was not meant simply for voyeuristic consumption.

Theatre's wariness at becoming involved with Cool Britannia was in retrospect a wise stance. While undoubtedly certain works from Britpop and Brit art will transcend the period in which they were created, perhaps the aesthetics of style over substance will more probably come to resemble the 'tawdry shell' of the Millennium Dome – a grand project often associated with New Labour at the end of the 1990s – where inside the flamboyant pleasure-dome was revealed to be a disparate and disappointing array of 'attractions'.

Whereas the Dome's aspirations were widely seen as being almost exclusively bound to the concerns of the nation's capital, the chapters in this volume aim to demonstrate that theatre during the 1990s went far beyond the narrow ambit of plays by young London-based in-yer-face dramatists. Intergenerational factors also operated throughout the decade whereby figures such as David Hare, Bonnie Greer, Harold Pinter and Ed Thomas jostled with new writers such as Sarah Kane, David Eldridge and Mark Ravenhill; the volume also gives equal prominence to regional voices, such as David Greig, David Harrower and Gary Mitchell, which were either denied or ignored at the time. The sheer plethora of different voices that emanated from the theatre during this period – although the novel arguably expressed more – produced the most authentic as well as representative impression of British culture and politics during the 1990s: less 'Cool Britannia', theatre nevertheless presented a nation that was both rumbustious yet also troubled and less at ease with itself than other sectors of the arts and media, but it was also a much truer one.

notes

1. A. Sierz, 'Outrage Theatres gave Young Writers Freedom – No Ideologies, No Rules, No Taste', *Daily Telegraph*, 17 February 2001.
2. D. Dromgoole, *The Full Room: An A–Z of Contemporary Playwriting* (London:

Methuen, 2000), p. v; A. Sierz, *In-Yer-Face Theatre: British Drama Today* (London: Faber, 2000), pp. xi–xii.

3. For accounts of the conference, see the following: A. Sierz, '"In Yer Face" Bristol', *New Theatre Quarterly*, vol. 19, no. 1 (2003), 90; A. Gonda, 'In-Yer Face?' http://www.writernet.co.uk/php2/news.php?id=324. Accessed 26 June 2005; S. Klimenko, 'Playing for Readers: Anxiety about the Written Word in Modern British Theatre', *Anglo Files: Journal of English Teaching*, no. 126 (2002), 27–34.

4. Sierz, *In-Yer-Face Theatre*, p. xii.

5. D. Edgar, 'Secret Lives', *Guardian*, 19 April 2003.

6. M. Ravenhill, *Shopping and Fucking*, in *Plays I* (London: Methuen, 2001), p. 66.

7. J. Reinelt, '"Politics, Playwriting, Postmodernism": An Interview with David Edgar', *Contemporary Theatre Review*, vol. 14, no. 4 (2004), 42–53 (44).

8. M. S. Clark, 'Against Pessimissm', in M. M. Delgado and C. Svich (eds), *Theatre in Crisis? Performance Manifestos for a New Century* (Manchester: Manchester University Press, 2002), pp. 82–8 (p. 83).

9. E. Sakellaridou, 'New Faces for British Political Theatre', *Studies in Theatre & Performance*, vol. 20, no. 1 (1999), 43–51 (46).

10. J. Bull, 'A Review of In-Yer-Face Theatre: British Drama Today', *Contemporary Theatre Review*, vol. 13, no. 1 (2003), 123–5 (123).

11. D. Eldridge, 'In-Yer-Face and After', *Studies in Theatre and Performance*, vol. 23, no. 1, 55–8 (55).

12. A. Sierz, 'In-Yer-Face Theatre: New British Drama Today', *Anglo Files: Journal of English Teaching*, no. 126 (2002), 8–14 (12).

13. Cited in Sierz, *In-Yer-Face Theatre*, p. 39; K. P. Müller, 'Political Plays in England in the 1990s', in B. Reitz and M. Berninger (eds), *British Drama of the 1990s* (Heidelberg: Universitätsverlag Carl Winter, 2002), pp. 15–36.

14. Eldridge, 'In-Yer-Face and After', 56; Sierz, 'In-Yer-Face Theatre: New British Drama Today', 10.

15. Sierz, 'In-Yer-Face Theatre: New British Drama Today', 4; 9.

16. Bull, 'A Review of In-Yer-Face Theatre', 123.

17. J. London, 'Dancing with the Dead Man: Notes on a Theatre for the Future of Europe', in *Theatre in Crisis?*, pp. 103–7 (106).

18. V. Gottlieb, 'Theatre Today – the "New Realism"', *Contemporary Theatre Review*, vol. 13, no. 1 (2003), 6–14 (9; 8).

19. Sierz, 'In-Yer-Face Theatre: New British Drama Today', 14.

20. D. I. Rabey, *English Drama Since 1940* (London: Longman, 2003), p. 202.

21. Sakellaridou, 'New Faces for British Political Theatre', 46.

22. P. Patrice, 'Ravenhill and Durringer, or the *Entente Cordiale* Misunderstood', trans. D. Bradby, *Contemporary Theatre Review*, vol. 14, no. 2 (2004), 4–16 (5; 6).

23. Müller, 'Political Plays in England in the 1990s', 16.

24. Ibid., 15.

25. Ibid., 18.
26. Sierz, 'In-Yer-Face Theatre: New British Drama Today', 12.
27. Reinelt, 'Politics, Playwriting, Postmodernism', 47.
28. A. Sierz, '"Me and My Mates": The State of English Playwriting, 2003', *New Theatre Quarterly*, vol. 20, no. 1 (2004), 79–83 (81).
29. Reinelt, 'Politics, Playwriting, Postmodernism', 48.
30. M. Ravenhill, 'A Tear in the Fabric: The James Bulger Murder and New Theatre Writing in the "Nineties"', *New Theatre Quarterly*, vol. 20, no. 4 (2004), 305–14 (310).
31. D. Edgar, 'New State of Play', *Guardian*, 1 March 1993.
32. R. Hewison, 'Rebirth of a Nation', *The Times*, 19 May 1996.
33. K. Urban, 'Towards a Theory of Cruel Britannia: Coolness, Cruelty and the 'Nineties', *New Theatre Quarterly*, vol. 20, no. 4 (2004), 354–72 (355).
34. M. Collin, *Altered State: The Story of Ecstasy Culture and Acid House* (London: Serpent's Tail, 1997), pp. 4–5.
35. Ravenhill, *Shopping and Fucking*, in *Plays I*, p. 39.
36. Ravenhill, *Some Explicit Polaroids*, in *Plays 1*, p. 269; p. 273; p. 270.
37. Ibid., p. 241.

part i
in-yer-face theatre: a reconsideration

introduction to part i

As mentioned, the group of young dramatists who made up the 1994–95 season at the Royal Court have been said to have expressed the dominant zeitgeist. Peter Ansorge commented at the time, 'the new regime at the Court has been cultivating a post-Thatcher brat-pack of writers in their early twenties who are undoubtedly in touch with the mood of young audiences', and Aleks Sierz in his chapter in Ansorge's book, 'In-Yer-Face and After: Reflections on New Writing in the 1990s', mounts both a defence and a reassessment of his existing work on this period.[1] He argues that, while never offering itself up as being a definitive account of the period, his narrative has come to be misrepresented and misunderstood in some quarters. By way of reminder, Sierz directs our attention to the very opening sentence of his book, which states quite unequivocally that it is 'a personal and polemical history of British theatre', and one that was created directly at the moment without the benefit of hindsight or distance.[2]

In his reassessment Sierz acknowledges areas where he has unconsciously marginalized, excluded and occasionally misrepresented. These primarily fall into two categories: an overly metropolitan bias and a disregard of plays by dramatists of colour. With regard to the former, Sierz readily acknowledges that the book is an account of London-based playwrights and understands that for playgoers in cities such as Birmingham, Cardiff and Edinburgh, 'the story of the 1990s would have been radically different'. As regards the latter, Sierz observes, 'In what looks like a freak spasm of orientalism' the period reads as almost 'exclusively paleface', where dramatists such as Roy Williams, Ayub Khan-Din, Parv Bancil, Kara Miller and Tanika Gupta get only a cursory mention.

Ken Urban's chapter, 'Cruel Britannia', provides not only a critique but a theoretical model for consideration in the face of such critical divergence; here he defends the in-yer-face dramatists from accusations of cynicism and political lethargy, and maintains that below the depthless surface of 'Cool Britannia' lurks what he terms 'Cruel Britannia'; a

form of nihilism predicated on allowing the possibility of transformation. Based on the writings of Nietzsche, Heidegger, Artaud and Bataille,
Urban argues that 'Cruel Britannia' displays a nihilism founded on an
ethical vision as opposed to a *moral* one. Despite appearing to adopt an
amoral position, he argues that the nihilism within plays such as *Blasted*
and *Phaedra's Love* is not a cynical one. While conceding that 'Cruel
Britannia is not radical or revolutionary in any traditional sense', at the
same time Urban believes that this does not necessarily mean that it is
politically lethargic or reactionary.

One major feature of the writing produced by the new generation of
dramatists in the 1990s was their deliberate rejection of older, self-
consciously political writing. Mel Kenyon, the literary agent who represented writers such as David Greig, Sarah Kane, Mark Ravenhill and
Judy Upton, summarized this generational difference in the following
way:

> To write these big political plays full of certainties and resolution is
> completely nonsensical in a time of fragmentation. When you want
> to create a political piece of drama, there's no point in mimicking the
> form of resolution and certainty in a time of complete uncertainty.[3]

Yet despite Sierz's belief that forms of 1980s political drama such as
the 'state-of-the-nation' play had 'mercifully . . . gone out of fashion
soon after the fall of the Berlin Wall', old habits die hard, and playwrights from the 1968 generation continued to write successful work
based around these supposedly redundant forms throughout the 1990s
and beyond into the millennial decade: examples included David
Edgar's *Pentecost* (1994), which looked at the 'New Europe' emerging
from the changing geographical and political boundaries following the
events of 1989; Michael Frayn's *Democracy* (2003), which looked at post-
war German politics, and David Hare's *The Permanent Way* (2003),
which examined the state of Britain's railways following privatization.[4]

Hare also began the 1990s with three plays that were closer to home:
Racing Demon (1990), *Murmuring Judges* (1991) and *The Absence of War*
(1993). Commonly known as *The Hare Trilogy*, these plays anatomized
three key English institutions – the Church of England, the judiciary
and the party-political system. Significantly, *The Hare Trilogy* also underwent a revival in a 2003 production at the Birmingham Repertory
Theatre, becoming a rare example of a new play from the 1990s enjoying a large-scale revival in the new millennium.

It is also worth remembering that 1997, arguably the year both Cool

Britannia and 'in-yer face theatre' were at their height, saw the winner of the Evening Standard Award for best play go to Tom Stoppard's *The Invention of Love*, with its principal subject the Victorian poet A. E. Housman. Thus playwriting in the 1990s sometimes demonstrated a stubborn resistance to the prevailing zeitgeist. As David Eldridge reminds us, such aberrations from a received narrative served to disrupt the understandable impulse that theatre critics and historians have to rationalize and contextualize, whereas in reality, 'the picture is one that is a messy, vivid streak of hues and colours, forming no coherent narrative'.[5]

Mary Luckhurst's 'Harold Pinter and poetic politics' also challenges such received views. Its starting point is a 1997 lecture given by David Hare entitled 'A Defence of the New': among other laments on the state of British theatre, Hare obliquely criticizes the in-yer-face generation for turning their backs on the broadly socialist continuum established since Osborne's *Look Back in Anger* in 1956. Hare's disappointment is also shared by other commentators such as Peter Ansorge and Vera Gottlieb, who saw the 1990s generation somehow retreating from a playwriting tradition that had lasted from 1956 until the mid-1970s: this they maintain represented the high point of British postwar political theatre.[6] Luckhurst argues that Hare's decision to also place the work of Harold Pinter and Caryl Churchill outside this continuum 'represents blindness': while Hare's mapping 'recognizes them as indisputable theatrical geniuses', they are excluded from the Osborne tradition as something 'other'.

Taking Harold Pinter as her main case study, Luckhurst argues that the 1990s continued a process already started during the previous decade with plays such as *One for the Road* (1984) and *Mountain Language* (1988), and which developed over the next two decades through work such as *New World Order* (1991), *Party Time* (1993), *Ashes to Ashes* (1996) and *Celebration* (2000). Luckhurst's chapter also serves to open up the ideological gulf that seemed to exist between the different playwriting generations and their own responses to politics; a situation Hare expresses in his self-performed monologue *Via Dolorosa* (1998), 'where no one believes in anything anymore'.[7]

notes

1. P. Ansorge, *From Liverpool to Los Angeles: On Writing for Theatre, Film and Television* (London: Faber, 1997), p. 59.
2. A. Sierz, *In-Yer-Face Theatre. British Drama Today* (London: Faber, 2000), p. xi.

3. Cited in K. Urban, '"An Ethics of Catastrophe": The Theatre of Sarah Kane', *Performing Arts Journal*, no. 69 (2001), 36–46 (39).
4. A. Sierz, '"Me and my Mates" The State of English Playwriting, 2003', *New Theatre Quarterly*, vol. 20, no. 1 (2004), 79–83 (83).
5. D. Eldridge, 'In-Yer-Face and After', *Studies in Theatre and Performance*, vol. 23, no. 1 (2003), 55–8 (56).
6. See, for instance, P. Ansorge, 'Really a Golden Age?' in D. Edgar (ed.), *State of Play Issue 1: Playwrights on Playwriting* (London: Faber, 1999), pp. 37–47; V. Gottlieb, 'Lukewarm Britain', in V. Gottlieb and C. Chambers (eds), *Theatre in a Cool Climate* (Oxford: Amber Lane, 1999), pp. 201–12.
7. D. Hare, *Via Dolorosa* & *When Shall We Live* (London: Faber, 1998), p. 4.

1
'we all need stories': the politics of in-yer-face theatre

aleks sierz

Near the climax of Mark Ravenhill's *Shopping and Fucking*, the character Robbie makes a speech that's designed to appeal to anyone in the audience who suffers from an 'incredulity toward metanarratives', that malady common to our so-called postmodern condition.[1] 'I think', says Robbie, 'we all need stories, we make up stories so that we can get by. And I think a long time ago there were big stories. Stories so big you could live your whole life in them. The Powerful Hands of the Gods and Fate. The Journey to Enlightenment. The March of Socialism. But they all died or the world grew up or grew senile or forgot them, so now we're all making up our own stories. Little stories.'[2] Since its premiere, *Shopping and Fucking* has become a canonical 1990s text: it has influenced other playwrights, it has received university approval and it has been parodied. For example, its title was winked at by Grae Cleugh in his *F***ing Games* (Royal Court, 2001); it's been published in a Methuen Student Edition; and in Christopher Douglas and Nigel Planer's satirical *I An Actor*, written under the pseudonym of Nicholas Craig, this 'Blowtorch of the Barbican' mentions one role in which he found himself 'wading through a sea of syringes and crème fraiche' in a play called *Fist F***ing* staged at, no prizes for guessing, the Royal Court.[3] If attracting parody is a clear sign that a new theatre sensibility has well and truly arrived, Robbie's speech also runs the risk of political confusion, of its author being seen as a postmodern joker, when in fact 'Ravenhill far from accepts the desirability of the soul-less post-modern landscape that his work explores'.[4] So Robbie's speech is both a knowing

23

joke about one of the classics of postmodern theory and also contains a truth about contemporary theatre history.

My book, *In-Yer-Face Theatre: British Drama Today*, which was first published in March 2001, responded to this need for contemporary stories by offering a narrative about new writing for British theatre in the 1990s. Creating a narrative is, of course, a political act, and its first step is an act of labelling, or branding. But every time work such as Ravenhill's is branded, its politics are concealed as well as proclaimed. For example, if you call such plays Neo-Jacobean, you trumpet their continuity with a tradition of British playwriting that stretches back to the Renaissance – but you also conceal the fact that the politics of this suggests a conservative approach to drama that emphasizes how things essentially always stay the same. Similarly, if you see Ravenhill and the like as New Brutalists, you are asserting that the brutality of the work is its most important feature. Given that, on one level, *Shopping and Fucking* is a retelling of the myth of the babes in the wood, brutality is surely not the right word. The term New Brutalism also suggests an essentialist reading of human nature: we are mere brutes, and true drama bears witness to that. Politically, this tends to emphasize the impossibility of changing human nature. A further drawback of the New Brutalist brand is that it implicitly compares theatre with architecture – the National Theatre is a New Brutalist building – and it is a terrible mistake to name a new theatrical sensibility after the architecture of an institution which, in the early 1990s, had such a poor record of championing new writers. Finally, if you see playwrights such as Ravenhill as examples of 'Cool Drama', then you're stressing not only their fashionable qualities, but also their detachment from passionate politics – in other words, you're arguing that they're basically cynical. Too cool to get angry.[5]

Since branding a new phenomenon is such a political act, perhaps it is worth reiterating why the term 'in-yer-face theatre' is still the best way of theorizing what has happened. When, in 1998, I asked Sarah Kane what she thought of the label 'in-yer-face theatre', she shrugged as if to say: 'That's your problem, mate, not mine.' Then she said: 'At least it's fucking better than New Brutalism.'[6] Unlike names such as New Brutalism, in-yer-face theatre describes not just the content of a play but the relationship between the writer and the public, or (more accurately) the relationship between the stage and the audience. Because of this, it powerfully suggests much more than a mere description of content. For example, it implies theoretical ideas about experiential theatre (a crucial concept for understanding the nature of 1990s drama); the question of what is taboo; the notion of what is a theatrical provocation – and it not only focuses on the sensibility, especially its confrontational aspects, of the writing but also on the way it seeks its theatrical expression: it spotlights theatre practice. In other words, the name in-yer-face theatre strongly suggests what is particular about the experience of watching extreme theatre – the feeling that your personal space is threatened. It gives a sense of that violation of intimacy that some forms of extreme drama produce in the audience. In other words, it is a tool with which to understand the relationship between play and audience.

In-yer-face theatre is also political. Firstly, this brand of theatre emphasizes the sense of rupture, a radical break, with the past – it stresses what was new and innovative about the dramatic voices which were heard for the first time in the 1990s. Secondly, this brand not only suggests a confrontational approach; it also implies the existence of an avant-garde: although cultural critics have announced the death of the avant-garde on more than one occasion in the past 50 years, in theatre its re-emergence in the 1990s took a classical form: innovation, scandal and then retrenchment. Nor is the idea of an avant-garde politically neutral: from the origins of the term in the anarchism of Mikhail Bakhtin, the avant-garde 'is still characterized by a radical political posture'.[7] Finally, the in-yer-face brand is fully resonant of the 1990s zeitgeist. The term was often used about other cultural forms and thus it links theatre to the wider culture of that decade (it nods at other 1990s phenomena, from shock jocks to Young British Artists).[8] But if the term really is political, what do its politics imply?

Politically, the story told by *In-Yer-Face Theatre* is now a familiar one. In the late 1980s, due to Thatcherite subsidy cuts, British theatre was in crisis, a state eloquently summarized by playwright David Edgar: 'A decline in audiences, financial cutbacks, a crisis of confidence, rampant commercialism, a hostile culture, a haemorrhage in the production of new work.'[9] Then, egged on by a handful of artistic directors – Ian Brown and Dominic Dromgoole, followed by Mike Bradwell, Stephen Daldry, Abigail Morris and Jenny Topper – a new wave of young writers arrived, pioneering a fresh theatre sensibility and reviving the fortunes not only of new writing but also of theatre in general. Within a couple of years, the names of Kane, Ravenhill, Jez Butterworth, Martin McDonagh, Phyllis Nagy, Rebecca Prichard and at least thirty others became familiar not only to British audiences but to European, and eventually American, ones. These writers took up a political project that is central to British theatre. Graham Saunders comments: '*Blasted* and *Look Back in Anger* in their own different ways served to reinvigorate the theatre once again as a place where new dissenting voices could be heard.'[10] And, as a cultural avant-garde, the dissenting new writers of the 1990s produced work that was on the extreme left, being fiercely, sometimes ferociously, critical of consumer capitalism, social inequality, sexual discrimination, violence and war. No social custom was left unturned. In cultural terms, the five-year period between 1994 and 1999 saw a victory of committed, provocative and confrontational new work by a new generation that was angry about the world they'd grown up in. But this victory also had its costs.

context: 'a personal and polemical history . . .'

In-Yer-Face Theatre is, first and foremost, a text, and its politics are the product of a time and place. In the mid-1990s, the debuts of playwrights such as Kane and Ravenhill were intensely controversial. Their plays were sites of cultural contestation, a struggle conducted as much on the news pages of newspapers as in their culture sections, as well as on the radio and on television. Although the emerging playwrights were cheered on by many theatre professionals, some critics, commentators, moralists and audience members opposed their work and would have been happy to censor it. From the start, the debates about in-yer-face theatre were highly partisan, and there was no knowing what the outcome might have been: there was even a possibility that the careers of these writers might have been strangled at birth.

Although it is a badge of pride that, since the abolition of censorship in 1968, British theatre is a free space, this narrative of liberation is not without its problems. As playwright John Arden once wrote: 'Since [the Lord Chamberlain's] time, there have always been more than enough people about to interfere in various unacceptable ways with a dramatist's scripts, ideas and intentions.'[11] The authoritarian model of censorship (censorship by the state) has simply been replaced by what could be described as the plaintiff model (censorship by interest group). Since 1968, the nation's moral guardians are no longer concentrated in the centre, but are diffused throughout society. They include pressure groups such as the National Viewers' and Listeners' Association (now Mediawatch), religious groups or other moral vigilantes, usually supported by the right-wing press. State censorship has been replaced by populist censorship, whose aim is the age-old reactionary one of mental closure and the imposition of restrictions. What the shift between these two models amounts to is a gradual move away from a traditional idea of moral guardianship to one of a populist morality (both believe in traditional absolute values). The resulting conservative discourse contrasts upright citizens who produce acceptable art with a perverted 'other' whose work is unclean, whose intentions are to corrupt and whose experiments always fail. The problem is that while in the past you could negotiate with the Lord Chamberlain, and playwrights and directors regularly did so, it's much harder to negotiate with fanatical religious groups or tabloid hysteria. Abolishing censorship hasn't stopped censoriousness, and the will to censor remains deeply ingrained in the puritanical side of Anglo-Saxon public culture. Mrs Mary Whitehouse is no more, but her spirit still wields the blue pencil.

This censorious atmosphere, in which *Blasted* was hounded by the press and *Shopping and Fucking* attacked simply because of its title, meant that it was essential, both politically and artistically, to defend this new theatre sensibility and make a case for its radical credentials. As Christopher Innes observes, 'Even though *Blasted* ran for barely two weeks, the newspaper scandal was perhaps more vociferous than for any other play during the century.'[12] *In-Yer-Face Theatre*, therefore, was both a report from the front line and an advocacy argument. It also aimed to counter academic hostility to the work of the new playwrights – led by Ravenhill and Kane – who had emerged in the 1990s. Dismissive comments such as 'Some critics view the plays of Kane, Ravenhill and Butterworth as examples of a renaissance in British theatre. I do not see a renaissance,' and 'I am not of the view that Kane was a great writer nor that her plays represented a defining moment' were commonplace.[13] The new was as much a scandal in the academy as in the stalls bar. Gradually, however, the work of these playwrights has become accepted, and the relevance of their work more widely appreciated. For example, in the aftermath of 9/11, perceptions have continued to change. As David Ian Rabey comments, in 'an alarmingly volatile world climate . . . plays such as Barker's *The Europeans* and *Judith*, Sarah Kane's *Blasted* and even Bond's *The Worlds* assumed ominous new immediacies of resonance'.[14]

So, from its inception, *In-Yer-Face Theatre* was intended to be a personal and polemical account of the explosion of new writing in the 1990s. Its polemical nature was expressed not only in its advocacy of the new but in its political thrust. The creation of the idea of 'in-yer-face theatre' emphasized the fact that this was a book about performance and not about literature, an obvious point which nevertheless still manages to elude Jen Harvie when she caricatures the book as an example of theatre history which sees plays 'principally as written text rather than integrally as theatre'.[15] Then, by using the tactic of grouping a number of different playwrights under one brand, the book aimed to create a critical mass of innovation and impact. The term 'in-yer-face' was never an outright invention, nor an imposition from above, but was derived from reviews of the plays in question by national newspaper critics in the mid-1990s. But if the term came from below, the book's act of branding allowed several different writers to be grouped together under one rubric. One of the problems that arises from focusing on writers, on their biographies and on their plays, is that this personalizes a theatre phenomenon and tends to obscure questions of power and issues about the theatre system. All the messy conflicts that lie behind the decision to stage a play – including competition between theatres, relationships between agents and managements, disagreements at script meetings, internal wrangling and questions of the allocation of resources – are all hidden. So is any sustained discussion of how memory is a battlefield, and of how theatre history makes concrete the triumph of one memory of events over another. Indeed, *In-Yer-Face Theatre* has been written as if the murmuring of everyday practices, as theatre-makers created plays, put them on, sat through press nights, read reviews and received cheques in the post, all happened without any economic relationships. Of course, money is mentioned in passing, but only in passing. And any silent subversion of the economic system (such as that by Ravenhill, who on a discussion panel confessed to shoplifting copies of the plays of Edward Bond) remains absent from the story.[16] *In-Yer-Face Theatre* is written from the point of view of the consumer: it sympathizes with the writer as producer but tends to downplay the role of theatres as institutions, and thus ignores much of the politics of theatre power. As a personal polemic, it may be subjectively exciting, but the excitement of an experiential approach to theatre history tends to thrust aside questions of objective power.

It is also worth emphasizing that although in-yer-face theatre was clearly a new theatre practice, it was never a movement. You couldn't buy a membership card, or read a manifesto, or join a march. It was a network, and the playwrights involved knew each other well. But although *In-Yer-Face Theatre* scrupulously avoids referring to the new writers of the 1990s as a movement, some of its readers have been less careful. They are not entirely to blame for this mistake – the structure of the book itself suggests such a reading.

structure: 'chapter 1 defines its characteristics . . .'

The politics of *In-Yer-Face Theatre* are inscribed in its structure. As a work of empirical contemporary history, it was evidently inspired by books such as Martin Esslin's *The Theatre of the Absurd* (1961) and John Russell Taylor's *Anger and After* (1962). Intertextual references abound: for example, Esslin's point – 'If a good play must have a cleverly constructed story, these have no story or plot to speak of' – is echoed by *In-Yer-Face Theatre*'s 'If a well-made play has to have a good plot, much provocative drama prefers to have a strong sense of experiential confrontation.'[17] Russell Taylor's phrase 'Then, on 8 May 1956 came the revolution. . . .' is clearly echoed by the reformulation, during a description of the explosion (itself an image of revolt) of creativity in the mid-1990s: 'Then came the resolution.'[18] Like these previous accounts, *In-Yer-Face Theatre* has a defiantly 'common-sense' structure – a teleological historical introduction, followed by a prelude, then three chapters on individual big-name writers, three thematic chapters and a polemical conclusion – that acts to make the new and the radical both familiar and comprehensible. How else would you write about a new theatre phenomenon except by profiling its playwrights and discussing their work? Here, the book's focus on individual writers acts as a kind of Trojan horse, quietly and insidiously urging the reader to admit these playwrights into their minds, and creating the impression that they are all in-yer-face shock-artists, all equally radical and all joined in a common purpose – to change the world.

At the same time, the clarity of the structure of *In-Yer-Face Theatre* conceals not only the messy reality of recent history; it also domesticates a concept that in reality tends to be fugitive, and it thus stabilizes what is inherently unstable. Whereas the book seems silently to suggest that in-yer-face is a brand of contemporary theatre and that you can divide the world into those playwrights who are in-yer-face and those who are not, and plays into those that are and those that are not, the reality was very different. As evidence of the inherent instability of the concept, it is worth looking at how the idea first came about. At first, it appeared as a menu of ingredients: does the play in question have explicit scenes of sex and violence? Do the characters use words like 'cunt', 'fuck' and 'shit' insistently? Is someone's arse being fucked, or a hammer being wielded in anger? The limitations of this approach were quickly exposed: as Kane pointed out, 'a list of contents is not a review'.[19] A broader way of thinking about in-yer-face theatre was needed and that was found by appreciating its emotional intensity. When theatre makes you squirm inside with its depiction of emotionally fraught relationships and extreme states of mind, then is it justifiably named 'in-yer-face'. Even this, however, might apply to only a

small number of plays. Finally, an even wider cast of the net conceptual-
ized the term as a general sensibility, one that is characterized by a new
directness and that carries a mix of personal feeling and public ideas typical of the 1990s. Understanding how the concept of in-yer-face theatre
mutated in this way underlines the fact that it is inherently unstable.

What is also insufficiently stressed is the fact that the term is a slip-
pery beast. One way of understanding it is to use a metaphor. The
book's conclusion points out that:

> In-yer-face theatre is less a school of writing or a movement than
> series of networks, in which individuals such as [Anthony] Neilson,
> Ravenhill and Kane formed temporary milieus. Perhaps the best
> metaphor for in-yer-face writing is that of an arena, an imaginary
> place that can be visited or passed through, a spot where a writer can
> grow up, or where they can return to after other adventures.[20]

This 'arena' is a very complex phenomenon because it is both a sensibility and a fistful of theatre techniques. As a sensibility, meaning a mix
of feeling and ideas, it blows through the work not only of young playwrights, but also of older ones, such as Martin Crimp, Caryl Churchill
and Harold Pinter. Because *In-Yer-Face Theatre* includes only playwrights
who made their debuts in the 1990s, it excludes older writers whose
recent work has also been affected by the 1990s. As a series of theatre
techniques – including a stage language that emphasizes rawness, intensity and swearing, stage images that show acute pain or comfortless
vulnerability, characterization that prefers complicit victims to innocent ones, and a 90-minute structure that dispenses with an interval –
in-yer-face theatre depends on certain material conditions. One is the
abolition of censorship; the other is the use of studio spaces. In fact, you
could characterize the 1990s simply as the onward march of the studio
play. Taken together, and seen as the complex phenomenon that it
truly is, the term is less of a monolith than the book implies. There is
no such thing as a simple 'in-yer-face playwright': some writers, such as
Neilson, Ravenhill and Kane, have written such identifiable plays;
others, such as Patrick Marber, David Greig, Gary Mitchell and Judy
Upton, have written plays which feature gruelling, emotionally fraught
scenes; some, such as McDonagh, have done both. Yet others, such as
David Eldridge or Joe Penhall, have written one shocker and then
moved on. The problem with inclusion in the book is that this may of
itself be taken to align a playwright with a particular style or theatre
practice when most of their work has been quite different. Eldridge, for

example, is now seen as one of Britain's 'most carefully and delicately naturalistic' writers, whose 'work occupies some space in the layered, emotionally rich territory of the everyday'.[21] Recently, Eldridge has shown an ability to move confidently across the theatrical territory, from his version of the non-naturalistic *Festen* (2004) to his adaptation of the high naturalism of Ibsen's *The Wild Duck* (2005).

Like any structure, that of *In-Yer-Face Theatre* operates on the basis not only of who and what is included, but also of who and what is excluded. From the start, the physical theatre and live art of the 1990s was excluded because the book's polemic concentrated on 'the Britishness of British theatre' and therefore on what Jen Harvie has misnamed 'traditional textual patriotism', focusing 'overwhelmingly on plays and playwrights'.[22] But although Harvie's book asserts this idea of Britishness, it fails to examine it. While not as bad as Englishness, with its connotations of little-islander bulldog localism, the Britishness of British theatre is actually quite an international phenomenon: London might boast of being the theatre capital of the world, but where would it be without the Irish, the Americans, and the French, Germans and Russians? British theatre, even when it exalts in its textual brilliance, is a mongrel beast, just as Britain is a mongrel nation. In this respect, *In-Yer-Face Theatre* cries out to be read against the grain.

For more obvious reasons, the book also excluded successful new writers, such as Greig, and successful plays, such as Diane Samuels's *Kindertransport* (1993), that did not fit the in-yer-face brand. Among other things, such exclusions tended to emphasize the laddishness of 1990s playwriting and its central theme of the crisis of masculinity.[23] Some significant plays – such as Jonathan Harvey's *Beautiful Thing* (1993) and Kevin Elyot's *My Night with Reg* (1994) – are marginalized because they lack in-yer-face aggression. Similarly, writers such as Billy Roche and Robert Holman are thrust aside. The book is also exclusively paleface. In what looks like a freak spasm of orientalism, new writers such as Roy Williams, Ayub Khan-Din, Parv Bancil, Kara Miller and Tanika Gupta make, at best, only a passing appearance. In the case of Williams, this was a mistake: some his work, especially *Lift Off* (1999), is a perfect example of the 1990s sensibility. So, at its worst, a concept such as in-yer-face theatre downgrades those writers who have worked in a variety of styles or whose work is only partly touched by this sensibility. Finally, the book prefers women writers – led by Kane – who don't accept being labelled as feminists to those that do. Despite the publication of *In-Yer-Face Theatre*, however, some of those excluded have received the monographs they deserve.[24]

Perhaps the most radical exclusion, however, was theatre outside London. Location is theatre's most exciting asset, and its greatest drawback. To experience live theatre, you have to be there. As playwright Tom Stoppard says, 'If you are not there, you miss it.'[25] In the late 1980s, living in London meant being in the middle of a crisis of new writing, one that was eventually overcome by the Royal Court, the Bush, the Soho, the Hampstead and the National theatres. But what if you lived in Scotland? What if your nearest theatre was not the Royal Court, but the Traverse or the Tron? Then the story of the 1990s would have been radically different. Ditto if you happened to live in Manchester, Leeds, Belfast or Cardiff. So while some of the most exciting passages of writing in *In-Yer-Face Theatre* describe the experience of going to the theatre, it is London theatres that are privileged over those outside the metropolis. Taking the capital as its centre, it marginalizes those writers – such as Greig, David Harrower, Moira Buffini, Kate Dean, Paul Lucas, Sarah Woods and many others – whose careers were made outside London. And it leaves the politics of an overcentralized British culture largely unchallenged.

myth: 'how meaning is created . . .'

As a discourse, *In-Yer-Face Theatre* works like a myth. Like other myths, it tells a seductive story which offers the consoling illusions of coherence and closure. The renaissance in new writing which it mythologizes began in the early 1990s, became a public scandal with the staging of *Blasted* in 1995 and more or less ran out of steam by the end of 1999, the year of Kane's suicide.[26] In its vision of new writers as an avantgarde pioneering a revolutionary new theatre sensibility, the book offers an Enlightenment narrative in a time of modernity in the theatre. On a mythic level, it tells the age-old story of the struggle to emerge from darkness into light; on an artistic level, it reasserts the power of theatre; on a political level, it describes how critical voices fought to create a space in which to be heard. The myth suggests that the metanarrative of the 'March of Socialism' is not dead. And, as Edgar adds, 'Far from celebrating the death of the class struggle, it seems to me that one of the great subjects of in-yer-face theatre is mourning its loss.'[27] At the same time, as myth, in-yer-face theatre is closely related to another brand of contemporary theatre, 'new writing'.

The implication of the 'new writing' brand is that, simply by being new, its products are good in themselves and therefore virtuous. Colin Chambers observes that since the *annus mirabilis* of *Look Back in Anger* in 1956, ' "New" came to stand for a significant, meaningful text that had "relevance" and new plays became the central platform in the emerging theatre.'[28] The promotion of the new, of course, assumes the existence of an 'other', which by definition has to be old, boring and passé. What's neatly sidestepped here is any consideration of how new and old interact, and of how good or bad individual plays are; what matters most is novelty, youth and hype. In our current culture, the myth of 'yoof' is widely accepted without question.

As well as excluding some writers, the concept of in-yer-face theatre creates an illusion of coherence – despite evidence of a much more messy reality – simply because such brands always encourage us to think of complex social realities in personal terms. Thus, over the years, in-yer-face theatre has come to acquire its own personality – as if this was not an elusive sensibility but a solid individual, not so much a cultural phenomena as a force of nature. As Roland Barthes observes: 'The world enters language as a dialectical relation between activities, between human actions; it comes out of myth as a harmonious display of essences.'[29] What in reality was an aspect of a sensibility, and a series of theatre practices, with all the artistic contradictions that implies, gradually became perceived as an individual. And in its guise as a myth-ical individual, in-yer-face theatre soon acquired a natural life cycle: he (yes, this was a lad) was born, rapidly grew to maturity, misbehaved himself a bit during his adolescence, and then died young. Stylish but doomed, in-yer-face theatre was the James Dean of 1990s drama. And once a theatre sensibility is turned into a person, this person can then become a movement, with all the muddled thinking that that involves.

Not only did *In-Yer-Face Theatre* help to personify what was essen-tially a narrative, but it also tidied up a messy reality. If the joke about today's journalists is that they don't let facts get in the way of a good story, it's surely not controversial to say that, although the general narrative of the renaissance of new writing in the mid-1990s is true, several key episodes need a touch of shading. As often told, the story goes that the Royal Court staged Kane's *Blasted* and Out of Joint produced Ravenhill's *Shopping and Fucking*. So far, so true. But if you talk to people who were actually there at the time, they'll tell you that there was so much hostility to *Blasted* at Court script meetings that it was almost not put on at all, and that Ravenhill rewrote *Shopping and Fucking* substantially to make it more the kind of play that director Max Stafford-Clark wanted. In fact, Thomas Ostermeier's German produc-tion at the Baracke in Berlin was based on Ravenhill's original draft, which was much wilder than the published English version.[30] Neither of these new facts changes the story but they do show just how fragile, how contingent and how complex contemporary history is. If a script meeting had made a different decision, if a director had rejected a particular play, history would have told another tale. But, after all, isn't it the function of myth to turn complex reality into a memorable story?

The myth of in-yer-face theatre now lives on independently of the *In-Yer-Face Theatre* book. For example, in an article about the Royal Court's celebration of its fiftieth anniversary, Dominic Cavendish refers to the 1990s as the era of 'the visceral writing of Sarah Kane and her so-called "in-yer-face" contemporaries, who rose up in revulsion during the torpid, depressed early '90s'.[31] Similarly, some academics have analysed its character further.[32] And, however unwillingly, theatre practitioners prefer the in-yer-face brand to its competitors. For example, in Act Two of April de Angelis's *A Laughing Matter* (2002), scene three has the title (which in the first production was read out on stage): 'In-Yer-Face Theatre'. As always, myth acts to make familiar the unfamiliar, to provide a category with which to understand a new experience – in this case, the experience of watching experiential plays – and to turn culture into nature. Isn't it 'natural' for 'yoof' to want to shock us?

Since 2001, however, as the effects of 9/11 work through the culture, things are rapidly changing. In his postscript to *The Full Room*, Dominic Dromgoole says that the 'great shudder' of 9/11, which occurred between the first and revised editions of his book, 're-configured the landscape completely', and had the effect of dating his book in a 'profound sense'.[33] Certainly, in the early years of the new millennium, new writing for British theatre has become more plentiful, more varied and more overtly political than ever. Although some playwrights, such as Philip Ridley, debbie tucker green and Dennis Kelly, use some of the techniques of in-yer-face theatre, the general scene has moved on. The 1990s are gradually receding into history. As contemporary history, they pose once again the question of the politics of representation. The problem with *In-Yer-Face Theatre* is that both its author and its readers have too often accepted uncritically its literalness as a representation of reality. In fact, what happened was messy and the concept of in-yer-face theatre is both complex in itself – a volatile mix of sensibility and theatre practice – and refers to a complex reality, in which there were certainly in-yer-face moments but equally certainly no simple in-yer-face writers, no unproblematically in-yer-face plays and no in-yer-face movement.

Maybe the time has come to radically reassess in-yer-face theatre. Certainly its relationship between stage and audience deserves more study, but perhaps now is the time to rethink its role as a brand for the 1990s. A good starting point would be to begin seeing in-yer-face theatre less as a literal representation of reality and more as a metaphor. As the latter, it combines many meanings: it celebrates the renaissance of new writing; it denotes an aggressive assault on theatre apathy; it promotes a radical theatre agenda; it implies a revival of a defunct art form; it asserts theatre's role in cultural contestation; and it suggests a polemic against censorship. The story told by *In-Yer-Face Theatre* is the best general narrative of the 1990s that we have so far, but clearly the fact that it has become so rapidly naturalized could only happen with the exclusion of many other aspects of British theatre. Taking a hint from Robbie in *Shopping and Fucking*, maybe the best thing to do is to carry on 'making up our own stories', although not necessarily little ones. The challenge is to do that without sacrificing the radical politics of the main narrative. But whatever happens to the history of the 1990s, it remains true that, in the wider world, 'a vital part of theatre's vocation is to push back the limits of language and representation, transgress decorum, crack open consensus', and that 'it is playwrights, rather than directors seeking their own kind of authorship, who lead this charge'.[34] Long may that continue.

notes

1. J. Lyotard, *The Postmodern Condition: A Report on Knowledge* (Manchester: Manchester University Press, 1984), p. xxiv.
2. M. Ravenhill, *Plays: 1* (London: Methuen, 2001), p. 66.
3. M. Ravenhill, *Shopping and Fucking*, D. Rebellato, ed. (London: Methuen Student Edition, 2005); N. Craig, *I An Actor*, rev. edn (London: Methuen 2001), p. xv. For more about the use of asterisks in titles see A. Sierz, *In-Yer-Face Theatre: British Drama Today* (London: Faber, 2001), pp. 125–6.
4. L. Tomlin, 'English Theatre in the 1990s and Beyond', in B. Kershaw (ed.), *The Cambridge History of British Theatre: Vol. 3 – Since 1895* (Cambridge: Cambridge University Press, 2004), pp. 498–512 (p. 504). See also A. Sierz, 'Cool Britannia? "In-Yer-Face" Writing in the British Theatre Today', *New Theatre Quarterly*, vol. 14, no. 4 (1998), 324–33.
5. For Ravenhill's politics see Dan Rebellato's introductions to Ravenhill, *Plays: 1* and *Shopping and Fucking* (Methuen Student Edn).
6. See A. Sierz, 'Raising Kane', *What's On*, 28 March 2001; and 'Sarah Kane: A Última Entrevista', *Artistas Unidos*, no. 14 (2005), 66–7.
7. C. Innes, *Avant Garde Theatre 1892–1992* (London: Routledge, 1993), p. 1.
8. For example, 'This was the nineties – the "lottery age" – the "in-yer-face" age', S. Napier-Bell, *Black Vinyl, White Powder* (London: Ebury, 2002), p. 390.

9. D. Edgar, 'Provocative Acts: British Playwriting in the Post-war Era and Beyond', in D. Edgar (ed.), *State of Play: Playwrights on Playwriting* (London: Faber, 1999), pp. 1–34 (p. 22). See also J. Bull, *Stage Right: Crisis and Recovery in British Contemporary Mainstream Theatre* (Basingstoke: Macmillan, 1994), pp. 14–36.

10. G. Saunders, 'The Apocalyptic Theatre of Sarah Kane', in B. Reitz and M. Berninger (eds), *British Drama of the 1990s* (Heidelberg: Universitätsverlag Carl Winter, 2002), pp. 123–36 (p. 124).

11. Cited in J. Johnston, *The Lord Chamberlain's Blue Pencil* (London: Hodder & Stoughton, 1990), p. 250. See also M. Billington, 'What Price the Arts?' in N. Buchan and T. Summer (eds), *Glasnost in Britain? Against Censorship and in Defence of the Word* (London: Macmillan, 1989), pp. 162–70, and A. Sierz, ' "The Element That Most Outrages": Morality, Censorship and Sarah Kane's *Blasted*', in E. Batley and D. Bradby (eds), *Morality and Justice: The Challenge of European Theatre* (Amsterdam: Rodopi, 2001), pp. 225–39.

12. C. Innes, *Modern British Drama: The Twentieth Century* (Cambridge: Cambridge University Press, 2002), p. 529.

13. V. Gottlieb, 'Lukewarm Britannia', in V. Gottlieb and C. Chambers (eds), *Theatre in a Cool Climate* (London: Amber Lane Press, 1999), p. 211; M. Luckhurst, 'An Embarrassment of Riches: Women Dramatists in 1990s Britain', in *British Drama of the 1990s*, pp. 65–77 (p. 72; p. 73). But see also Luckhurst, 'Infamy and Dying Young: Sarah Kane, 1971–1999', in M. Luckhurst and J. Moody (eds), *Theatre and Celebrity in Britain 1660–2000* (Basingstoke: Palgrave, 2005), pp. 107–26; A. Sierz, ' "To Recommend a Cure": Beyond Social Realism and In-Yer-Face Theatre', in H. U. Mohr and K. Mächler (eds), *Extending the Code: New Forms of Dramatic and Theatrical Expression* (Trier: Wissenschaftlicher Verlag Trier, 2004), pp. 45–62.

14. D. Rabey, *English Drama Since 1940* (London: Longman, 2003), p. 192.

15. J. Harvie, *Staging the UK* (Manchester: Manchester University Press, 2005), p. 115.

16. M. Ravenhill, 'Reputations: Edward Bond', Theatre Voice webcast, www.theatrevoice.com. Accessed 11 March 2005.

17. M. Esslin, *The Theatre of the Absurd*, rev. edn (London: Methuen, 2001), p. 21; and Sierz, *In-Yer-Face Theatre*, p. 243.

18. J. Russell Taylor, *Anger and After: A Guide to the New British Drama*, 2nd edn (London: Eyre Methuen, 1969), p. 28, and Sierz, In-Yer-Face Theatre, p. 234.

19. H. Stephenson and N. Langridge, *Rage and Reason: Women Playwrights on Playwriting* (London: Methuen 1997), p. 132.

20. Sierz, *In-Yer-Face Theatre*, pp. 248–9.

21. D. Rebellato, 'New Theatre Writing: Simon Stephens', *Contemporary Theatre Review*, vol. 4, no. 1 (2005), 174–8 (174).

22. Harvie, *Staging the UK*, pp. 114–15.

23. Edgar, *State of Play*, pp. 27–30.

24. For example, E. Aston and J. Reinelt (eds), *The Cambridge Companion to*

Modern British Women Playwrights (Cambridge: Cambridge University Press, 2000); E. Aston, *Feminist Views on the English Stage: Women Playwrights 1990–2000* (Cambridge: Cambridge University Press, 2003) and G. Griffin, *Contemporary Black and Asian Women Playwrights in Britain* (Cambridge: Cambridge University Press, 2003).

25. T. Stoppard, interview with A. Sierz (22 September 2005).
26. See G. Saunders, *'Love Me or Kill Me': Sarah Kane and the Theatre of Extremes* (Manchester: Manchester University Press, 2002), pp. 4–6, pp. 117–18.
27. D. Edgar, 'Unsteady States: Theories of Contemporary New Writing', *Contemporary Theatre Review*, vol. 15, no. 3 (2005), 301.
28. C. Chambers, *Inside the Royal Shakespeare Company: Creativity and the Institution* (London: Routledge, 2004), p. 132.
29. R. Barthes, *Mythologies*, trans. A. Laves (London: Vintage, 1993), p. 142.
30. Interview with director James MacDonald (30 September 2005) and public platform with Mark Ravenhill at the National Student Drama Festival, Scarborough (11 April 2003).
31. D. Cavendish, 'Whatever Happened to Anger?', *Daily Telegraph*, 11 January 2006.
32. For example, K. Urban, 'Towards a Theory of Cruel Britannia: Coolness, Cruelty, and the 'Nineties', *New Theatre Quarterly*, vol. 20, no. 4 (2004), 354–72.
33. D. Dromgoole, *The Full Room*, rev. edn (London: Methuen, 2002), p. 300.
34. M. Kustow, *theatre@risk*, rev. edn (London: Methuen, 2001), p. 209.

2
cruel britannia
ken urban

On 18 January 1995, the British theatre world got what it least expected: a kick in the arse, a jab in the eyeball and a punch in the gut. It came not a moment too soon. That night, Jack Tinker and his fellow critics took their seats in the Royal Court Theatre Upstairs for a performance of Sarah Kane's *Blasted*, a play featuring scenes of cannibalism, eye-gouging and anal rape, a play so disturbing one critic thought he would part with his supper. Set in 'a very expensive hotel room in Leeds – the kind [that] is so expensive it could be anywhere in the world', the play documents an abusive relationship between Ian, a dying journalist, and Cate, a naïve young woman.[1] The play's realism is literally blasted apart when a soldier breaks his way into the room and a mortar bomb strikes the hotel. The hotel room becomes a battlefield, Leeds becomes Bosnia. Critics attacked both the play and the author, and the tabloids weighed in on the controversy: 'Rape Play Girl Goes Into Hiding', read a headline in the *Daily Express*. Writers such as Caryl Churchill, Harold Pinter and Edward Bond came to Kane's defence, and there was a growing sense that *Blasted* heralded a shift in the culture of new writing. As a postscript to the controversy, the *Observer* published a short column on *Blasted* the day after the production closed; its final sentence prophetically read, 'I can hardly wait to see what Ms. Kane does next.'[2]

In the months that followed the press night of *Blasted*, the critics' scepticism and hostility gave way to a deluge of praise and catchphrase. Equally shocking plays by Jez Butterworth (*Mojo*) and Mark Ravenhill (*Shopping and Fucking*) followed *Blasted* at the Court and both garnered strong notices. By 1996, critics as diverse as Michael Billington, Aleks Sierz and Benedict Nightingale heralded a new golden age of British drama, naming Kane as one of its leading voices. The early 1990s had seen new writing fade from its prominent place, with directors and collaborative work taking centre stage, but in a few short years, things went from crisis to renaissance, thanks to writers such as Kane, Ravenhill, Butterworth, Joe Penhall and Martin McDonagh, to name but five of the many new writers who emerged during this time. The plays of these writers were shocking, full of drug use, graphic violence and simulated sex, and tended towards formal experimentation, shying away from critical realism, the mainstay of British drama since 1950s naturalism was married to 1960s political theatre during the 1970s and 1980s. Rather than a fringe movement, however, this aesthetic became a dominant sensibility during the 1990s. Ravenhill's *Shopping and Fucking*, a play whose title couldn't even be printed on publicity or written in full on a theatre's marquee, was running in the London's West End before the decade's end. This aggressive theatre became known across the globe as 'in-yer-face'.

These new writers emerged during a particular moment in British cultural history: the reign of 'Cool Britannia', when Tony Blair's New Labour Party rebranded London as the global capital of coolness, and when the British advertising industry heralded the return of Swinging London. Playwright David Edgar noted that theatre had become the 'fifth leg of the new Swinging London', and in-yer-face theatre took its place alongside pop music, fine art, fashion and food as the products of a revitalized Britain.[3] Rather than being co-opted by this rebranding, however, Kane and Ravenhill are part of what I call 'Cruel Britannia', a youth-based counter-politics to the cynicism and opportunism of Cool Britannia. This chapter argues that Kane's generation, rather than turning its back on British theatre's political tradition, as some critics have charged, use cruelty as a means of both reflecting and challenging the despair of contemporary urban life, shaped by global capitalism and cultural uniformity. The cruel displays found in their plays, I would suggest, represent the ethical possibilities of an active nihilism.

coolness and new labour

Tony Blair didn't invent Cool Britannia. By the time New Labour came to power in May 1997, the phenomenon was quickly moving toward its terminal phase. But New Labour, under Blair's stewardship, seized a golden opportunity. As early as 1994, the media began to take notice of the sudden revitalization of British arts and culture. By 1996, the media hype machine had kicked into full gear. When *Newsweek* anoints London the 'coolest city in the world', and Ben and Jerry's launches a new ice cream called 'Cool Britannia', *and* both events occur within seven months of each other, the cultural signposts are impossible to ignore: Swinging London is back. And for a brief span of time, it was. Oasis and Blur, the Spice Girls and Girl Power, Charles Saatchi and the Young British Artists (the YBAs), Alexander McQueen and the clothes of 'Highland Rape': this cocktail of British culture was sold across the globe as Cool Britannia.

Blair not only wanted the world to guzzle this distinctively British brew; he wanted New Labour and Cool Britannia to be synonymous. Blair wrote in 1997 that England was 'leading a creative revolution', much like the Industrial Revolution of the nineteenth century, but rather than exporting the fruits of industry, 'New Britain' was taking America and Europe 'by storm' with '*our* rock music', '*our* musicals'.[4] By aligning itself with this youthful movement, New Labour was able to distinguish itself generationally from both Old Labour and the Tories, and in the process, court younger voters. This act of distinguishing the parties became increasingly important since Blair's Third Way economic policies muddied such differences, leaving the party open to accusations that Blairism amounted to little more than Thatcherism-lite. In truth, what New Labour and the Clintonian Democrats in the USA succeeded in doing was marrying free-market economics and social liberalism, or to put it more succinctly, they created a vision of counter-cultural individualism – the 1960s without the stink of the collective.

To sell a revamped Left, New Labour emphasized a love of youth culture by joining the cosmopolitan rebranding of Britain. England had never been able to shake off completely the image that it is a backwards-looking island of genteel tea parties and frumpy monarchs. By placing 'creative industries' and 'lifestyles' at the centre of a government-sponsored campaign, Blair hoped that Britain's image would change, accentuating a vitality and creativity at odds with any nostalgic visage of Merrie England. Instead, New Labour looked at England as a brand, as a commodity, to be marketed and managed.

Since the mid-1980s, there has been a steady shift from an *economy of production* to a *culture of brands*. Companies no longer see their primary function as selling sneakers, personal computers and mugs of coffee; they now sell a 'lifestyle', a 'business solution', an 'experience'.[5] Rather than a product with which consumers have a utilitarian relationship, a brand forges a connection with consumers by representing ideals and values, giving a faceless commodity an aura of social value and cultural importance, thus fostering 'brand loyalty' on the part of consumers.

New Labour took note of this economic shift and developed a theory of culture to accompany it. In the 1990s, Blair's public vision of England's return to glory was not rooted in economic or geographic expansion, but in the language of advertising and popular culture. Anneke Elwes, then Planning Director for the ad agency BMP, wrote, 'The cultural output of countries is like a large advertising campaign on behalf of that country.'[6] New Labour saw possibilities in fully embracing the consumer culture of American capitalism for specifically British ends, making England's 'cultural output' a brand that could be sold to the world at large. Taking the advice of the ad execs to heart, New Labour wound up, in the words of John Gross, 'elevating the commercial to the ideological', applying 'supermarket language to a whole society'.[7] No longer would England be the land of bad food and crooked teeth; London was now the epicentre of a cultural renaissance, its inhabitants no longer citizens of a fading imperial power, but vital members of a country blazing into the new millennium high on a rush of newness. The fruits of British cosmopolitanism would be an alternative, a rival even, to American culture, which has been the maker and breaker of all things cool since the 1950s, and it could be marketed to the world like the Nike swoosh or the McDonald's Golden Arches. Thus a few weeks following Blair's victory over John Major in the general election, Cultural Secretary Chris Smith proclaimed that Cool Britannia was here to stay.

selling the cool

That in-yer-face drama could become part of a marketable cultural identity may seem odd at first, but the 1990s were all about peddling the provocative. This was the decade when the alternative went mainstream. Thanks to the band Nirvana and the 'grunge' movement that followed them in American pop music, punk rock broke into the mainstream during the 1990s. In the UK, 'indie' was transformed from a philosophy of making music opposed to corporate rock into a mere codeword for 'guitar-based pop'. Being 'indie' or punk no longer meant that you couldn't sign with Sony or have a Top-40 hit. What was once deemed a contradiction in terms – a punk 'hit' on the radio or an 'indie' band on a major label – was now perfectly acceptable. Writer Michael Bracewell calls this phenomenon 'the gentrification of the avant-garde', where 'experimentalism' becomes the 'new conformism'.[8] The 'in-yer-face' playwrights were a 'Britpack' modelled on pop musicians – Ravenhill referred to *Shopping and Fucking* as a 'piece of Brit-pop' and

McDonagh thought theatre should be like 'a really good rock concert' –
and the plays' radical aesthetics, or at least challenging subjects, were
not an anathema to the marketplace, but highly marketable, thanks to
catchy slogans and the allure of the dangerous.

The artistic home for many of the 'in-yer-face' playwrights was the
Royal Court, then run by Stephen Daldry. During his first year as
Artistic Director, Daldry asked, 'Why is [the Court's] audience so fucking middle-aged? We are not telling the right stories.' His solution: 'We
have to listen to the kids.'[9] Daldry worked hard to create a 'cult of
youth', and in light of the controversy surrounding Kane's *Blasted* and
the ensuing ticket sales, he did his best to keep the Court in the press.
Daldry's philosophy can be summed up: do lots of new work, do it for
short runs so that houses are full every night, always invite important
people, and if a play tanks, remember that it will close before the Court
loses too much cash. The result: new plays become events and producing new writing is no longer deemed risky.

Daldry was not alone in his desire to make the theatre cool again.
The Bush's Dominic Dromgoole and the Traverse's Ian Brown were
equally excited by the prospects of a new writing culture which was
unfettered by ideology or mainstream tastes, and both of these theatres
debuted the work of an impressive number of new writers.

While theatre benefited from its new-found cool status, the hoped-
for political union between New Labour and Cool Britannia met a sour
end. There would be no fraternal bond between Tony and the brothers
from Oasis. Nothing is crueller than coolness when it feels exploited by
those in power. Coolness, as Dick Pountain and David Robins succinctly
define it, is 'a permanent state of private rebellion'.[10] Marked by a liber-
tarian attitude of 'whatever', cool is highly individualistic, preferring
the role of detached onlooker to the passionate commitment of politics,
and the 1990s saw this attitude become the 'dominant mindset of
advanced consumer capitalism'.[11] New Labour used 'coolness' as the
means by which to reconcile the basic contradiction of capitalism:
the need to work and the desires of the individual. 'Cool', Pountain and
Robins write, 'dissolve[s] the categories of left and right by decoupling
economic and social assumptions that have been more or less fixed
since the French Revolution.'[12] In the 1990s, being *laissez-faire* in
economics *and* social issues makes complete sense to politicians, but to
voters, the boundaries separating the party of Thatcher from the party
of Harold Wilson and James Callaghan were no longer clear.

The culture of Cool Britannia demonstrates this erosion of Left and
Right. Britpop – the music of bands such as Oasis, The Verve and Blur –

often resembles little more than cultural recycling, the styles and sounds of the 1960s without any oppositional content, and they are often fuelled by a nostalgia for a Swinging London that is most assuredly white. Like the Young British Artists, the 'in-yer-face' play-wrights often embraced coolness and courted celebrity, while their work erased any remaining separation between art and the marketplace. Unsurprisingly, the critics of in-yer-face theatre claimed that it had nothing to say and that the plays verged on being reactionary. Vera Gottlieb, a vocal critic of in-yer-face, thought the 'the plays of the nineties [gave] up any attempt to engage with significant public issues' and summed up the whole of Cool Britannia this way: 'The media and the market "named" something, then "made" something – and subse-quently "claimed" something.'[13] But in the end, plays like *Blasted* and *Shopping and Fucking* are not the same as *Men Behaving Badly* and the Spice Girls' 'philosophy' of Girl Power.

cruelty and nihilism

The defining feature of 1990s drama is its cruelty. While critics were quick to note the prevalence of violence in new writing, understanding the plays of Ravenhill and Kane as simply violent renders them one-dimensional; they become about shock and shock alone. The cruelty of 'in-yer-face' drama shares a kinship with the writings of Antonin Artaud and Georges Bataille, two Surrealists who envisioned the transformative power of cruelty. Cruelty is the wilful causing of pain to others and, often, the self. For Artaud and Bataille, it is the force that violently awakens consciousness to a horror that has remained unseen and unspoken, or wilfully repressed.[14] Bataille and Artaud share a belief that cruelty's unmasking of pain makes a space for ethical possibility, for change, even joy, but such possibility does not allow any escape or metaphysical hope. Cruelty is not redemptive: it scars. Kane's *Blasted*, for instance, brings the horrors of Bosnia to a banal hotel room in Leeds, and James MacDonald's 1995 production of the play was a far cry from the dismissive 'whatever' associated with Cool Britannia.

While coolness is associated with a cynical state of disinterestedness, cruelty is a very different affect. Though it may appear cold, cruelty carries with it the possibility of transformation, but – and this is what disturbs many critics of in-yer-face theatre – it does so without any moral framework or ideological certainty: no redemptive message, no socialist empowerment, no women running off to form a collective. Cruelty's bringing-to-consciousness is a nihilistic one. In fact, *Variety's* critic Matt Wolf initially dubbed writers such as Kane and Ravenhill the 'New Nihilists'.

Nietzsche, in a note from 1887, gives nihilism a handy gloss: 'What does nihilism mean? That the highest values devaluate themselves. The aim is lacking; "why?" finds no answer.'[15] Where one expects to find something – a god, a higher power, a unity, a reason – one instead finds an absence. Since Plato, value is bestowed on material existence through a true, unchanging metaphysical system. This is how morality interprets the world. We judge material existence in relation to an ideal world. But over time comes the realization that the 'true', idealized world is a fabrication, nothing more than a comforting fable. When the comfort of unity, of the higher goal, is revealed to be false, it leaves one with the feeling that the world is valueless, without meaning, and this sense of meaninglessness could *not* be experienced as such had it not been for morality's interpretation of the world in the first case.

Concomitant with Nietzsche's discussion of nihilism are two other influential uses of the term: first, as a pathology, the psychiatric–medical community deems nihilism 'a psychical factor', a symptom of severe depression. This use, first appearing in a medical journal in 1888, is where the pedestrian sense of nihilism as a synonym for 'depressing' or 'hopeless' derives. Second, as a political designation: the Russian Nihilists. The radical anti-Czarists of the 1850s and 60s, made famous in Ivan Turgenev's novel *Fathers and Sons* (1862), these nihilists were the precursors to our modern-day terrorists and anarchists who see destruction as the basis for change.

In this genealogy, nihilism appears as a three-fold concept: it is a *philosophical problem* about value and meaning in a godless world, an *affect* of hopelessness, and an *ethical stance* where change comes from destruction. For Nietzsche, all nihilism can take two forms. In its reactive state, nihilism appears as the most life-hating of enterprises, giving rise to fascist or totalitarian worldviews: because there is nothing, then nothing matters. An active nihilism, on the other hand, is an affirmation of life; suffering becomes a way to extol existence, not denigrate it. The recognition of the valuelessness of the world, while painful, is also the opportunity to create new values, rooted not in metaphysics, but in materiality. Such an affirmation can provide the ground for goodness to emerge from cruelty. But unlike the 'true' good of metaphysics, nihilism's conception of goodness is grounded in the here and now, as that which, to quote Bataille, 'belongs only to the person for whom there is no beyond'.[16] This is nihilism's ethical potential, which opposes the rule of morality. Morality functions as a stand-in for the judgement of God, while ethics can be understood as a set of possibilities that help us assess how we act, but without the aid of any transcendental truth.[17]

In an unfinished note from 1887, Nietzsche sums up nihilism this way: 'It is ambiguous. . . . As active nihilism . . . it can be a sign of strength . . . a violent force of destruction; . . . nihilism could be a good sign'.[18] Nihilism for Nietzsche is always uncertain, always in a struggle between active and reactive forms. Nietzsche's hope was that nihilism would defeat nihilism, that active forces would overpower reactive ones. Nihilism, then, was the final phase before the achieving of pure affirmation, or what he calls in *Ecce Homo* 'the affirmation of annihilating and destroying'.[19] This desire to transform annihilation into affirmation is at the core of this dominant strand of 1990s British theatre known as 'in-yer-face'. These plays do not merely represent suffering on the stage as a way to mirror urban life; instead, the ethical possibilities of cruelty – like those discussed in Nietzsche's philosophy – become the means by which the playwrights of the 1990s critique and intervene in their historical moment.

ravenhill and kane's cruel ethics

The playwrights most associated with in-yer-face were Mark Ravenhill and Sarah Kane. Their two plays, *Shopping and Fucking* and *Phaedra's Love*, were produced at the height of the Cool Britannia phenomenon, and both share an investment in cruelty and nihilism, evidence of a Cruel Britannia existing within the moment of the cool.

First produced by the Royal Court in 1996, Ravenhill's *Shopping and Fucking* was an instant sensation, if not for the title alone. By 1998, the play was running in the West End and more than twenty productions were occurring around the globe, including one featuring film star Philip Seymour Hoffman in New York. The play concerns a group of barely functioning urban dwellers, three of which are named after members of boy band Take That. Its episodic fourteen scenes, more filmic than Brechtian, show a world of rampant consumerism, of Thatcherism writ large. Like the genre of paperback fiction that gives the play its title, *Shopping and Fucking* shows a world reduced to shopping and fucking.

Mark is a drug addict kicked out of rehab for having sex, and he returns to his flat to find Lulu and Robbie, the young woman and man whom he 'bought' at a store, trying to continue their lives without him. Mark has been a father figure for these twenty-nothings and Robbie hopes Mark has come back to reclaim that place in their lives. But as part of his twelve-step programme, Mark is not allowed to 'form an attachment' with another person, and sensing Robbie's love for him, he leaves the flat. Mark then hires Gary, a fourteen-year-old rent boy who left home after being repeatedly raped by his stepfather. Mark falls in love with Gary, but since he is paying Gary, he tells himself, 'it won't mean anything'.[20] Lulu and Robbie try to live a 'normal' life without Mark, but after a botched Ecstasy deal, the pair owes a gangster money. If they cannot repay him, they will pay with their lives. Mark's purchasing of Gary, Lulu and Robbie's vain attempts at earning a living: Ravenhill's characters are overdetermined by economics. But while money is crucial for survival, it has paradoxically robbed the world of its meaning, of its value.

In the play's most extreme moment, Mark realizes that he wants Gary's love, but the boy will never give that because the boy's true desire is for his absent father. But rather than paternal love, Gary's fantasy is to have this absent father sodomize him with a knife. Gary tells Mark:

> I've got this unhappiness. This big sadness swelling like it's gonna burst. I'm sick and I'm never going to be well. . . . I want it over. And there's only one ending. . . . He's got no face in the story. But I want to put a face to him. Your face.[21]

Gary demands that Mark fulfil his wish because Gary is paying him, and as Mark himself has said, when money is exchanged, an act becomes a 'transaction', not an emotional attachment, and therefore, the act 'doesn't actually mean anything'.[22] But Max Stafford-Clark's production, full of neon lights and loud club music, left Gary's fate a mystery: has Mark satisfied the desire and killed Gary, or has it just left Gary wounded, but still alive? Or could Mark even perform such a violent act? Ravenhill and Stafford-Clark refused to reveal the answer.

The melding of coolness and cruelty is clear in Ravenhill's play, where irony gives way to terrifying violence. The play demonstrates nihilism as a *philosophical problem* and as an *affect*. There is a crisis of meaning and it produces a profound state of psychological turmoil. Robbie tells Gary:

> I think a long time ago there were big stories. Stories so big you could live your whole life in them. The Powerful Hands of Gods and Fate. The Journey to Enlightenment. The March of Socialism. But they all died or the world grew up or grew senile or forgot them, so now we're

all making up our own stories. Little stories. It comes out in different ways. . . . It's lonely.[23]

Where something *should* be, there is an absence. Robbie mourns the loss of the metanarratives of God, Enlightenment and Socialism, taking comfort in the 'little stories' we make, though he tells Gary, we are still left feeling 'lonely'. Gary understands this loneliness all too well as he suffers from a nihilistic desire for self-destruction. His 'little story' that he wants to 'put a face to' involves a violent patriarch whose cruelty ends his sadness.

The *ethical* possibilities of nihilism become clearer in Stafford-Clark's production, where a more active nihilism takes shape, allowing an image of the good to emerge as a surprisingly visceral experience. Though it is unclear whether Gary's desire kills him, now that Gary is gone, Mark can again become emotionally attached. The play's final scene shows Mark, Lulu and Robbie feeding each other a microwave dinner, an echo of the play's first scene; unlike the play's opening where Mark vomits up the gift of food, still too sick on heroin to keep anything down, in the final scene, the trio has become a family of sorts, sharing a meal with each other. Stafford-Clark emphasized this development by having identical staging for both moments. But if this is a moment of ethical possibility, it is, of course, a very fraught one, for this kindness would not be possible without Gary's sacrifice. His gift is two-fold: the money that Gary gives Mark allows Robbie and Lulu to pay off the gangster; Gary's literal disappearance allows the threesome to act with kindness toward each other, but these things are only achieved through violence. To put it crudely, the play acknowledges the horror of Gary's wish, while also suggesting that, in this instance, it might be potentially ethical to fuck someone up the arse with a knife.

With *Shopping and Fucking*, Ravenhill and Stafford-Clark created a theatre event that was pure Cool Britannia, a media spectacle where the play was almost upstaged by the publicity of the title and subject matter, and the rave-like atmosphere of the production designed to entice younger viewers. But at the same time, the play's exploration of nihilism connects it to the world of Cruel Britannia, to the possibilities of an active nihilism.

A second example of this Cruel Britannia is *Phaedra's Love*, Sarah Kane's adaptation of Seneca, presented at the intimate Gate Theatre the same year as *Shopping and Fucking*. Kane's play is a series of scenes where Hippolytus is cruel to both the people who love him and those who claim to have his interests at heart. Hippolytus's cruelty, however, comes not out of maliciousness, but out of a desire for complete honesty. But since there is no unsoiled truth in the world, Hippolytus suffers a crippling depression. All this changes when his stepmother Phaedra accuses her stepson of rape and kills herself. Hippolytus did not technically rape Phaedra; Phaedra was obsessively in love with her stepson. Hippolytus, aware of this fact, allowed his stepmother to give him oral sex. But afterwards, he tells Phaedra that her daughter Strophe had more technique, and that she should go see a doctor because he has gonorrhoea. His cruelty, perversely, is ethical. He wants Phaedra to hate him and get over her obsession, but instead, she kills herself and calls Hippolytus a rapist in her suicide letter. Rather than reveal what occurred, an act he fears would render him a fraud, since he feels responsible for Phaedra's death, he allows the charge to go unchallenged, even though it means certain death.

Hippolytus can be seen as an example of Nietzsche's 'last man', who has killed God and substituted himself in God's place. Yet the 'last man' refuses to act, fearing risk and preferring comfort, and as a result, he is trapped by reactive nihilism, by 'a will to nothingness' that makes him hate life. Hippolytus tells the Priest, who begs Hippolytus to confess: 'I can't sin against a God I don't believe in. . . . A non-existent God can't forgive. . . . I've lived by honesty let me die by it. . . . I've chosen my path. I'm fucking doomed.'[24] While Hippolytus has shed himself of metaphysical comfort, he remains enamoured of a romantic notion of truth and is willing to die in its name. His hatred of hypocrisy has led him to hate life and he passively watches events unfold around him. But Hippolytus finally acts in the play's closing moment. Outside the courthouse, he hurls himself into a crowd of angry plebeians who tear him to bits. Just before a vulture feeds off his corpse, Hippolytus looks up at the sky and says, 'If there could have been more moments like this.'[25] The final moment of the play in Kane's production at the Gate was a mess of stage blood and fake intestines.

Hippolytus, by embracing a violent end, finally experiences an embodiment that cures him of his hatred of life. Kane's play and her production use humour to reveal how ridiculous it is that Hippolytus can only experience a life-loving sensation through self-destructing. A lifetime of disembowelments would be, to a rational person at least, hardly a life worth living. Yet that moment of extreme cruelty creates a sensation of pleasure for Hippolytus; he now understands the value of physical existence. The humour of Hippolytus's final line comes from the way it reduces the metaphysical to the bodily. This juxtaposition – between Hippolytus's ethereal longing for 'more moments like this', and a stage covered in bloody limbs and innards – reveals that idealism cannot escape the ultimate truth of the body. For if death is the only thing that gives life meaning, Hippolytus's realization comes too late: you can only die once. Yet in willing his own destruction, Hippolytus is able to defeat reactive nihilism, if just for that brief moment before his death when the vulture descends to make a meal of him. The 'last man' transforms himself into the 'man who wants to perish'.[26] While the first is a reactive personality for Nietzsche, the second wants to overcome, to transform destruction into affirmation.

In the confines of a theatre, the experience of moments like Hippolytus's death or Gary's violent fantasy makes an impact that is tragic in the Nietzschean sense. The tragic, for Nietzsche, is that which turns suffering into an affirmation of life. But this ethos comes about only as a result of a cruelty that strips away any metaphysical fiction, as in Hippolytus's 'joy before death' – to use Bataille's phrase – where destruction affirms. In *The Gay Science*, Nietzsche writes:

> The desire for destruction, change, and becoming can be an expression of an overflowing energy that is pregnant with the future . . . but it can also be the hatred of the ill-constituted, disinherited and underprivileged, who destroy . . . because what exists . . . outrages and provokes them.[27]

A choice therefore exists between an active and reactive nihilism; and in the case of its active form, nihilism serves as the ground in which an ethics can take root. Active nihilism, therefore, is a stage that one passes *through* in order to achieve what Nietzsche variously calls the 'Dionysian', the 'tragic', or the *Übermensch*; and that same, perhaps romantic, desire to move *beyond* while also remaining *bound* to this existence is found in Ravenhill's and Kane's plays: an impossibility that art strives toward even in its impossibility. At the end of *Phaedra's Love*, Hippolytus does shed his nihilism, finding joy in pain, but at the cost of his life.

nihilism as *verwindung*

If this reading of Ravenhill and Kane demonstrates the ethical investments of their work, it is important to note that Cruel Britannia is not politically radical or revolutionary in any traditional sense. It is a counter-politics existing within the moment of Cool Britannia; it is not 'outside' or 'above' the historical moment from which it emerged.

While Cruel Britannia is engaged in the significant ethical issues of the day, its cruelty and nihilism do not espouse any clear or partisan ideology. Rather, the phenomenon that I am calling Cruel Britannia can be understood as the 'twisting' or 'turning away', in a Heideggerian sense, of Cool Britannia.

Heidegger, in his 1955 essay *Über 'die Linie'* (*Concerning 'the Line'*, which he later slightly expanded and re-titled *The Question of Being* in 1960), weighed in on contemporary debates about nihilism in postwar Germany. He was suspicious of the claims of his friend and writer Ernst Jünger that nihilism could be overcome, that Germany could 'cross the line' from its present state of nihilism into a post-nihilistic one.[28] Less optimistic than either Jünger or his philosophical forefather Nietzsche, Heidegger argued that thought could not move beyond or cross that demarcation between our nihilistic world and one that has overcome nihilism. 'Such overcoming [of nihilism] takes place in the area of the restoration of metaphysics', Heidegger writes, and 'the attempt to cross the line [out of 'complete nihilism'] remains inhibited in a conception which belongs in the area of the dominance of the oblivion of Being'; it remains trapped within the prison of Western metaphysics, and to Heidegger, an anti-metaphysician, 'that is a repelling thought'.[29]

Heidegger's advice: 'Instead of wanting to overcome nihilism, we must first try to enter into its *essence*.'[30] In other words, rather than crossing over the line, we must consider the line itself. As Elliot Neaman notes, 'For Heidegger, nihilism is not an external phenomenon, but . . . part of human practices in the modern world.'[31] This move to consider the line itself is what philosopher Simon Critchley characterizes as a 'delineation' of nihilism that 'forbids us . . . the gesture of transgression'.[32] Instead of overcoming, Heidegger advocates 'twisting' or 'turning aside' (*Verwindung*), a 'delineation' of nihilism that transforms but does not wish to transcend. In short, it is Heidegger's call to immanent critique. It is a call to a critical self-awareness that does not eradicate what it calls attention to, because that would do little more than give false comfort; but instead this calling attention to itself makes us reflect on the possibility of change, even if, as in the case of nihilism, such change cannot be imagined as a complete escape or overcoming. The logic of *Verwindung*: change is possible; redemption is not.

Heidegger's concept helps us rethink the paradigm that views art as either radical or compromised, as either outside the mainstream and therefore authentic, or popular and therefore a 'sell- out'. The displays of cruelty found in certain strands of Cool Britannia culture, particularly 'in-yer-face' theatre, perform an immanent critique. The culture of

Cruel Britannia is not oppositional in the sense of being outside 1990s commodity culture. It exists within that phenomenon, but through its invocation of cruelty and its exploration of an active nihilism, it is able to comment upon the historical moment. It works, to borrow Critchley's reading of Heidegger, as a *delineation* of the moment occurring within the moment itself. But that delineation is, by its very nature, anti-transcendental, and therefore cannot be considered truly 'transgressive'.

cruel britannia's legacy: debbie tucker green

Cool Britannia is now over. *Newsweek* rescinded its earlier proclamation that London was 'the world's coolest city' (4 November 1996) by giving an issue less than two years later the headline, 'Uncool Britannia' (6 July 1998). The weekly began to dismantle the mythology it had a hand in creating. Blair and his New Labour government slowly dissociated themselves from their early policies that placed 'creative industries' at the centre of their political vision. By the end of the decade, Blair would no longer be inviting heads of state to concerts by British girl-bands like All Saints. In this decade, Blair made a new friend in George W. Bush, and in the years following the World Trade Center disaster in New York City, the two had more pressing international matters to discuss.

Though it enjoyed a shelf life longer than most fads, the popular phenomenon that defined the 1990s was over before the new millennium had even begun. Concomitant with the death of Cool Britannia was the waning of 'in-yer-face'. Aleks Sierz, in a 2002 article, argues that the suicide of Sarah Kane in February 1999 and the West End success that same year of Conor McPherson's 1997 redemptive play *The Weir* marked the end of the aesthetic he provocatively named.[33] In a 2005 survey of British drama, Sierz laments the new timidity that has followed in the wake of writers such as Kane and Ravenhill. After the period of dramatic experimentation, British new writing, according to Sierz, was again dominated by 'social-realist plays' about 'me and my mates'.[34]

It might be too early to define what characterizes new writing in this decade, but Sierz is right: the diverse and nihilistic energy of 1990s drama is noticeably absent, replaced by a renewed interest in documentary drama (David Hare's *Stuff Happens*, 2004 and the Tricycle Theatre's *Justifying War: Scenes from the Hutton Inquiry*, 2003) and naturalistic plays set in council flats and working-class pubs (Jamie Linley's *Dirty Works*, 2005) and Roy Williams's *Sing Yer Hearts Out for the Lads*). But the state of new writing is not as grim as such an assessment may imply.

Many of the 1990s playwrights continue to explore provocative themes in their current work. Philip Ridley's 2005 play *Mercury Fur*, about a world of amnesiac teens addicted to butterflies and violence, was greeted by a press hysteria that echoed the reception of *Blasted* a decade ago. Mark Ravenhill's latest *The Cut* explores the mechanics of torture. It opened in London at the Donmar Warehouse in February 2006 in a production starring Sir Ian McKellen, better known to some as Gandalf. And in the space of a year, Martin McDonagh had two plays on Broadway: *The Pillowman*, about a writer in a totalitarian state, ran to rave reviews in the summer of 2005; and his bleak comedy about the IRA, *The Lieutenant of Inishmore*, opened on the Great White Way in May 2006. Perhaps unlike the Cool, Cruel Britannia is not dead, but instead has been absorbed into the fabric of British theatrical culture, now a popular export for other theatre centres.

More interesting is how the project of Cruel Britannia, with its co-mingling of coolness and cruelty, of nihilism and ethics, continues to affect new writing. debbie tucker green's *stoning mary*, which premiered at the Royal Court Theatre Downstairs in 2005, is a good example of Cruel Britannia's continuing influence. A language-driven play, *stoning mary* follows three interconnected narratives: a husband and wife fighting over which one of them can have the retroviral prescription that will slow the effects of AIDS; two parents terrified of their son who has become a child soldier in a militia; and a young woman awaiting her public stoning after confessing to the murder of a child soldier who had killed her parents. The play's storylines suggest contemporary Africa: the AIDS crisis of South Africa, the use of child soldiers in the Congo and the Sudan, and the stoning of women in Nigeria. Yet green specifies that 'the play is set in the country where it is performed in', and that 'all characters are white'.[35] In doing this, green's play transposes the crises of South Africa to England in a way similar to Kane's *Blasted*, which brought Bosnia to Leeds. The narratives of *stoning mary* conjure up Africa, while the voices of the characters locate the play specifically in urban Britain, and that combination creates a third space for the audience, a space of dislocation that is neither location and yet both. In a real sense, green's play envisions the consequences of Blair's widely reported statement made to the World Economic Forum in January 2005. There, Blair told his audience, 'If what was happening in Africa today was happening in any other part of the world, there would be such a scandal and clamour that governments would be falling over themselves to act in response.'[36]

That sense of dislocation and alienation is acutely literalized in the

play's characters, who exist in a state of nihilistic despair, most dramatically, the title character who awaits execution for murdering a child
soldier. Mary hopes that her sister has brought good news regarding a
petition that might deliver a stay of execution. The sister stalls, teasing
Mary about her thick glasses, and chides her for her decision to stop
smoking. But the sister eventually reveals the grim truth: instead of the
6,000 signatures needed, Mary received twelve. Where Mary expected
solidarity among women, she found instead that no one stood up for
her. Her lengthy outburst describes how, in the end, it's not that 'the
womanist bitches', 'the feminist bitches', and 'the burn the bra bitches'
wouldn't support a 'bitch'; these 'professional bitches' won't support a
'bitch' like her: someone who can't read or count, someone who is
deemed ugly, and someone who is considered expendable.[37] green's
hypnotic repetition of 'bitch' becomes an accusation, a mantra that
exposes female collectivity to be a myth, for women turn a blind eye
when it comes to someone like Mary. Such a strategy clearly implicates
a Western audience because in crucial ways, we have turned a blind eye
to the problems of Africa, particularly the plight of African women.
Instead of 'sistas' helping each other, there's only a bunch of bitches
that can't be bothered to help out another bitch when she's down.

green's desire to bring the cruelty of the 'developing world' into the
everyday setting of the 'first world' connects her writing to another
young playwright whose shocking first play opened ten years earlier.
That earlier play imagined what would happen if the horrors on the
evening news were brought into Leeds hotel room. The Cruel Britannia
imagined by Kane and Ravenhill in plays like *Blasted*, *Phaedra's Love* and
Shopping and Fucking seeks possibilities in an ethical nihilism. The plays'
cruelty – like the cruelty theorized in the writings of Nietzsche, Artaud
and Bataille – challenges the cynicism and opportunism of the historical
moment. For Kane and Ravenhill, that moment was the reign of Cool
Britannia, when London sought to become the global capital of cool.
While that moment has passed, that ethical project continues in the
work of writers of a new generation, writers like debbie tucker green.

18 January 1995: Press night for *Blasted*.
1 April 2005: *stoning mary* opens.
The Cool is dead. Long live the Cruel.

notes

An earlier version of this piece was published as 'Towards a Theory of Cruel

Britannia: Coolness, Cruelty, and the 'Nineties', in *New Theatre Quarterly*, vol. 20, no. 4 (2004), 354–72. Thanks to Simon Trussler, Elin Diamond, Rebecca D'Monté, Aleks Sierz, Graham Saunders, Dan Rebellato and Janelle Reinelt for their advice and encouragement.

1. S. Kane, *Complete Plays* (London: Methuen, 2001), p. 3.
2. *Observer*, Review of *Blasted*, 5 February 1995.
3. D. Edgar, 'Provocative Acts: British Playwriting in the Post-War Era and Beyond', in D. Edgar (ed.), *State of Play, Issue One: Playwrights on Playwriting* (London: Faber, 1999), pp. 1–34 (p. 28).
4. T. Blair, 'Britain Can Remake It', *Guardian*, 22 July 1997.
5. See N. Klein's *No Logo* (New York: Picador, 2000) for an insightful analysis of the new economy of brands as well as the growing resistance to it.
6. Cited in J. Lloyd, 'Cool Britannia Warms Up', *New Statesman*, 13 March 1998.
7. J. Gross, 'The Emperor of Ice Cream', *New Criterion*, June 1998.
8. M. Bracewell, *When Surface Was Depth: Death by Cappuccino and Other Reflections on Music and Culture in the 1990s* (Cambridge, MA: De Capo, 2002), p. 159.
9. In January 1993, the *Evening Standard* quoted Daldry as saying, 'Why is our audience so f****** middle-aged? We are not telling the right stories . . . We have to listen to the kids. A younger audience – that's vital.' It is unclear if Daldry ever said exactly that, but he carried such sentiments into his time at the Court. Cited in W. Lesser, *A Director Calls* (London: Faber, 1997), p. 90.
10. D. Pountain and D. Robins, *Cool Rules: Anatomy of an Attitude* (London: Reaktion, 2000), p. 19.
11. Ibid., p. 161.
12. Ibid., p. 172.
13. V. Gottlieb, 'Lukewarm Britannia', in V. Gottlieb and C. Chambers (eds), *Theatre in a Cool Climate* (Oxford: Amber Lane, 1999), p. 212, p. 209.
14. See A. Artaud, 'The Theatre and the Plague' and 'Letters on Cruelty', in *The Theatre and Its Double*, trans. M. C. Richards (New York: Grove Press, 1958), pp. 15–32 and pp. 101–4; G. Bataille, 'The Practice of Joy Before Death', in *Visions of Excess: Selected Writings, 1927–1939*, trans. A. Stoekl, with C. R. Lovitt and D. M. Leslie, Jr (Minneapolis, MN: University of Minnesota Press, 1985), pp. 235–9.
15. F. Nietzsche, *The Will to Power*, W. Kaufman and R. J. Hollingdale, eds (New York: Vintage, 1968), p. 9
16. Bataille, 'The Practice of Joy', p. 239.
17. This distinction between morals and ethics comes from philosopher Gilles Deleuze:

    The difference is that morality presents us with a series of constraining rules of a special sort, ones that judge actions and intentions by consider-ing them in relation to transcendent values (this is good, that's bad . . .);

ethics is a set of optional rules that assess what we do, what we say, in relation to the ways of existing involved. *Negotiations*, trans. M. Joughin (New York: Columbia University Press, 1995), p. 100.

See also Deleuze, 'On the Difference between the *Ethics* and a Morality', *Spinoza: Practical Philosophy*, trans. R. Hurley (San Francisco, CA: City Lights, 1988), pp. 17–29.

18. Nietzsche, *The Will to Power*, p. 17, p. 18, p. 69.
19. F. Nietzsche, *Ecce Homo*, in *On the Genealogy of Morals and Ecce Homo*, trans. W. Kaufmann (New York: Vintage, 1967), p. 273. Translation modified.
20. M. Ravenhill, *Plays: 1* (London: Methuen, 2001), p. 25.
21. Ibid., p. 85.
22. Ibid., p. 24.
23. Ibid., p. 66.
24. Kane, *Complete Plays*, p. 95.
25. Ibid., p. 103.
26. See F. Nietzsche, *Thus Spoke Zarathustra: A Book for All and None*, in *The Portable Nietzsche*, ed. and trans. W. Kaufmann (London: Penguin, 1954), pp. 103–439.
27. F. Nietzsche, *The Gay Science*, trans. Walter Kaufmann (New York: Vintage, 1974), p. 329.
28. See E. Jünger, *Über die Linie* (Frankfurt-am-Main: Vittorio Klostermann, 1958).
29. M. Heidegger, *The Question of Being*, trans. W. Kluback and J. T. Wilde (New York: Twayne, 1958), p. 93, p. 101, p. 87.
30. Ibid., p. 103.
31. E.Y. Neaman, *A Dubious Past: Ernst Jünger and the Politics of Literature after Nazism* (Berkeley, CA: University of California Press, 1999), p. 180.
32. S. Critchley, *Very Little . . . Almost Nothing: Death, Philosophy, Literature* (London: Routledge, 1997), p. 17.
33. A. Sierz, 'Still "In-Yer-Face"?: Towards a Critique and a Summation', *New Theatre Quarterly*, vol. 19, no. 1 (2002), 17–24.
34. See A. Sierz, 'Beyond Timidity?: The State of British New Writing', *Performing Arts Journal*, vol. 27, no. 3 (2005), 55–61.
35. d. t. green, *stoning mary* (London: Nick Hern, 2005), p. 2.
36. Cited in L. Elliott, 'Blair urges "Quantum Leap" on Aid to Africa as Debate about Finance Rages', *Guardian*, 28 January 2005.
37. green, *stoning mary*, pp. 61–3.

3
harold pinter and poetic politics

mary luckhurst

double-blindness

On 17 February 1997, the year of Blair's election as Prime Minister, David Hare gave his now famously ill-tempered lecture at the Royal National Theatre, entitled 'A Defence of the New'. A more appropriate title might have been 'A Defence of the Old' as he wondered at the dogged conservatism of artistic directors and new writers:

> If you examine the overall repertory of plays which are currently performed, in London at least, then it seems in its essential mix remarkably little changed from the middle-brow, unambitious selection which attracted so much contempt even forty years ago.[1]

He pointedly did not name Sarah Kane or Mark Ravenhill, expressed surprise at Stephen Daldry and Nicholas Wright's claim that there was a boom in new writing talent as well as astonishment that so many might choose a profession in the 'poor, beleaguered theatre', and was bitterly 'disturbed' that none of these new playwrights had offered 'that kind of rallying point which every theatre-going generation needs to provide a focus for its own wishes and dreams'.[2] Critics had nothing to recommend them, cultural commentators had churned out 'a load of nonsense', and academicism in the theatre was an outright 'threat' to the industry's very survival.[3] But worse was to come: the supposedly new breed of director was positively evil (especially if she was called Deborah Warner), and British theatre was facing a deadly invasion:

> Up until recently in Britain we had happily escaped the wilder excesses of Director's Theatre with all its naff ideas and its opportu-

nities for largely arbitrary pieces of self-advertisement. We liked to regard a play as something which worked in an intended area of meaning . . . – a play was not just a toy with which a director might mess around at will.[4]

Hare, then in his fiftieth year, was suffering a crisis which seemed to be rooted in a fear that theatre might not survive what he thought were ever-increasing attacks on its relevance. He was also losing his great champion and power-base, Richard Eyre, the director of his trilogy *Racing Demon*, *Murmuring Judges* and *The Absence of War*, who stepped down as artistic director of the RNT a few months later. And he was about to fail to write the political play about Palestine commissioned by the Royal Court, producing *Via Dolorosa* instead, a monologue both about his failure as writer and performer and about his profound sense of unease that theatrical realism and traditional purveyors of it like himself might indeed be redundant.[5] Given his self-styled status of national playwright, his loss of faith in the facility of theatre to engage with contemporary issues is odd, especially in the same decade as the trilogy, but though the plays were interesting commentaries on the church, the state and the judiciary, they were essayistic and theatrically unadventurous. They hardly experimented with aesthetic limits in the mode of Kane's *Blasted*, nor touched a chord with younger, less seasoned theatregoers as had Ravenhill's *Shopping and Fucking*. They were also politically pallid.

Yet Hare's perturbation is instructive and his lecture encodes continuing confusions and assumptions about a certain tradition of political theatre in England which has been elevated at the cost of other traditions and experiments – which in turn suffer from a poverty of descriptive and theoretical languages that might chart them with more sophistication. Hare's insistence that the contemporary claim for the New can only be asserted by John Osborne and the generation of (largely socialist) dramatists whom he alleges took their cue from *Look Back in Anger* (which he sees as revolutionary) in the late 1950s and the 1960s, is familiar.[6] His contestation that his own generation is somehow more legitimately engaged with political theatre than others is equally familiar. That authenticity of the Angry Young Man generation is clearly visible, Hare argues, in the clarity of its mission:

To us, the theatre existed mainly for political purposes, to try to dramatise, more tellingly than any piece of reportage, what we took to be the irrevocable decline of our culture. . . . The purpose of the

whole complex ecology of British theatre . . . was in order that new
works might be produced which truly played to the current concerns
and interests of the audience that attended them. The theatre should
not just reflect life. It should represent it.[7]

I don't in this chapter want to expound on the disturbing fiction of *Look
Back in Anger* and the way it has been used as a vehicle to peddle myths
about representativeness and the Royal Court – Dan Rebellato and
Humphrey Carpenter have begun the task of unpicking those particular
knots.[8] Most new and already established playwrights of the 1990s
engaged with contemporary concerns; but given post-imperial crisis and
the break-up of Britain, many new playwrights had difficulty identifying
at all with what Hare phrased 'our culture' – a term that, in this context,
includes and excludes so surgically. And whereas Hare seems nostalgic
for a time when politics meant socialism or capitalism and when the
Royal Court had few competitors for new work, for many in the 1990s
'politics' had become infinitely more complicated not just in terms of
ethnicity, gender and class, but also in terms of the purpose of theatre
and the dilemma of claiming to 'represent' anyone. The Labour government has persistently addressed issues of representation and audience
and new writers have been eagerly served by the revolution in literary
management.[9] The Labour government certainly agree that theatre
should reflect life, and they seem to agree that realism has a dominant
role to play, but what reflecting life might mean, whose life exactly, *how*
it should be represented, and what sort of status the theatre writer should
have in theatre-making, is currently a matter of healthily fervent debate.
What is perplexing about Hare's lecture is his claim that playwrights in
the 1990s, and especially new playwrights, were not writing political
plays – that there is no political theatre in England that cannot be traced
in its heritage back to Osborne. Caryl Churchill and Harold Pinter, the
two great playwrights, are mentioned in passing, but they are not apparently writing political theatre. I am using Hare's lecture as an example of
a certain kind of double-blindness which is all too prevalent – a blindness that recognizes them as indisputable theatrical geniuses, yet cannot
place them in the Osborne tradition, and positions them in categories
apart from political theatre, and as something 'other' than mainstream.
I am by no means suggesting that this started to happen in the 1990s but
examining the work of Pinter in this decade yields much food for
thought. I do not, in the remit of this essay, have the space to interrogate Churchill too: her poetics and politics are very different to Pinter's
and she goes even further in challenging the forms of the political play.

pinter as anomaly

In a thoughtful essay entitled 'Theatre and Politics', Simon Shepherd seeks to plot a course through the relationship between theatre and politics in the 1990s and the preceding decades. Wisely he avoids the term 'political theatre', which has come to stand as a synonym for the dominant form of social-realist drama in the Osborne tradition, and is a term that suggests an unassailable claim to authority in the representation of the political. Using the plays of Arden, Edgar, Brenton, Hare and McGrath from the 1960s to the 1980s as examples, he demonstrates their qualities as chronicle or state-of-the-nation plays with their effort to describe and explain the causes of contemporary life in England: 'The characteristic tone is cynical, the plays confront their art-theatre audience with the demolition of the liberal middle ground.'[10] The agenda of enlightenment is clear, the dramaturgy of these plays containing what Shepherd terms an inherent 'quality of politicality', but 'no guarantee that the play will work politically on its audience'.[11] By comparing these plays with Ravenhill's *Shopping and Fucking* and Roy Williams's *Sing yer Heart Out for the Lads* (2002), Shepherd argues that state-of-the-nation dramaturgies were perceived as a redundant form by new playwrights in the 1990s:

> Their attempt to chronicle social change was seen as naïve. For the more fashionable intellectual now espoused a belief in relativism. Through a selective attention to the work of such philosophers as Foucault and Lyotard, a generation of students thought that they learnt that power was constituted not as a monolith but as a set of micro-negotiations and that attempts to make sense of society through overarching grand narratives were misleading. The explanatory interlocking of private behaviours and larger social changes was associated with unfashionable philosophies such as Marxism, now proved ineffectual by the overthrow of Communist regimes in Eastern Europe. State-of-the-nation dramaturgy no longer seemed credible.
>
> While the political issues themselves remain very similar – the sense of a competitive, greedy, sexploitative, racist society – the instrument for thinking about them changed. For part of the work of this dramaturgy is not so much to imitate the feeling of life in the modern UK as to demonstrate an awareness of how properly to think about this life.[12]

Shepherd's scepticism about the political integrity of new plays in the 1990s is evident from his distrust of what he sees as the 'fashionable intellectual' behind the work. His jibe is most clearly levelled at Ravenhill and the so-called in-yer-face dramatists who reaped the benefits of the sensation surrounding *Blasted* in 1995. Shepherd implies that the ground shifted from political engagement to moral diagnosis and implicitly he regards this stance as a less than admirable retreat. But at the same time, Shepherd also appears to agree with Hare's assertion that there is little that is new about the work of 1990s dramatists. Aleks Sierz, the inventor of in-yer-face theatre, is contradictory about any didactive political agenda among his problematically diverse collection of playwrights, though he contends that the fact that they are 'Thatcher's Children' places them 'in a direct line with the powerful leftist tradition in British theatre'.[13] The logic does not follow, but Sierz, like Hare, positions his in-yer-face pretenders within the establishment canon, implying that they share a political agenda which he seems to regard as antithetical to their preoccupation with representing political anomie and 'questioning of moral norms'.[14] Sierz sees these playwrights as part of a continuum; Shepherd and Hare see them as part of a continuum but find them guilty of sitting on a political fence.

While Hare failed to recognize the fashion for new plays, his implicit anxiety about the reluctance to engage overtly with big- picture political scenarios was not misplaced. But if an aversion to political ideology and the party line is clear in plays of the 1990s, then so is the arrival of a new kind of politically correct consumer-led theatre marketplace with its own ferocious development industry attached to it, one which Nicholas Wright sounded ominous warnings about at the end of the decade:

> The race is on to discover new writers, and any theatrical institution which neglects to do so or scores too many conspicuous misses will soon find itself roundly attacked, with all the consequent damage to its ego and its funding. . . . As management culture seeps into every level of our lives, so will dramaturgical help become more managed and more intrusive.[15]

For art funders, politics came to signify the politics of a constituency rather than a single dominant culture. Writers from every conceivable constituency have been 'developed' in the last ten years, and Kane and Ravenhill were certainly catalysts in the new writing boom in the mainstream, on the fringe, and in community arts projects. Whatever the sinister aspects, the development culture has produced a far greater diversity of playwrights and introduced a very wide range of issues to the stage.[16] The broad brushstroke of the state-of-the-nation play has been replaced with the interrogation of identity politics and for many companies currently working with new media an interrogation of what theatrical representation itself might mean. What commentators agree on is that the in-yer-face pretenders and the majority of new play-wrights who came to the fore in the 1990s were not, for the most part, overtly engaged with questions of governance, nor did they make radi-cal experiments with form. Kane's *Crave* (1998) and *4.48 Psychosis* (2000) are notable exceptions in terms of formal dramaturgy but they also delineate a shift from an exterior to an interior world, and are set at a far remove from external political structures. As David Edgar has said of Kane and her followers, it looks very much as if 'a drama which sought to mourn the end of politics has biodegraded into a drama which demonstrates it'.[17] Against this backdrop Pinter looks more and more anomalous.

the writer and the citizen

Interviewing Pinter in 1989, the American critic Mel Gussow expressed his view that Pinter had 'always been a political playwright': 'One can trace a serious interest in your art in the world of politics from *The Birthday Party* and *The Hothouse* all the way through to *One for the Road* and *Mountain Language*.'[18] Pinter gave a carefully qualified response, arguing that he saw his early plays in the 1950s and 1960s as political in the sense that they were concerned with 'social and political struc-tures', but spoke of a hiatus between the late 1960s and mid-1980s, during which time he wrote plays primarily focused on more private worlds, and gave *Landscape* (1968), *Silence* (1969), *Old Times* (1971) and *Betrayal* (1978) as examples. *One for the Road* and *Mountain Language* certainly marked a phase of more overt engagement with political issues, inspired as they were by human rights abuses in Turkey and by the Kurdish question.[19] No doubt the English critical establishment will begin to reframe Pinter as a political playwright in the wake of his Nobel Prize for Literature and his extraordinary acceptance speech in 2005, but I expect that reframing to be very slow. The Nobel Prize took by surprise only the English, whom, as I have said, regard Pinter as producing work that is not seen as centrally important to the prejudicial construct of political theatre, but as something effete and apart from it.[20]

A major reason for the estranging of Pinter's works from the dominant idea of political theatre has been his refusal of realist conventions, especially in relation to issues of cause and effect. Drew Milne is right to assert that 'political specificity [is] usually associated with political drama', and Pinter has frequently been criticized for refusing to locate his dramas more precisely.[21] Furthermore, realism is associated with certain kinds of play structure which Pinter ultimately rejected.[22] The picture has also been complicated by Pinter's statements about his stance on the relationship between politics and his own theatre writing in the early part of his career.

In a sensitive interrogation of his hostile statements about social-realist writers in the 1960s and 1970s, Austin Quigley has argued that Pinter was wary of a 'reductive social analysis' that emulated the simplistic rhetoric of political institutions and politicians themselves.[23] Pinter's dislike of drama as a crude political vehicle is also well documented:

> I always have hated propaganda plays . . . agit-prop . . . But I still feel that there is room, there is a role somewhere for a work that is not following, pursuing, the normal narrative procedure of the drama, and it's to be found and I'm trying to find it.[24]

Whilst Pinter rejects agit-prop, he believes in directness, as his poems, sketches and short plays demonstrate. But there is also a contradiction between his desire to be direct and his conviction that to be effective, drama must be allusive. In the 1990s this contradiction is manifest in his return to his sketch-writer roots in *The New World Order*, performed at the Royal Court in 1991, and in *Party Time*, a forty-minute play performed at the Almeida Theatre in the same year. Just over seven pages long, *The New World Order* portrays a blackly comic duo, Des and Lionel, who are reminiscent of Goldberg and McGann in *The Birthday Party* and Ben and Gus in *The Dumb Waiter* (1959). The sketch represents the initial stages of the interrogation of an unnamed, blindfolded man seated on a chair, who is referred to only in the third person, is directly addressed twice – through expletives – and taunted both by the prospect of what horrors his interrogators may inflict on his wife and by what form of brutalization will be perpetrated against him in the space of the next half an hour.[25] What Pinter so brilliantly exploits in this skit is the gap between what might be construed from the interrogators' attitudes and linguistic registers as a jovial piss-take and the reality of imminent and extreme physical violence. Des and Lionel speak as if enacting a music-hall gag routine. Lionel sobs with elation as the thought of destroying the blindfolded victim fills him with an overwhelming sense of moral purity and righteousness:

DES: Well, you're right. You're right to feel pure. You know why?
LIONEL: Why?
DES: Because you're keeping the world clean for democracy.
[*They look into each others' eyes.*]
DES: I'm going to shake you by the hand.
[*Des shakes Lionel by the hand. He then gestures to the man in the chair with his thumb.*]
And so will he . . . [*he looks at his watch*] . . . in about thirty-five minutes.[26]

The obscenely flippant punchline underlines both the delusional grandiosity of Lionel's emotional outburst and the shocking expendability of the victim. We do not know with any precision what ideology the interrogators espouse, nor their origin, but their names and their manner suggest that they might act as cyphers for Western democracies that pursue aggressive foreign policies cloaked in a rhetoric proclaiming justice or peace. (The Gulf War was as much on Pinter's mind at this time as his long-term contempt for American invasions of parts of Asia, the Middle East and Latin America.) For Pinter this carefully constructed distance between words and action allows for the operation of policy, whether brutal suppression or genocide; and the fact that the victim is nameless and silent only highlights the absolute authority of his oppressors. It is the political rhetoric itself – the rhetoric that propels the fabrication of those illusions/delusions that perpetrators use to justify their actions – that Pinter sees as the most effective weapon in the pursuit of total domination. It is precisely the rhetorical language-patterns used by politicians that Pinter suspects may be anathema to the kind of drama he is trying to explore. For him a straightforward realist representation of a politician would close down dramatic possibilities. And yet there is, and always has been, a dialectical tension between what Pinter calls his duties as a citizen and his task as an artist, a matter he alludes to in his Nobel speech:

As a citizen I must ask: What is true? What is false?
Truth in drama is forever elusive. You never quite find it but the search for it is compulsive . . . But the real truth is there never is any such thing as one truth to be found in dramatic art. There are many. . . .

Political language as used by politicians, does not venture into any of this territory since the majority of politicians, on the evidence available to us, are interested not in truth but in power and the maintenance of that power. To maintain that power it is essential that people remain in ignorance.[27]

This is a very interesting comment in relation to *Party Time*, where it becomes important to understand that Pinter, who directed the premiere, provided a political backdrop for the actors. Roger Lloyd Pack, directed by Pinter in *One for the Road*, played Fred in *Party Time* and was struck by the director's greater openness about location and character.

With *One for the Road* no one ever raised publicly the question of where it was set. But with *Party Time* we all assumed it was set in England and that the club referred to was a particularly trendy place, with a gym and a swimming pool, in west London. Harold was also much more explicit both in terms of character detail and in how he wanted the play done. He gave everybody a background saying 'You're probably someone in the City' or 'You're someone high up in the Civil Service'. He knew how he wanted everything to be.[28]

Similarly Gawn Grainger, who played Douglas, noted that Pinter always connected *Party Time* to current events taking place during the rehearsal period.[29] This is an unusual example of Pinter operating as 'citizen' in the rehearsal room, providing political contexts for the mysteries of his text.[30]

Set in a luxury flat, *Party Time* focuses on a social gathering of the elite jet-set and explores the chilling 'society of beautifully dressed people', connoisseurs of 'elegance, style, grace, taste'.[31] The party is hosted by Gavin, a man of political influence, who is clearly at the heart of government decision-making. It is Gavin who explains, in confidence, that the 'traffic problems' experienced by his guests that evening are the result of 'a bit of a round-up'.[32] His words are more than euphemistic: another guest has already revealed that 'there's nobody on the streets' and that the army have set up checkpoints and roadblocks.[33] Nor do we miss the irony of his surname, White, with its Pinteresque associations of white-washing and dangerously inverted morality. Douglas, Terry and Fred might be described as henchmen of the regime, all approving of the unseen violence outside, attempting to bury disturbing allusions to Dusty's missing brother Jimmy and censoring the subject of Charlotte's deceased husband, apparently tortured to death. Dusty refuses to observe the codes of silence and repeatedly invokes Jimmy, asking what has become of him, her husband eventually threatening to kill her for her resistance to conformity. At the end of the play Jimmy enters the party unexpectedly. A survivor of horrific torture, and no doubt one of the 'problems' which Gavin indicates will be 'resolved very soon', he delivers a monologue in a poetic register which contrasts in tone and content to the ruthless gaiety of the party-goers and the barely disguised bloodlust of the men:

What am I?

Sometimes a door bangs, I hear voices, then it stops. Everything stops. It all stops. It all closes. It all closes down. It shuts. It all shuts. It shuts down. It shuts. I see nothing at any time any more. I sit sucking the dark.

It's what I have. The dark is my mouth and I suck it. It's the only thing I have. It's mine. It's my own. I suck it.[34]

Politically Jimmy's monologue is very significant in Pinter's *oeuvre* – he is the only character who enunciates what has become of him after excessive torture. Stanley in *The Birthday Party* loses his powers of articulation, like Lamb in *The Hothouse* (1980). In *One for the Road* we simply learn that Victor's son has been killed, while Victor himself uses silence as resistance while his wife Gila slowly loses her sanity in the face of gross physical abuse. In *The New World Order* we know nothing of the state of mind of the blindfolded victim, nor do we know if he is even able to talk, but the interrogators, practised at their art, anticipate that he will be abused into a state of complete abjection. The blindfolded man is the elusive truth of Pinter's drama, the poetic image. Standing 'thinly dressed' in the doorway in a 'burning' light, the other partygoers 'still, in silhouette' around him, Jimmy's physical frailty and disorientation are highlighted with eerie intensity.[35] Like the blindfolded man, Jimmy represents, both physically and verbally, another reality – the reality politicians and their supporters seek to suppress and cover, and the thing that must be denied so that – to return to Pinter's Nobel speech – power can be maintained and 'people remain in ignorance'. Jimmy's curious poetry may not deliver precise memories or a clear-cut narrative of where exactly he has been, who has done this to him and why, but it is still devastatingly eloquent in its dramatic and political import. The very fact that he is able to function at all and that, against all the odds, he has negotiated the situation on the streets and turned up at the party, is an action of extraordinary individual protest. He may have secured his ultimate fate in doing so but his broken presence is an uncontestable truth and flies in the face of all attempts at suppression, of Dame Melissa's determined moral self-blinding, and of Gavin's quiet insistence moments before that: 'the service this country provides will run on normal, secure and legitimate paths' and that 'the ordinary citizen' will 'be allowed to pursue his labours and his leisure in peace'.[36] Jimmy's body and voice are the evidence of an alternative truth and of the world that lies behind the 'door which is never used, is half open', just as the blindfolded man, whom Des sneeringly describes as 'a man of principle', symbolizes all the other resisters beyond the confines of the torture chamber who will need to be overcome.[37]

Both *The New World Order* and *Party Time* are politically engaged in ways that eluded David Hare's definition of 1990s political theatre. They were certainly elusive texts, as Pinter might describe them, but they were far from being texts that a director might 'mess around with at will'. Indeed, they were texts which the writer himself directed, and in the case of *Party Time* in particular the direction itself provided critical political clues. As Pinter demonstrates, politics constitutes both word and action but the relation between the two can be far from straightforward, and it is that sinister gap which continues to obsess him. Though he rhetorically separates the artist from the citizen, the matter, as Pinter very well knows, is more complicated than that: the paradox of art is that it must be both truth and fiction. At the end of his Nobel speech Pinter talks of the writer's duty to 'smash the mirror' to get at the truth, but at the same time he is aware of the moral danger this presents: 'a writer's life is a highly vulnerable, almost naked activity. . . . You find no shelter unless you lie, in which case, it could be argued, you become a politician.' But he is also clear that it must be the responsible citizen who is the conduit for the artistic fiction:

> I believe that despite the enormous odds that exist, unflinching, unswerving fierce intellectual determination, as citizens, to define the real truth of our lives and our societies is a crucial obligation which devolves upon us all. It is, in fact, mandatory.
>
> If such a determination is not embodied in our political vision, we have no hope of restoring what is so nearly lost to us – the dignity of man.[38]

notes

1. D. Hare, 'A Defence of the New', in *Platform Papers 9* (London: Royal National Theatre, 1997), pp. 5–17, p. 11.
2. Ibid., p. 14. Daldry was the Artistic Director at the Royal Court from 1992 to 1996 and Nicholas Wright was Literary Consultant at the RNT.
3. Ibid., pp. 13–16.
4. Ibid., p. 15.
5. See M. Luckhurst, 'Contemporary English Theatre: Why Realism?' in M. Rubik and E. Mettinger-Schartmann (eds), *(Dis)Continuities: Trends and Traditions in Contemporary Theatre and Drama in English* (Trier: Wissenschaftlicher Verlag, 2002), pp. 73–84.
6. Dramatists such as Arnold Wesker, David Edgar, Howard Brenton, David Storey and Edward Bond.
7. Hare, 'A Defence of the New', p. 9.
8. Dan Rebellato, *1956 And All That: The Making of Modern British Drama* (London: Routledge, 1999); Humphrey Carpenter, *The Angry Young Men: A Literary Comedy of the 1950s* (London: Penguin, 2003).
9. M. Luckhurst, *Dramaturgy: A Revolution in Theatre* (Cambridge: Cambridge University Press, 2006).
10. S. Shepherd, 'Theatre and Politics', in L. Marcus and P. Nicholls (eds), *The Cambridge History of Twentieth-Century English Literature* (Cambridge: Cambridge University Press, 2004), pp. 635–52 (p. 637).
11. Ibid., p. 639.
12. Ibid., p. 637.
13. A. Sierz, *In-Yer-Face Theatre. British Drama Today* (London: Faber, 2000), p. 238.
14. Ibid., p. 4.
15. Cited in *State of Play. Issue 1: Playwrights on Playwriting*, D. Edgar, ed. (London: Faber, 1999), pp. 104–8 (p. 106).
16. See Luckhurst, *Dramaturgy*, pp. 200–267.
17. D. Edgar, 'Unsteady States: Theories of Contemporary Writing', *Contemporary Theatre Review*, vol. 5, no. 3 (2005), 297–308 (302).
18. M. Gussow, *Conversations with Pinter* (London: Nick Hern, 1994), p. 81.
19. Ibid., p. 82; M. Billington, *The Life and Work of Harold Pinter* (London: Faber, 1996), pp. 309–13.
20. The same is true for Caryl Churchill in this decade with her plays *Mad Forest* (1990) and *Far Away* (2000): both are highly political and eschew realism in favour of poetic registers and poetic images, though Churchill's forms and registers are very different to Pinter's.
21. D. Milne, 'Pinter's Sexual Politics', in P. Raby (ed.), *The Cambridge Companion to Harold Pinter* (Cambridge: Cambridge University Press, 2001), pp. 195–211 (p. 197).
22. L. Gordon (ed.), *Pinter at 70: A Casebook* (London: Routledge, 2001), p. 148.

23. A. Quigley, 'Pinter, Politics and Postmodernism', in *The Cambridge Companion to Harold Pinter*, pp. 7–27 (p. 9).

24. Gordon, *Pinter at 70*, p. 150.

25. Torture, as I have argued elsewhere, is a major and life-long preoccupation for Pinter, and as ever he represents it purely verbally, leaving the physical atrocities to the spectator's imagination. See M. Luckhurst, 'Torture in the Plays of Harold Pinter', in M. Luckhurst (ed.), *A Companion to Modern British and Irish Drama: 1880–2005* (Oxford: Blackwell, 2006), pp. 353–70.

26. H. Pinter, *Plays: 4* (London: Faber, 1993), pp. 277–8.

27. H. Pinter, 'Nobel Prize Acceptance Speech', *Guardian*, 8 December 2005, pp. 9–10.

28. Cited in Billington, *The Life and Work of Harold Pinter*, p. 333.

29. Ibid.

30. Pinter, like Beckett, is generally associated with a reluctance to provide context and character exposition when directing. See interview with I. Varma in M. Luckhurst (ed.), *On Acting* (London: Faber, 2001), pp. 147–8.

31. H. Pinter, *Plays: 4*, p. 299.

32. Ibid., p. 313.

33. Ibid., p. 286.

34. Ibid., p. 313; pp. 313–14.

35. Ibid., p. 313.

36. Ibid.

37. Pinter specifies that there are two doors, ibid., p. 281; ibid., p. 276.

38. Pinter, 'Nobel Prize Acceptance Speech', p. 13.

part ii
thatcherism and
(post-)feminism

introduction to part ii

Writing in 1999, the playwright David Edgar argued that if the 1980s belonged to the so-called 'third wave' of predominantly female dramatists, and with it plays that addressed a feminist politics, then the 1990s belonged to a group of writers whose work 'address[ed] masculinity and its discontents as demonstrably as the plays of the early 1960s addressed class, and those of the 1970s the failures of social democracy'.[1] By the 1990s women playwrights from this generation felt a sense of exclusion. Timberlake Wertenbaker, for instance, saw this period of 'male violence [and] homoerotica' as both restrictive and reactionary, while Charlotte Keatley saw the drama to be both empty and disturbing, with Jez Butterworth's *Mojo* as 'yet again another play about a bunch of men doing nothing much'.[2]

The 1990s for women's drama provides a notable paradox in that, while the dominant playwright of the period was Sarah Kane, her work did not seem directly to address feminist politics, and she has been quoted as saying, 'I have no responsibility as a woman writer because I don't believe there's such a thing.'[3] In one respect this situation was analogous to British politics throughout the 1980s, where the activism and resistance of feminism took place under a woman prime minister who was virulently dismissive of feminism in general. The three chapters in this section go some way to presenting an alternative discourse and reminder that female voices in 1990s theatre had not been dissipated under a shower of testosterone.

As has been mentiond, the political events of the 1980s very much shaped the culture of the 1990s. The effects of Thatcherism on theatre have been well charted in work such as John Bull's *Stage Right: Crisis and Recovery in British Contemporary Mainstream Theatre* and Dominic Shellard's *British Theatre Since the War*. Rebecca D'Monté's chapter, 'Thatcher's children: alienation and anomie in the plays of Judy Upton', takes this playwright's work as a case study to explore the lingering effects of Thatcherite politics on the small seaside communites that form the locus for Upton during the latter part of the 1990s.

Klaus Peter Müller, while making a case for Upton's play's being political, at the same time maintains that she is not truly a political playwright as nowhere in her work 'suggests any possibility for change': in its place is merely 'a strong sense of frustration that life is not as splendid as it is usually presented in the jargons of politics or advertizing'.[4] D'Monté's chapter provides a historical framework in which she argues that the election of Mrs Thatcher in 1979 and the successive Conservative administrations lasting until 1997 had a profound effect: not just upon the work of Upton, but on the in-yer-face playwrights in general; she also maintains that Gottlieb's and Müller's definitions of British political theatre, rooted in the events of 1968 and continuing until the mid-1970s, had long since become redundant for Upton's generation. Ken Urban succinctly characterizes the features associated with these self-consciously 'political' plays:

> [This] school of critical realism approaches political subjects with a journalistic eye . . . For an issue to be presented properly within this dominant theatrical model, one side must be confronted with its opposing viewpoint and through conversation lies the hope that dialectical reconciliation may be achieved. An individual character serves as a stand-in for a political ideology, a symbolic 'talking head', and the dramatic form best suited to this forum of ideas was, hands down, a realistic narrative.[5]

While dramatists such as Edgar and Hare continued to write successfully and develop on variations of this model well into the 1990s and beyond, D'Monté contests that the legacy of Thatcherism no longer made this a viable option for Upton and her generation, with a rejection of political party allegiance and reluctance to submit to a form of ideology. While Upton's work frequently shows its protagonists trapped and unable to leave the seaside towns that form the backdrop to much of her work, she maintains that while 'unable to posit an agenda for transformation or revolution . . . this in itself becomes a political message'.

With regard to black women's writing in the 1990s, there was more of an optimistic sense at the beginning of the decade in that the gains – paradoxically made during the height of the Thatcherite 1980s – would be maintained and built upon during the remainder of the decade. Writing in 1995, Mary Karen Dahl enthusiastically commented that 'energetic development continues despite deep cuts in public funding'; empirical signs such as the launch of new anthologies on black women's plays and a corresponding increase in academic writing on the subject demonstrated some truth behind this enthusiastic forecast.[6]

However, Lynette Goddard's chapter,'Middle-class aspirations and black women's mental (ill) health in Zindika's *Leonora's Dance*, and Bonnie Greer's *Munda Negra* and *Dancing on Blackwater*', maintains that 'the 1990s shows a depressing lack of momentum for black women's theatre in Britain'. Certainly with the advent of Cool Britannia, the previously favourable climate for black women's drama seemed to dissipate rapidly. Whereas Brit art represented black artists such as Isaac Julien, Steve McQueen, Chris Ofili and Yinka Shoribane, in theatre it was only the Asian dramatist Ayub Khan-Din's *East is East* (1996), and its subsequent film adaptation, that enjoyed anything like mainstream success in the 1990s. Despite the West Yorkshire Playhouse presenting two seasons devoted to black writing during the autumn of 1996/97, audiences were poor and seemed to mark a decline in the development of black British writing that had emerged and grown throughout the 1970s and 1980s.

This anomalous situation was even more pronounced within the offshoot movement in Cool Britannia termed Britpop. Here (with the notable exception of British/Asian combo Cornershop), new beat groups such as Oasis and Blur promoted themselves not only through a quintessentially 'English' sensibility, but one that also seemed to ignore demographic changes brought about by postwar immigration. Jon Savage called this disparity to account at the time:

> Welcome to the curiously hermetic, over-mediated world of Britpop ... Within a multicultural metropolis, where the dominant sounds are swingbeat, ragga or jungle, Britpop is a synthesis of white styles with any black influence bled out.[7]

As Savage also observes, a paradox emerged in that the period of Cool Britannia was marked by simultaneous developments in black electronic dance music; although largely ignored at the time, its overall dissemination, accompanied by black 'street' fashion and language, has arguably made the deepest inroads into mainstream British culture. In terms of theatre in the 1990s, Winsome Pinnock observes that this process was already under way with several plays associated with in-yer-face theatre, such as Rebecca Prichard's *Yard Gal*, Che Walker's *Been so Long* and David Eldridge's *Serving it Up*, which appropriated the rhythms and discourse of black speech where 'the characters, both white black, rich and poor, share a common street patois'.[8]

Klaus Peter Müller argues that part of the reason for a general decline in British black and Asian playwriting during the 1990s came about due to established figures in the 1980s such as Hanif Kureishi and Winsome Pinnock undergoing a change of emphasis and tone in their writing – moving away from overtly political treatments of ethnicity to an exploration of 'private worlds', in plays such as *Sleep With Me* (1999) and *Water* (2001).[9] Yet this reading proves unsatisfactory if one also considers that many of the most successful plays of the 1990s such as Conor McPherson's *The Weir*, Patrick Marber's *Closer* and Sarah Kane's *Crave* (1998), equally revolved around such privately constructed worlds. While Goddard sees this changing emphasis 'on the interpersonal relationships between characters in urban multifarious (multicultural, multiracial, multifaith) communities', yielding more success for millennial black women dramatists (such as Doña Daley and debbie tucker green), the more problematic state of affairs in the 1990s might be attributed in part to the ongoing expectations that black and Asian writers should adopt a heightened politicized engagement towards self-identity. Failure to engage with the expectations set down by artistic directors, audiences and critics risked alienation. Bernadine Evaristo also believes that black audiences themselves have increasingly turned away from political drama to the less demanding concerns of popular imported Caribbean comedies, with their mix of raucous humour and music.[10]

Goddard argues that during the 1990s black women dramatists started to move towards work that could 'account for the experiences of upwardly mobile and middle-class black women in the UK', yet these plays also demonstrated a form of *psychomachia* for their protagonists as they struggled with the dichotomy produced through 'their quest for individual success, acquired in Eurocentric terms of wealth and social status'.

The theme of mental illness was a popular one during the period, with plays such as Joe Penhall's *Some Voices* (1994) and *Blue/Orange* (2000) (notably about black male schizophrenia) as well as Sarah Kane's last play *4.48 Psychosis*. However, such drama (with the notable exception of *Blue/Orange*) shows the effects of mental illness on both the individual and those around them; in contrast, Goddard argues that the plight of women in the plays by Zindika and Bonnie Greer 'extend ideas of black women's cultural identity as a complex negotiation between lives in Britain and African-Caribbean heritages and account for the longer-term psychological effects of migration on people separated from their cultural roots'.

Near the end of Penhall's *Blue/Orange* the psychiatrist Bruce goads his black patient Christopher, telling him that his account of being victimized by white neighbours is delusional: 'They're black! All your neighbours are. It's a *Black Neighbourhood*. You you you *moron*. You stupid fool. Are you *retarded?*'[11] However, it is Bruce's callous and easy dismissal of Chris's illness as arising from societal forces that is shown to be the principal cause of illness in Zindika's and Greer's plays. Here Goddard argues that 'representations of mixed race and/or middle-class black female characters . . . allude to fragmentations of cultural identity as class consciousness collides with race and gender in nineties Britain'.

While Goddard notes an improvement in the fortunes of millennial black playwriting, with the emergence of names such as Roy Williams, Kwame Kwei-Armah and debbie tucker green, even here gender disparity still appears to exist. The success of plays such as *Fallout* (2003) and *Elmina's Kitchen* (2003) has seen subsequent work by Williams and Kwei-Armah premiered on the main stages of the Royal Court and National Theatre respectively. In contrast, despite the critical acclaim of plays such as *dirty butterfly* (2003), tucker green's work (with the exception of *stoning mary* in 2005), is still largely confined to studio spaces such as the Soho and Theatre Upstairs at the Royal Court.

Women's writing and performance in the 1990s is also the subject of Elaine Aston's 'A good night out, for the girls'. Aston, like Goddard, also concurs that women's writing underwent a process fragmentation and marginalization during the 1990s; yet Aston notes that in one sphere of performance women literally took centre stage – namely the realm of popular commercial theatre. Although generally regarded with suspicion and largely ignored to date by feminist theatre scholarship, Aston contests that her three case studies – Eve Ensler's *The Vagina Monologues* (1999), Catherine Johnson's *Shang-a-Lang* (1998) and *Mamma Mia!* (1999), and Jenny Eclair's stand-up comedy show *Prozac and Tantrums* (1995) – not only encompass a wide range of performance styles, but also offer their female audiences rewarding and empowering experiences.

Ensler's *The Vagina Monologues* is a rare example from an off-Broadway show making the cross-over to commercial theatre. However, its inception at the fringes of theatrical culture informs Aston's observation that *The Vagina Monologues* 'offers a curious mix of the pleasurable and the painful', whereby popular forms such as stand-up comedy and audience participation are interspersed with confessional monologues such as 'my vagina was my village', which discusses the policy of mass rape that took place against Bosnian Muslim women during the civil war in the former Yugoslavia.

Catherine Johnson's *Shang-a-Lang* also started out at another fringe venue – London's Bush Theatre. However, despite the success of a national tour in the autumn of 1999, the popularity of *Shang-a-Lang* was later far eclipsed in what Dominic Dromgoole describes as 'the equivalent of winning the lottery', when Johnson wrote the book that accompanied the phenomenal global success of the Abba-inspired musical *Mamma Mia!*[12] In Jenny Eclair's show *Prozac and Tantrums*, Aston argues that the popular form of stand-up comedy is used to attack constructions of the 'Beauty Myth' and the domestic feminine in a confrontational performance style that she terms a 'shock-fest of cellulite-ridden comedy'. The persona Eclair's adopts, described by Aston as 'teddy-boy-punk-feminine', gives licence to indulge 'in an excess of swearing, drinking and comic stories of outrageously promiscuous behaviour'. In this way Aston believes that Eclair's show invites its largely female audience 'to take pleasure from the opportunities it offers for the cathartic release of her Rabelaisian body that farts, vomits, shits and overindulges in sex, booze and cigarettes'.

Jenny Eclair's observation, 'there's nothing more scary than a bunch of 40-year-old women on the razz', forms the basis of Aston's advocacy of what she calls a 'white trash feminine', which through its embrace of the excessive and parodic can act as a liberating force for female audiences who experience Eclair's and Johnson's work *en masse*. While acknowledging that *The Vagina Monologues* provides evidence of a continuum, stretching back to the work of experimental feminist theatre in the 1970s, Aston argues that out of her case studies Ensler's play might be the least successful due to 'its inability to pay attention to the local difficulties with and struggles against violence and oppression', and 'a problematic belief in the power of the individual (woman) to speak out and overcome systems that threaten to or do indeed abuse and oppress her'.

Surprisingly, it is the work of Catherine Johnson and Jenny Eclair that Aston believes not only to be the most effective in providing 'a good night out', but also in refiguring negative connotations associated with '"trash" behaviour in the spirit of celebration, not condemnation'. This advocacy of a 'monstrous feminine' not only reclaims the misogynist overtones of John Knox's infamous *First Blast of the Trumpet against the Monstrous Regiment of Women* (1558), in a spirit of female solidarity, but at the same time performs a similar act of reclamation against the moral panic stirred up by its 1990s counterpart, 'the ladette'.

The recent success of the stage show *Grumpy Old Women Live* serves as a practical illustration of Aston's ideas. Originally, a spin-off television series to *Grumpy Old Men* (2003–), each programme features a selection of middle-aged malcontents in the public eye who are given licence to rail at the petty injustices and annoyances that a given aspect of contemporary life presents. However, the spin-off book and stage show (again with Jenny Eclair as co-writer and performer) perhaps serve to illustrate that female experiences have been more popular with audiences. Following the success of a national tour in autumn 2005, culminating in a West End residency, *Grumpy Old Women Live* is still touring the UK in 2007. Jenny Eclair describes the show as 'the antidote to the *Vagina Monologues*', and Kathryn Flett's description of the almost-all-female audience at a performance in the Lancashire town of Bolton bears close similarities with Aston's impressions of the matinee audience at *Mamma Mia!*: 'They are here in their twenties, accompanied by their mothers, posses of thirty- and forty-somethings on girls-nights-out, grey-coiffered wearers of denims with stretch waistbands seated next to Botoxed ladies with expensive-looking highlights and Mulberry handbags, in short a gobsmackingly impressive cross-section of Greater Mancunian womanhood'.[13]

Flett describes the show as 'empowering', an aspect which its co-creator (and producer of the television series) Judith Holder attributes to the fact that previously 'middle-aged women didn't really have a voice'.[14] The success of *Grumpy Old Women Live* also illustrates Aston's view that such shows offer both pleasure and catharsis: they also venture into the realms of the political by attempting to 'articulate the desire for women's sexual and familial lives to change'.

Aston's chapter also does much to challenge the obsession 'Cool Britannia' had with youth culture. Winsome Pinnock observes that its various cultural manifestations such as Brit art and in-yer-face theatre were 'led by the desires of the young', and while dramatists such as Kane and Ravenhill were keen to acknowledge the influence of older writers (particularly the work of Harold Pinter and Edward Bond), plays by contemporaries such as Nick Grosso's *Peaches*, Helen Blakeman's *Caravan* (1997) and Che Walker's *Been so Long* seemed to be aimed exclusively at younger audiences.[15] The themes they explored – sex, relationships, hedonism and consumerism – made them *seem* very contemporary. Yet paradoxically, below the raffishness and bravado a more conservative bent emerged. David Ian Rabey points out that in contrast to the more abstract forms used by older dramatists such as Pinter and Bond, who explored the interface between both social realism and private worlds, much in-yer-face theatre was based around a form of domestic social realism, often found in soap opera.[16]

notes

1. D. Edgar, *Issue 1: Playwrights on Playwriting* (London: Faber, 1999), pp. 27–8.
2. H. Stephenson, and N. Langridge, *Rage and Reason: Women Playwrights on Playwriting* (London: Methuen 1997), p. 73.
3. Ibid., p. 134.
4. K. P. Müller, 'Political Plays in England in the 1990s', in B. Reitz and M. Berninger (eds), *British Drama of the 1990s* (Heidelberg: Universitätsverlag Carl Winter, 2002), pp. 15–36 (p. 27).
5. K. Urban, '"An Ethics of Catastrophe": The Theatre of Sarah Kane', *Performing Arts Journal*, no. 69 (2001), 36–46 (39).
6. M. K. Dahl, 'Postcolonial British Theatre': Black Voices at the Center', in J. E. Gainor (ed.), *Imperialism and Theatre: Essays on World Theatre, Drama and Performance* (London: Routledge, 1995), pp. 38–55 (p. 39).
7. Cited in S. Borthwick and R. Moy, *Popular Music Genres* (Edinburgh: Edinburgh University Press, 2004), p. 188.
8. W. Pinnock, 'Breaking Down the Door', in C. Chambers and V. Gottlieb (eds), *Theatre in a Cool Climate* (Oxford: Amber Lane Press, 1999), pp. 27–38 (p. 29).
9. Müller, 'Political Plays', p. 19.
10. B. Evaristo, 'Black Women in Theatre', in K. George (ed.), *Six Plays by Black and Asian Women Writers* (London: Aurora Metro Press, 1993), pp. 5–7.
11. J. Penhall, *Blue/Orange* (London: Methuen, 2000), p. 106.
12. D. Dromgoole, *The Full Room: An A–Z of Contemporary Playwriting* (London: Methuen, 2000, repr. 2002), p. 153.
13. D. Maxwell, 'Why so Grumpy Ladies? Your Tour's a Hot Ticket', *The Times*, 8 April 2006.
14. K. Flett, 'We're Old, Grumpy and Proud', *Observer Review*, 13 November 2005.
15. Pinnock, 'Breaking Down the Door', p. 27.
16. D. Rabey, *English Drama Since 1940* (Edinburgh: Longman, 2003), p. 193.

4
thatcher's children: alienation and anomie in the plays of judy upton
rebecca d'monté

As for other dramatists associated with the 'new wave' in the 1990s, Judy Upton's most formative years took place during Margaret Thatcher's governments. In 1979, when Thatcher became Britain's first female prime minister, Upton was 13; at the end of her reign, Upton was 24. The Tory Party held on to power for seven more years, under the leadership of John Major, although Thatcher's influence dominated British politics until New Labour's landslide victory in 1997, and some would argue even beyond.[1] Thatcherite policies affected the theatre, not just in the gradual erosion of subsidization and implementation of the market-driven economy, but also in the subject matter and use of dramatic form. Whilst it was initially suggested that many of the playwrights of the 1990s – especially the in-yer-face dramatists – were essentially apolitical, a fresh look at Judy Upton's work shows her marked concern with the effects of Conservative rule, and her plays can be seen to provide a coruscating denunciation of the political strategies of the 1980s and 1990s. Moreover, whilst Upton can quite rightly be classified as one of 'Thatcher's children', the importance of her role as a *female* dramatist also needs to be further addressed, something that is not possible when viewing her solely as part of the in-yer-face generation.[2]

thatcherism and theatre

This is not the place to explore the way in which Thatcherism came into being. Suffice to say, this 'ism' (the only one attached to a British prime minister) was an attempt by several right-wing thinkers to forge a coherent policy based on monetarism.[3] The welfare state started to be dismantled in order to loosen what was termed the dependency culture – the 1983 manifesto posited that the state should do less and the individual should do more – and there was no longer a belief in full employment.[4] More treacherously, 'it had become thinkable' that the homeless and jobless 'might be at least in part responsible for their plight, that they had perhaps failed or even refused to look for other possibilities', an ethos that Alan Bleasdale challenged in his ground-breaking television drama *Boys from the Blackstuff* (1982).[5] Living standards did rise for a significant proportion of the country, but this type of 'popular capitalism' also deepened the disparity between rich and poor. Perhaps Thatcher's most controversial statement came when asked her views on society. She parried: 'What society? . . . We don't belong to society, we are all just individuals, doing the best we can for ourselves.'[6] This belief in self-serving individualism rather than caring collectivism came to stand for the Thatcherite, and indeed Reaganite, years, particularly when allied to notions of the free market. The rise in unemployment and reduced job opportunities, even given the many 'youth schemes' put into place during the 1980s, had the effect, therefore, of dividing the country into one of 'haves' and 'have-nots'.

By necessity, the many changes wrought to society by Thatcherism also helped to change the tenor of British theatre. During the 1970s, traditionally seen as the high point of British political drama, there had been a great increase in alternative theatre companies, engendered by political activity during the previous decade – an era, incidentally, seen by Thatcherite followers as the begetter of social ills in the 1980s. Subsidized touring companies such as Cheek by Jowl, Out of Joint, 7:84, and Hull Truck produced exciting and innovative drama that often challenged the status quo. The focus was upon the competing discourses of capitalism, socialism and communism, relayed in the work of a clutch of prominent playwrights: John McGrath, Trevor Griffiths, David Hare, Howard Brenton, David Edgar and Caryl Churchill. Whilst the technique and form may have varied, there was a commonality of view; an acute disappointment about the inability to create a broadly socialist country based on egalitarian principles established during the 1945–51 Labour government. The events of the 1970s – union demands, strikes, increasing welfare demands – made this seem even further from being implemented. With his political views firmly rooted in the collectivism of the 1960s, Hare believed in 'a committed theatre movement', where he could be 'part of a struggle for something more important and larger than my own work'. However, by the end of the

1970s, with the power structures undergoing radical change, he found himself unable to satisfy either political side:

> the right loathed me because they claimed I was doing the very thing of which the left was meanwhile claiming I wasn't doing enough: turning the theatre from a place of harmless, corroborative entertainment into a boring dissenters' pulpit. Inevitably, one side wanted me to preach more; the other less.[7]

Under Thatcher, theatre companies were financially and artistically discouraged, and the arts were increasingly required to prove themselves as 'a successful industry that offered a good return on public investment'.[8] Funding was subtly used as a form of censorship: companies deploying political content that criticized governmental policy ran the risk of subsidy cuts during the next financial year. Some playwrights, though, tackled Thatcherism head-on, as in Churchill's *Top Girls* (1982), which brought together issues of historical and cultural gender stereotyping with a 'celebration' of the Iron Lady's policies through her fictional admirer, Marlene. The play is a 'socialist-critique of bourgeois-feminist values', which allows for a scathing attack upon a society that values power, ambition and the creation of wealth, but rejects personal relationships, as expressed in that between Marlene's daughter, Angie, and working-class sister, Joyce.[9] David Hare's *The Secret Rapture* (1988) also plays off pro- and anti-Thatcherite characters against one another, once more in terms of two sisters. Isobel works for a design company, and is eventually ousted from her business by Marion, a junior Conservative MP, who describes the new era: 'The gloves are off. That's what's great. That's what's exciting. It's a new age. Fight to the death.'[10] Those who are unable to 'fight' go under, like Isobel, and Churchill's Angie and Joyce. The link between the personal and the political persists in Griffiths's *Thatcher's Children* (1993), which provided 'a panoramic polemic on the effects of fourteen years of extreme conservative rule'.[11] Unlike in his earlier plays, he emphasizes here the individual experience, or the 'politics of feeling', by following a group of schoolchildren who find themselves living out the sweeping changes put forward during the 1980s, with some achieving financial success, at the expense of their moral and personal lives, whilst others struggle to survive.[12] Plays such as Churchill's updating of a city comedy, *Serious Money* (1987), went further in looking at political structures of society. This concerned itself with the Tory deregularization of the City, where old financial controls were abolished and replaced by a system that encouraged aggressive individualism, but also presaged the makeover culture and spin of New Labour. *Pravda* (1985), Howard Brenton and David Hare's epic play, portrays a Robert Maxwell-like newspaper magnate, whose management style emulated that of the government's pursuit of capitalism by any means. Truth becomes yet another commodity to be exploited, as in the ironic titular reference to the Russian state-owned newspaper. D. Keith Peacock suggests that 'The play's action, while appearing somewhat simplistic, may in fact be seen as an accurate representation of the impotence felt by the Left in the face of Thatcherism.'[13] The theatre was beginning to founder under the weight of satirical critiques of the government and a debate over what tactics the Left should now employ.

thatcher's children

Ironically, the government cutbacks and free-market policies brought forward a new group of playwrights in the 1990s, showcased by a series of experimental seasons at fringe theatres in London, Edinburgh and Glasgow. Judy Upton was named one of the ten best dramatists in 1996, with others including Jez Butterworth, Nick Grosso, Sarah Kane, Martin McDonagh and Joe Penhall.[14] These were young playwrights, says Benedict Nightingale, whose work has premiered at one of the London fringe theatres: 'Each of them has a distinctive voice, although behind the diversity there are similarities of style and content. Together they express the feelings of a generation formed by the 1980s.'[15]

On another occasion, he noted that 'The majority of "In-yer-Face playwrights" are vastly entertaining – yet they radiate moral concern. They are Mrs Thatcher's disorientated children.'[16] This view is echoed by Aleks Sierz, who imagines those born in 1970 (only four years younger than Upton) as 'Thatcher's Children'.[17] Their worldview, he suggests, has been shaped by being brought up under a Tory govern-ment that lasted eighteen years, and this in turn generates the general feeling of anomie, alienation and aggression underpinning otherwise dissimilar plays like Upton's *Ashes and Sand* (1994), Ravenhill's *Shopping and Fucking*, and David Eldridge's *Serving it Up* (1996). Here there is an interrogation of the Prime Minister's assertion that there is no such thing as society, particularly through the way in which 'consumers' are themselves 'consumed' in a world governed by market forces. Authority figures are corrupt, social relationships have broken down, and the country's youth have found that their disillusionment has increasingly hardened into anger or dissipated into apathy. These playwrights appear to eschew Howard Brenton's socialist utopianism and David

Hare's political concern. Rather, they present a theatre of crisis, in which political questions can be asked, but not necessarily answered. Whilst the appearance of in-yer-face drama cannot be put down solely to a denunciation of all-things Thatcherite – for example, the so-called crisis of masculinity had, in part, been caused by the fracturing of gender roles in a post-feminist world – the concentration upon a mainly youthful 'underclass' mirrors exactly the age group of those brought up under Tory rule.

As a playwright, Judy Upton has been subsumed into this group of Thatcher's generation, and, out of all the playwrights considered under the epithet of 'in-yer-face', she is the one to expand most fully upon the consequences of Thatcherism. The disparity between politicians' promises and the reality experienced by the young was most explicitly expressed by Upton when she commented on the genesis of *Ashes and Sand* in the spring of 1994: 'The play just poured out. I was angry for myself and my friends, dragged kicking and screaming through a hell-hole of a comprehensive school, to end up living lives that fell short of our dreams.'[18]

Yet the importance of Upton's work goes beyond this. Sarah Hemming noted that the Bush Theatre championed the 'bad boys', with playwrights such as Tracy Letts and Nick Ward, 'while the Royal Court's Theatre Upstairs hosts the bad girls Judy Upton and Sarah Kane'.[19] Certainly, we can see many of the qualities of in-yer-face drama in Upton's plays: high levels of physical, emotional and mental brutality, the dysfunction of the family unit, rebellion against authority figures (and authority figures seen as lacking in morals), consumerism, and an episodic, visually shocking style. Yet this was a form of theatre dominated by male playwrights. Their plays present a distorted take on homosociality, where the bonds between men became pre-eminent, and women are given a tokenistic or nurturing role, when indeed they are present at all. Upton's *oeuvre* deals with how Thatcherism has affected both men and women, whether working or middle class. However, the experiences of teenage girls and young women are often foregrounded, showing how the politically watered-down feminism of the 1990s, with its 'girl power' and female self-assertion, is both informed by, and proves an inadequate defence to, the lasting legacy of the Thatcherite years.

judy upton's theatre of crisis

Several of Judy Upton's plays were first performed at The Red Room in

Kentish Town, North London, or at the Royal Court's Theatre Upstairs. These were spaces dedicated to new writing, and to new forms of staging. Upton's plays are character-based, rather than issue-driven or ideologically motivated. Yet several of her plays confront governmental policies, and all are pervaded by a sense of personal and social failure, with strong images of physical and mental illness, violence, loss of control and an inability to form fulfilling relationships. The focus is upon the individual rather than the collective, and society offers only threat rather than protection.

Education, once the foundation of the postwar Labour government, is no longer seen as a vehicle of change. Two plays from 1995, *Bruises* (Joint Winner of the Verity Bargate Award) and *The Shorewatchers' House*, portray education as pointless, or even lethal. Kate tells her mother about college: 'I don't think I'll go back after the holidays. I don't fit in, I don't understand half the stuff they're trying to teach me, or why I should need to know those things.'[20] We're told that Conrad 'thinks he's such a clever sod, but what has his fancy education brought him? Head of security for an ageing nuclear reactor. A beach house with death as a view at Time-Bomb-On-Sea. And contamination.'[21] Throughout, characters display the gap between their aspirations and the reality of their lives, which then leads to frustration and anger. In *Ashes and Sand*, for which Upton won the George Devine Award, all the characters, whether of the under- or ruling class, are failing. Of the female gang, only Lauren fleetingly refers to school; the others are truants from a system that has lost interest in them. In a brutal parody of capitalism, the gang members act as both entrepreneurs and consumers: their lives are prescribed by getting money (through robbing male tourists on the pier) and by spending it (on goods they do not need). It is posited that an education becomes meaningless anyway when the only jobs that are available lead nowhere: washing up in restaurants, working in shoe shops, joining futile youth schemes. Experiencing too much too young, but not having any sense of achievement, these characters are worn out before their time: Hayley comments, 'I look like an old tart. I'm going to be sixteen soon', a sentiment also used about Deniz in Rebecca Prichard's *Yard Gal*, whose 'face was old – she look about thirty, but she was fifteen like the rest of us'.[22]

The question is posed: what happens if the government puts the emphasis on the individual rather than the state, but that individual is then unable to cope? Upton looks at both the haves and have-nots of society, but often blurs the boundaries between the two. *Sunspots* (1996) brings together two such parallel worlds through sisters Pola and Aimee,

who are originally from suburban Sydenham. Pola now lives in an abandoned amusement arcade in Hastings, with graffitied walls, and sneers
at anything to do with the Establishment. She has only one ambition,
to tag every wall on the south coast (tellingly, with the word SISS). It is
suggested that she is a manic depressive, who goes from great enthusi-
asms to sadness, and has been sectioned before. She steals sunglasses (to
hide behind) and pieces of soap taken from one-night stands (to wash
herself clean). Aimee, whose life is more conventional, but is still drawn
to the energy of her sister, comes to visit with the older, richer Sam, on
their way to a new life in Cyprus. He is so shocked by Pola's life that he
suffers an epileptic, or catatonic, fit, and it is over his comatose body
that the battle for the soul of Aimee begins. Whilst Pola seems like a free
spirit, with her cheeky retorts and rejection of all the trappings of
'normality' – education, home, job, relationships – her life is made up
of the 'sunspots' of the title, dark spots on the sun, which only appear
dark in contrast to the brightness around them.

Although Daniel is part of the Establishment, in *Ashes and Sand* his
life is spiralling out of control, as he struggles to balance his public and
private faces. Like Hayley, he is an adrenaline junkie who wants 'my
future to hold something I can't predict'.[23] His shoplifting and fetish for
women's clothing are partly because 'Life's so dull. You have to take
risks.'[24] Having deliberately marginalized himself, he is now unable to
partake in a normal social life, eschewing Glyn's offer of dinner parties
with his family for hanging around the seafront arcades with under-age
girls. Shot once by a man, and stabbed three times by women in the
course of duty, he is literally and symbolically right when he tells Glyn,
'Life here's killing me.'[25]

The heroine of the significantly named *Sliding with Suzanne* (2001) is
even more traumatized by life. She has been unable to make a success
of any relationship, provide herself with a decent home, or find
anything but dead-end jobs. This escalation of disastrous events has led
to her becoming pregnant by her foster son, Luka. Several critics
misread this play when it was first performed, none more so than
Charles Spencer. Convinced that Margaret Thatcher would 'be appalled
by the language and much of the action but would, I suspect, end up
applauding its sentiments', he goes on to betray his own political viewpoint: 'The Suzanne of the title is one of life's feckless no-hopers', and
her inability to be happy is because 'The idea that she might have to put
in a bit of effort or moral responsibility to achieve that goal appears to
be beyond her.'[26] Upton, though, has deliberately portrayed a woman
who could have 'succeeded' in society's terms, but was unable to do so.

It is suggested that Luka's problems of violence – the play starts with him stamping on a hedgehog and battering a young shop assistant – stem from a disrupted family background. However, Suzanne's malaise seems to come from a different place. As part of the Thatcher generation, she has been assured so much, but finds a mismatch between the promise and the reality. Although she achieves A levels, there are no jobs available to her, except working in a coffee bar, where she is scalded by the machines and assaulted by the supervisor and customers. Her mother, Theresa, wanted her daughter to go further than work in an underwear factory, but her optimism seems shockingly disengaged from political reality:

> SUZANNE: No one wants my fucking A levels. If you've never had anything but shit jobs, you'll never get anything but shit jobs. You know that if anyone does.
> THERESA: I enjoyed my job . . .
> SUZANNE: Even though it's left you doubled up with sciatica and blind as a bat.[27]

Along with *Ashes and Sand* and *Sliding with Suzanne*, perhaps the other most politically motivated of Upton's plays is the one-act *Know Your Rights* (1998). This consists of parallel monologues by Bonnie, a black single mother, and Jane, an older woman who has been accidentally injured on the stairs in their block of flats by Bonnie's young son. With echoes of Jeremy Sandford and Ken Loach's 1966 TV play, *Cathy Come Home* (1966), one seemingly trivial event escalates into disaster as Jane struggles to pay her rent and care for her senile husband. Her concentration on survival forces her to legally pursue Bonnie, who is left at the end jobless, homeless, and in danger of losing her child. Here the poverty trap and changing social and political environment – the Citizens' Advice Bureau has been turned into a Dunkin' Donut – means that those at the bottom of the heap find themselves trapped in an uncaring and faceless system. Government directives to 'get on your bike' or to stop being a drain on resources are shown as pointless and unforgiving. The play, part of Red Room's political 'Seeing Red' season, was written in the early days of New Labour, when Upton felt that little had altered. She writes, 'While examining litigation culture I was also looking at a wider issue: the powers that be and the way in which they encourage us to blame those immediately around us when things go wrong, in order to prevent us seeing the bigger picture.'[28] The phrase that springs to mind here is 'the personal is political', where people's lives are formed and controlled by wider power structures, a frequently used dramatic device since the 1970s, but here there is a concentration upon the reality for individuals, rather than a critique of the specific structures themselves.

There is only one character in Upton's main *oeuvre* who is successful at manipulating events for her own purposes. This is Ella, in *Confidence* (1998), who identifies, and then exploits, the chain of power on a seedy seafront. Mr Bayliss, who has just got out of prison for tax fraud, owns the kiosks, Ben is his 'hard man' who runs these, Ben's brother Dean is a naïve teenager who works on one of the ice-cream stalls, and Ruby is at the bottom of the pile as a not-too-clever waitress. Ella sees a gap in the market for dolphin tours, and even the fact that they don't inhabit nearby waters doesn't put her off as she manages to con the punters by using remote-controlled facsimiles instead. This seemingly lightweight comedy actually presents the audience with a Thatcherite model of society, where cut-throat competitiveness and manipulation of the truth are rewarded with success. In fact, Ella's rapid rise, helped partly through the granting (or at least promise) of her sexual favours, also leads to a rapid fall when her scheme to run a club on the pier goes awry, but she bounces back through her confidence, used in both senses of the word.

Prepared to use people, particularly men, to get money and power, Ella is symptomatic of a society that has eschewed personal relationships in favour of a consumerist dream. This inability for the sexes to relate to one another, except, often, in the most violent or detached of ways, takes a variety of forms in Upton's work. The eponymously named protagonist in *Temple* (1995) studies human feelings through a videotape, echoing the perverse, but 'sanitary' relationships in Stephen Soderberg's film for the AIDS age, *Sex, Lies and Videotape* (1989). Temple's confused sexuality, where he takes on a female role at the end, is similar to Daniel's proclivity for female accoutrements in *Ashes and Sand*. In this brutal play, there are few tender moments, and the rejection of affection is stressed by Daniel's comments that 'I don't want to be touched any more . . . I don't want company.'[29] His idea of sexual connection is to pass a mint from his mouth to that of his female recipient, with this physical distance tellingly conveyed in one scene when Daniel and Hayley, both aching for tenderness, can only communicate by touching fingertips through a letterbox.

It is significant that Daniel is a policeman, as through these plays runs a lack of respect for authority, which does not act as a moral arbitrator or protector, and family relationships are seen as either brutally dysfunctional or non-existent. Violence has become a way of life, a means of communication. So, at the beginning of *Ashes and Sand*, one of the police officers, Glyn, throws darts at a pin-up of a woman, whose 'cunt' is the bull's-eye and later talks with nonchalance about the rising number of suicide drivers.

Women are as violent as men, taking up the attitudes of the 'Riot Grrrl Movement' which flooded into Britain in the 1990s. Grunge/punk rock bands like Hole, fronted by Courtney Love, attacked and parodied conventional notions of femininity, drawing on fetishized items of clothing and pornographic images to throw back at the audience.[30] With a feminist directive distorted through capitalism, 'girl power' seems to be about the group, but is in fact about the individual. The girl gang feels no pity for its victims, not even for its members, for 'It's a jungle out there. Survival of the fittest and all that.'[31] More directly, Hayley states: 'Let's spill some blood . . . I feel angry. If I don't hurt someone I don't know what I might do.'[32] This depiction of a girl gang on the rampage, already utlized in Philip Ridley's *Ghost from a Perfect Place* (1994), and later in Prichard's *Yard Gal* and Kia Corthron's *Breath, Boom* (2000) also picked up on a contemporary media debate about the rising tide of female violence; this was further fuelled by an incident a week before the opening night of *Ashes and Sand*, when celebrity Elizabeth Hurley was mugged by a group of teenage girls. Ian Rickson, the director of *Ashes and Sand*, has noted that Upton's 'anger is the impacted aggression of people from a socially deprived area', and that the play 'builds up to a violent release of energy that is upsetting but also purging'.[33] This can be seen in the penultimate scene, in which the girls ritualistically 'rape' Daniel in revenge for what they see as his betrayal. They pin him to the ground, and smear him with make-up, as they are '*shrieking, screaming obscenities or making pig noises, sometimes murmuring softly and caressing him, as he struggles*'.[34] This short scene echoes the climax of Edward Bond's *Saved* (1965), where a gang of youths stone a baby in a pram, before leaving the stage '*making a curious buzzing*'.[35] Whilst Upton's women are more articulate than those of Bond's men, they similarly take on an animal quality that is almost primeval, also employed by William Golding in his dystopic novel *Lord of the Flies* (1954). In both plays, the violence becomes an orgiastic release of aggressive instincts, caused by a society that has perpetuated or ignored conditions of social and cultural deprivation. Upton has not extended this into an evolved political discussion, as Bond outlined in the 'Author's Note' which prefaces his play, where he describes violence as a controlling element of his vision of capitalist society.[36] Nevertheless, the same qualities are there, this time as an expression of the way in which women have become alienated from any sense of political framework: the collectivism of early feminism had given way to a form of female self-assertion, which in turn had collapsed into an unfocused aggression against self and society.

Upton's social commentary is also intensified through calculated forms of staging. Scenes are frequently short and sharp, almost televisual in their impact. Graffiti, loud music and violent colloquialism express the language of the disenfranchised. The limited use of settings has been criticized, most notably by Mary Luckhurst, but there are several points to be made here.[37] Perhaps most obviously, Upton delineates a world in which the characters find themselves trapped, but equally represents the brutality and the fragmentation of society. Broken down by a society that promises so much and yet delivers so little, these characters find themselves enacting a cycle of repetition, also explored in *Yard Gal*. In Prichard's play, the prison that Boo is sent to is just another version of the violent streets of Hackney, and the impossibility of escape is driven home in the last lines, with its echoes of Beckett's *Waiting for Godot* (1955):

> MARIE: Can we go now?
> BOO: Can we go?[38]

This is also indicated in Upton's *The Shorewatchers' House*, where Nik, Conrad and Brigida are locked into a sado-masochistic *ménage-à-trois*. The house, on a stony beach, overlooks a nuclear power plant, and the characters' bizarre and brutal relationship is mirrored in the environment, where Brigida's obsessive fears about contamination, and Conrad's nightmares and defective hearing of the plant's wailing sirens run counter to their inability to leave. Conrad's family have all died of radiation-related illnesses, but he desperately clings to his childhood home; locked into a mutually cruel relationship, Brigida and Nik are thus also forced to remain. Their will has been drained away by a political system that allows such places to stay open, even given the high level of danger, and they are now no longer in a position to change how their lives are led. Again, the domestic violence meted out in *Bruises* is represented as a vicious circle that takes place between father and son, and is then passed on to their respective girlfriends, Phoebe and Kate. All this happens in a Bed & Breakfast, run mainly for the DSS, with the 'lights and beach hut backs of Worthing Prom' in the distance.[39] The setting, with its connotations of the underclass, replicates the characters' sense of disappointment and inability to grasp life's potential. Dave is a failed musician who uses alcohol and violence as a way to sublimate his shortcomings, whilst his son, Jay, finds himself working for a father he both fears and despises. The seamless movement between different parts of the stage, indicating rooms of the B&B, the bar where Jay works, his flat, and the house of Kate's mother, ensnares them in a web where the language of everyday existence is that of mental, physical and emotional brutality. Like *Bruises*, most of Upton's plays are set in the dilapidated coastal resorts of southern England; Upton herself was brought up in Shoreham-by-Sea, Sussex. Whilst male playwrights such as Alan Bleasdale looked at the landscapes of the industrial North in the 1980s, and 'in-yer-face' male dramatists of the 1990s focused upon gritty urban reality, Upton uses the microcosms of unfashionable southern seaside resorts (especially in *Bruises*) as a means to show how much society has changed under Thatcherism. These are 'places on the edge . . . where language runs out and is replaced by violence'.[40] Economic instability in these coastal areas, caused by seasonal work, often ill paid, a skills shortage and a migrant population, was made worse by governmental policies during the 1980s and 1990s. This included the use of B&B places for benefit claimants and asylum seekers, dubbed by the press the 'Costa del Dole'.[41] As a visitor to a seaside flat in Clare McIntyre's *My Heart's a Suitcase* (1990) says, it 'feels like the whole place has been left here to rot'.[42]

Overlaid with this in Upton's work is a more metaphorical meaning. Elaine Aston suggests that 'seaside towns gone to seed are especially evocative of good times gone wrong'.[43] The seaside holiday is a British tradition, evincing nostalgia and a sense of innocence. In its place, though, Upton has created a nightmarish world of tawdriness, corruption and cruelty, evoked in another period of instability in Graham Greene's *Brighton Rock* (1938). Upton's characters are not pleasure-seeking tourists but rather damaged inhabitants or seasonal workers trying to eke out an existence. John K. Walton has described how the seaside is a place where 'the genteel, controlled symmetrical front of the resort finds itself invaded by the disorder, untidiness and misrule of the back'.[44] Upton's plays, like Greene's book, explore this dark underside, where characters – particularly young women – attempt to create a world apart from social institutions like family, work and the law.

The location, therefore, functions in a variety of ways. It shows how the British seaside has suffered from disinvestment, as has much of Britain. It also delineates the decline in the relaxing qualities of the seaside and its concomitant rise as a place of consumption, so cynically exploited by Ella in *Confidence* when she says of the tourists' almost-compulsive need to spend money: 'Look at them – frittering it on ice cream, burgers, beers, arcade games, sticks of rock, palm readings, post-cards of bums and tits . . . Any old shit really, to convince themselves they've had the whole seaside experience.'[45] Again, Upton's visual display of slot machines represents capitalism's empty consumerist promises, also explored in terms of sex and violence in plays such as Mark Ravenhill's *Shopping and Fucking*. It is telling that Pola, in *Sunspots*, keeps her frugal supplies inside a machine, and that Sam collapses when the techno music and flashing lights in the arcade provide a sensory overload. The seaside has become debased into a 'cacophony of crude electronic noises and jerky graphics'.[46]

Paradoxically, the seaside can also represent escape. The sea is, of course, the furthest place that characters can run to; it is, literally, the end of the line. In *Ashes and Sand*, Hayley wants to steal enough money to go to Bali, only 19 hours away, but a 'different world. Dramatic land-scape, golden sandy beaches, a unique culture and some of the friend-liest people you will ever be fortunate to meet.'[47] Her sentimental and idealistic view of this place contrasts with the reality of the tawdry loca-tion where she lives, and the sea is an impassable barrier that her social situation prevents her from crossing. Inexorably, her plan is thwarted when members of her gang use the money to spend on short-term diversions like drink, drugs and clothes. Anna is surely echoing her contemporaries when she says, 'You just can't do anything these days. Whatever your dream is, someone comes along and smashes it to bits.'[48] Equally, Daniel desires a transfer to Gibraltar, but his arrest for shoplifting and attack by the girls lead the police psychologist to believe that he has deliberately sabotaged this plan. There is more than an element of truth in this, for to deaden his feelings of being half-alive, Daniel has become addicted to thrill-seeking and violence, which disturbingly he finds 'almost comforting'.[49] These are characters who find it impossible to keep still, as they move from seafront to arcade, and from police station to therapist's chair. Yet, paradoxically, the harder they try to get away, the more they remain entrapped by their situation. Filled with a sense of social dis-ease, their attempts to reach a life beyond 'this crappy country' remain a chimera.[50]

The same can be said to be true of Pola and Aimee in *Sunspots*. Aimee's plan to move to Cyprus founders when she rejects Sam. Although she pushes the dream into reality by stealing Jake's boat, Pola's fantasy of empowerment through her bohemian lifestyle is finally shattered by Sam just before they leave, when he observes that her inability to feel for anyone or anything renders her incapable of happiness. In handing her his own bar of soap, Sam brings down Pola's artfully constructed world. So, whilst the sisters may leave, carrying the boat, the implication is that they are not going anywhere. Again, it is left to Ella, in *Confidence*, to escape. She sees Hollywood, that traditional purveyor of dreams, as a way out of Britain, and although this is as unlikely for her as Bali is for Hayley, and similarly her 'get-rich-quick' schemes ultimately fail, she is one of Upton's few characters who manage to leave at the end. Yet this is also tinged with irony. She rebukes Dean for living at home with his parents, and having a dead-end summer job. However, her own ambition is fuelled by media-created aspirations of empty consumerism: 'If you're not interested in earning a new pair of Nikes by the end of the day . . . complete designer wardrobe by the end of the week . . . all the beers you can drink, and all the dope you can smoke . . . then OK, you stay here, as King of the Slackers, that's fine by me . . . *She stops, looks back* . . . I don't need you. I don't need anyone.'[51] Thus Ella's *confidence* in the Thatcherite system is shown by Upton to be a false path that leads to fraudulent and amoral behaviour. For others, living under governmental policies fashioned during the 1980s and 1990s, destruction of the mind, body and spirit is the inevitable consequence.

It has been much debated whether playwrights like Judy Upton and other in-yer-face dramatists can be called political. Klaus Peter Müller argues:

> There is a strong element of pessimism, often mixed with a strange sense of relish in the destructive and dehumanising worlds depicted. The amount of direct political statements is accordingly rather small in these plays, even though they can easily be interpreted as reflecting a specific cultural and thus also political climate.[52]

This is echoed by Benedict Nightingale, who comments that these dramatists 'have no obvious political credo, no social agenda'.[53] The problem, as far as he sees it, is that the audience is left to draw their own conclusions, and no moral is pressed home. More specifically to the point here, Sierz claims that Upton's inability to provide a political answer in her plays leads to 'drama becoming mere reportage', even if her plays 'fiercely illustrate[s] the culture of victimhood'. He concludes, 'The problem is that her work often lacks any sense of the possibility of empowerment or of change. There is neither tragic destiny nor social rehabilitation, but instead a series of cycles of deprivation.'[54]

Certainly, many other playwrights writing at this time have dealt directly with political events, but it is significant that these have tended to turn towards the continent, as in Brenton's *Berlin Bertie* (1992), Churchill's *Mad Forest* (1990) and *Far Away* (2000), which 'suggests that an absence of social and political responsibility will lead to global catastrophe'.[55] Both Brenton's *Collateral Damage* (1999, co-written with Tariq Ali and Andy De La Tour) and Kane's *Blasted* focus upon the ramifications of Yugoslavia's destruction, with Kane integrating foreign politics with the social collapse of Britain when she imagined what would happen if the battlegrounds of Bosnia arrived in a Leeds hotel room. In light of this, the work of other in-yer-face playwrights can seem atrophied.

Judy Upton has been placed firmly within the new generation of dramatists in the 1990s. While young and angry, her characters seem to lack faith in the democratic system, and even to veer towards political apathy: the utopian socialist visions of the 1970s and the satirical critiques of the 1980s no longer have any relevance. In line with this, it can be said of Upton that she provides a 'snapshot' of Britain during this decade. Thatcher's children have become disenfranchised, reflecting the alienation and anomie created by governmental policies. Upton is unable to posit an agenda for transformation or for revolution, and this in itself becomes a political message. Her awareness of gender politics, the loss of a shared female experience and language seems fitting for an age where equality for women is supposed to have been won, and therefore no longer seen as politically acute. Ultimately, Upton's plays seem to represent, therefore, not so much a crisis in masculinity as a crisis in feminism.

notes

1. For example, in a much-publicized speech, Michael Portillo argued for the Conservative Party to stay right of the centre line in order to put 'clear blue water' between themselves and other parties: M. Portillo, *Clear Blue Water: A Compendium of Speeches and Interviews Given by the Rt. Hon. Michael Portillo* (London: Conservative Way Forward, 1994).
2. I am, of course, here continuing on from Elaine Aston's pioneering work in this field, most notably *Feminist Views on the English Stage: Women Playwrights, 1990–2000* (Cambridge: Cambridge University Press, 2003).
3. John Major believed that Sir Keith Joseph, Sir Geoffrey Howe and Nigel Lawson were the driving force; see J. Sergeant, *Maggie: Her Fatal Legacy* (Basingstoke: Macmillan, 2005), p. 351. Others have put the onus on the Centre for Policy Studies, of which Joseph was a key member.

4. In a TV interview during 1981, Edward Heath denounced 'massive unemployment' as morally wrong. However, Thatcher refused to back down from her policies, famously confronting her party at their annual conference in 1980 with the words, 'You turn if you want to. The lady's not for turning.'

5. S. R. Letwin, *The Anatomy of Thatcherism* (London: Fontana, 1992), p. 315. For a discussion of Bleasdale's TV drama, see L. Cooke, *British Television Drama* (London: BFI Publishing, 2003): 'Yosser, immortalised by Bernard Hill . . . became an iconic character in the series whose repeated refrain, "Gizza job, I can do that", became a national catchphrase . . . the phrase entered into popular currency, a defiant cry capturing the desperation and disenfranchisement of a whole class', p. 132.

6. Cited in J. McGrath, *The Bone Won't Break: On Theatre and Hope in Hard Times* (London: Methuen, 1990), p. 3. Hugo Young notes that by this she meant that 'society had no meaning save as a grouping of individuals and families. These were the units that really mattered, whereas "society" was some kind of abstraction and alibi for individual responsibility. When the phrase became famous, official efforts were made to defuse its significance and insist that it didn't mean what it seemed to mean. But it did . . .'; *One of Us: A Biography of Margaret Thatcher* (London: Pan, 1990), p. 490.

7. D. Hare, 'Enter Stage Left', *Guardian*, 30 October 2004.

8. D. K. Peacock, *Thatcher's Theatre: British Theatre and Drama in the Eighties* (London: Greenwood Press, 1999), p. 54.

9. E. Aston, *Caryl Churchill* (Tavistock: Northcote House, 2001), p. 42.

10. D. Hare, *The Secret Rapture* (London: Faber, 1988), p. 38.

11. C. Innes, *Modern British Drama: The Twentieth Century* (Cambridge: Cambridge University Press, 2002), p. 367.

12. Peacock, *Thatcher's Theatre*, p. 66.

13. Ibid., p. 76.

14. B. Nightingale, 'Ten With the Playwright Stuff', *The Times*, 1 May 1996.

15. Ibid., p. 33.

16. B. Nightingale, cited in G. Saunders, *'Love Me or Kill Me': Sarah Kane and the Theatre of Extremes* (Manchester: Manchester University Press, 2002), p. 20.

17. A. Sierz, *In-Yer-Face Theatre: British Drama Today* (London: Faber, 2000), p. 237.

18. J. Upton, 'Afterword', in P. Edwardes (ed.), *Frontline Intelligence 3: New Plays for the Nineties* (London: Methuen, 1995), p. 261.

19. S Hemming, 'The Best of Time, the Worst of Time', *Independent*, 22 February 1995.

20. J. Upton, *Bruises & The Shorewatchers' House* (London: Methuen, 1996), p. 8.

21. Ibid., pp. 64–5.

22. Upton, *Plays: 1* (London: Methuen, 2002), p. 14; R. Prichard, *Yard Gal* (London: Faber, 1998), p. 21.

23. Upton, *Plays: 1*, p. 27.

24. Ibid., p. 36.

25. Ibid., p. 38.
26. C. Spencer, 'A Grown Up Portrait of Immaturity', *Daily Telegraph*, 5 September 2001.
27. J. Upton, *Sliding with Suzanne* (London: Methuen, 2001), pp. 39–40.
28. J. Upton, 'Introduction', *Plays: 1*, pp. vii–viii (p. vii).
29. Upton, *Plays: 1*, p. 12.
30. See I. Whelehan, *Overloaded: Popular Culture and the Future of Feminism* (London: Women's Press, 2000), p. 43.
31. Upton, *Plays: 1*, p. 11.
32. Ibid., p. 13.
33. Cited in Sierz, *In-Yer-Face Theatre*, p. 216.
34. Upton, *Plays: 1*, p. 64.
35. E. Bond, *Plays: 1* (London: Methuen, 1977), p. 82.
36. E. Bond, 'Author's Note: On Violence', in ibid., pp. 9–17.
37. See M. Luckhurst, 'An Embarrassment of Riches: Women Dramatists in 1990s Britain', in B. Reitz and M. Berninger (eds), *British Drama of the 1990s* (Heidelberg: Universitätsverlag Carl Winter, 2002), pp. 65–77.
38. Prichard, *Yard Gal*, p. 59.
39. Upton, *Bruises & The Shorewatchers' House*, p. 1.
40. S. Croft, *She Also Wrote Plays: An International Guide to Women Playwrights from the 10th to the 20th Century* (London: Faber, 2001), p. 258.
41. See J. K. Walton, *The British Seaside: Holidays and Resorts in the Twentieth Century* (Manchester: Manchester University Press, 2000), p. 143.
42. C. McIntyre, *My Heart's A Suitcase* (London: Nick Hern, 1998), p. 3.
43. Aston, *Feminist Views on the English Stage*, p. 67.
44. Walton, *The British Seaside*, p. 4.
45. J. Upton, *Confidence* (London: Methuen, 1998), p. 31.
46. Upton, *Plays: 1*, p. 99.
47. Ibid., p. 4.
48. Ibid., p. 46.
49. Ibid., p. 18.
50. Ibid., p. 59.
51. Upton, *Confidence*, p. 95; pp. 95–6.
52. K. P. Müller, 'Political Plays in England in the 1990s', in *British Drama of the 1990s*, pp. 15–36 (p. 15).
53. Nightingale, 'Ten With the Playwright Stuff', p. 33.
54. Sierz, *In-Yer-Face Theatre*, p. 218.
55. Aston, *Caryl Churchill*, p. 116.

5
middle-class aspirations and black women's mental (ill) health in zindika's *leonora's dance*, and bonnie greer's *munda negra* and *dancing on blackwater*

lynette goddard

black women's playwriting in the 1990s

The 1990s saw a sharp downturn in black British women's writing for the professional stage, in contrast to the previous decade during which plays by Trish Cooke, Yazmine Judd, Jackie Kay, Jenny McLeod, Maria Oshodi, Winsome Pinnock, Jacqueline Rudet and Zindika were produced by prominent black and women's theatre companies at key London venues.[1] When compared with the preceding decade, the 1990s shows a depressing lack of momentum for black British women's playwriting. However, the start of the twenty-first century has seen a re-energized surge, with productions of Winsome Pinnock's *Water* and *One Under* (2005), Doña Daley's *Blest Be the Tie* (2004), and debbie tucker green's *dirty butterfly* (2003), *born bad* (2003), *stoning mary* (2005), *trade* (2005) and *generations* (2007).[2] Millennial black women's plays have shifted away from the explicit concerns with cultural identity that were typical of earlier black women's theatre, and tend to focus more on the interpersonal relationships between characters in urban multifarious (multicultural, multiracial, multifaith) communities to ask complex questions about the world we live in now.

The groundwork for the move away from 'issue-plays' to the foregrounding of individual stories was laid throughout the 1990s in plays that started to account for a broader range of black women's experiences in the UK. Black women's plays of the 1980s dealt primarily with questions of black cultural identity and were mostly set in self-contained black families and communities in Britain or the Caribbean.[3] The characters were typically first- and second-generation black people – usually working class – and the generational conflicts between those who migrated from the Caribbean and their British-born children was a key theme. As Pinnock outlines, 'issues of identity were of pressing concern, the idea of being trapped between certain dualities: migrant/native, "black" culture/"white" culture; being caught between two cultures and belonging to neither'.[4] The importance of writing about identities and experiences that were hardly seen on the British stage meant that the plays reiterated similar stories that amounted to rather essentialist archetypes of black women's lives.

Gabriele Griffin observes that

> [w]hereas during the 1980s plays were dominated by inter-generational conflicts as expressive of the difference between the adult subject who migrated and the child who . . . *was migrated*, and their different accommodations to that situation, by the 1990s plays tended to focus much more on how to live in Britain now, beyond the experience of the moment of migration, as part of a generation that had grown up in the UK.[5]

By the 1990s, essentialist assumptions were challenged in plays that highlighted complexities, contestations and contradictions within black women's identity. Significantly, these plays started to account more substantially for the experiences of upwardly mobile and middle-class black women living in multicultural communities to explore the effects of the breakdown of separatist communities and the immediate challenges of developing a life in the post-Thatcher Britain.

Elaine Aston's 'feminist view' of the 1990s describes the emergence of a new 'girl-power' feminism, a 'contradictory mix of feminist and anti-feminist discourses that promoted an image of aggressive "sisterhood" and feminine glamour through a creed of selfish individualism designed to "get what you want out of life"'.[6] The 'new feminism' of the 1990s supplants the radical feminist principles of the 1970s and 1980s with ideas of the potential for individual success that are premised on assumptions that young women share equal freedom and choice with their male counterparts. Aston argues that such an individualistic feminist rhetoric 'has no political agenda to change the social structures within which girls live their lives, and merely suggests that by taking an aggressive stance together, girls will get what they want'.[7] Black women's plays of the 1990s demonstrate how ideas of individualistic attainment are problematic because education, career choices and overall self-esteem affect one's potential to actualize notions of freedom and choice in an institutionally racist society. The playwrights explored the effects of Thatcherite individualist principles on notions of black Britishness, accounting for issues of racism, sexism and diaspora in the context of the contemporary landscape 'Cool Britannia'. Assumptions of black communities and characters unified by shared experiences of oppression were unsettled as ruptures and discontinuities were evoked to examine ways of reconciling the individual with the collective. New concerns such as the growth of interracial communities, global capitalism, and ideas of changing class-consciousnesses in the context of 'New Europe' were raised and explored alongside demonstrations of how individualistic principles affect black women in an institutionally racist and sexist culture.

One apparent theme of 1990s black women's plays is the depiction of characters with mental health issues and breakdowns that are shown to be symptomatic effects of the quest for individual success in Eurocentric terms of wealth and social status. One of the black women characters in Pinnock's *Talking in Tongues* (1991) virtually has a nervous breakdown as a result of trying to maintain a successful upwardly mobile career and relationship in Britain.[8] Bonnie Greer's *Dancing on Blackwater* (1994) shows two black sisters dealing with unresolved issues surrounding their mother's suicide and reconciling their middle-class upbringing with their black cultural identity. One of the sisters suffers a number of neuroses that result from her lack of confidence as a black woman in Britain. In Greer's *Munda Negra* (1995) a professional African-American woman visiting Britain experiences hallucinations and hears voices and racist taunts of her inner child. The central character in Valerie Mason-John's *Brown Girl in the Ring* (Oval House Theatre, 1999) has a mental breakdown as her aspirations to enter the upper classes and be accepted as Queen Regina are thwarted by racism and heterosexism.[9] In Zindika's *Leonora's Dance* (1993) a black woman's mental health difficulties are caused by delusions of grandeur and aspirations that are impeded in England.[10] These representations of mental illness account for the longer-term psychological effects of migration on people separated from their cultural roots. The negotiations for identity prevalent in black women's playwriting are heightened by representations of mixed race and/or middle-class black female characters whose disjointed minds allude to fragmentations of cultural identity as class consciousness collides with race and gender in 1990s Britain.

split psyches and spirit worlds: zindika's *leonora's dance*

The main programme note for Black Theatre Co-operative's (BTC, now Nitro) production of Zindika's *Leonora's Dance* refers to the 'growing controversy surround[ing] the disproportionate number of black, mainly Afro-Caribbean people in Britain diagnosed as mentally ill, leading to questions about the very theory and practice of psychiatry itself'.[11] Figures suggest that 'Black people make up nearly a third of patients in secure services [and] they're six times more likely than their white counterparts to be sectioned under the Mental Health Act.'[12] Transcultural psychiatry and research on black mental health explores the effects of racism on psychiatric disorders among black people, and seeks specifically to problematize eugenicist notions of an inferior biological disposition, and foreground cultural explanations for the disproportionate numbers of black people within the mental health system.[13] One suggestion is that misunderstandings and misdiagnoses occur as a result of cultural differences, which leads to some behaviours and rituals that might be considered normal in 'black' cultures being seen as signs of mental disorder.[14]

Women are also thought to be disproportionately represented in the mental health system. Helen B. Lewis identifies the claim that 'two-thirds of agoraphobic patients seen by psychiatrists are women', but she suggests that these figures are more reflective of the fact that women are more open about their anxieties, 'reporting more symptoms of nervousness, nightmares and other anxiety experiences than men'.[15] Jane Ussher's feminist genealogy of women's mental health identifies how feminists have reinterpreted nineteenth-century concepts of hysteria, historically 'the accepted diagnosis of all aspects of female madness', as 'an expression of women's anger, women's oppression, and of the power of a misogynistic discourse to define what "woman" means, and to exert control over women's lives'.[16] Women's madness has been reconceived in feminist terms as a resistance to patriarchy, a refusal to enter into the symbolic world where the laws of the father prevail.

Articulations of black mental illness on stage contribute to the sociological debates about mental health and the care of black people in the psychiatric system.[17] An acknowledgement of how cultural racism *and* (hetero-) sexism affects black women's psyches is central to under-standing the depiction of black women's mental illness in 1990s plays.[18] *Leonora's Dance* explores black women's lives in 1990s London, focusing on the central character Leonora's agoraphobia and mental illness. Patrick Marmion's production preview in *What's On* describes the play as 'about how being black in a predominantly white society can literally drive you round the bend with its cultural exclusion zones'.[19] Leonora's mental health issues are related to black history and histori-cal perceptions of race to show how racism functions in the context of 'Cool Britannia'.

The play is set in Leonora's house, where she lives with two female lodgers – her niece Daphine and a young Chinese medical student Melisa Chung. Leonora, a Jamaican woman who migrated to England with dreams of becoming a professional ballet dancer, talks to her plants and ponders her failed ambitions. Daphine is an unemployed and illiterate young single mother who has moved to London from her home in Liverpool and left her young daughter behind. Melisa is from Hayward's Heath, running away from being forced into an arranged marriage. Each character occupies her own stage space and they meet each other as they pass through the communal space. Leonora's house is a metaphor for life in urban British communities, where diverse cultures live side by side but are separated by cultural and religious beliefs. Gabriele Griffin argues that 'geographical space and psychic location are mapped onto one another, reflecting the difficulties of leading a diasporic life in a postcolonial culture'.[20] The internal spatial divisions are emblematic of multiple identities co-habiting a shared geographical space, yet divided by cultural boundaries between them, and the conflicts between the characters when they enter each other's spaces suggest a lack of tolerance for each other's cultural beliefs.

The outside world is conceived as a dangerous place where the char-acters' difficulties as black and South East Asian women are compounded. Daphine and Melisa's tales about their experiences outside the house evoke their fears of a place where they are at odds with the system – Daphine struggles with literacy and is finding it diffi-cult to get employment, and Melisa is on the run from being forced into marriage. Leonora's anxieties about London as a big city to be feared almost materialize towards the end of the play when her only venture outside results in her nearly being run over and killed by a truck.

Leonora's mental anxieties are figured as a direct consequence of her mixed-race identity and cultural affinities. She rejects her maternal Caribbean ancestry in favour of identification with her white father's cultural heritage, identifying with a racist value system where she is excluded from full participation. The play invokes the tragic mulatta archetype to evoke notions of a double-conscious split psyche, which manifests in mental illness that is caused by the difficulties of reconciling both sides of her racial heritage.[21] The representation of mixed-race identity brings the trope of the tragic mulatta to the contemporary stage to invite questions of how stereotypical perceptions of race coalesce with the politics of 1990s Britain.

Barbara Tizard and Ann Phoenix indicate that the 'one-drop-of-black-blood' rule historically meant that mixed-race children were immediately classified as black, and sociological research has therefore suggested that 'a positive image for mixed-parentage people can come only from assuming a black identity and identifying with other black people'.[22] The possibilities for identifying as mixed race, as a particular identity, have been brought into question in recent years, with the 2001 British Census including mixed-race categories for the first time. Tizard and Phoenix highlight a growing popularity for mixed-race children to classify themselves as '"black with one white parent" [or] "black mixed parentage" [to] maintain solidarity with black people and potentially give recognition to racisms as affecting people of "mixed parentage" and "black" people in similar ways while recognizing that some issues are particular to people of mixed parentage'.[23] Anne Wilson also suggests that '[c]ontrary to the popular stereotype of mixed race people as torn between black and white, many children seemed to have found a happy and secure identity for themselves as "black mixed race".'[24] Wilson argues that many mixed-race children tend to 'consider themselves full members of the black community, since any attempt to adopt a white identity is likely to bring conflict and rejection'.[25] These ideas are illustrated by Leonora's exclusion from fully integrating with white culture and her rejection of her black heritage in favour of identification with white culture, causing her low self-esteem and consequent mental breakdown.

Leonora's mental health issues could be understood through W. E. B. Du Bois's concept of black 'double-consciousness . . . always looking at one's self through the eyes of others, of measuring one's soul by the tape of a world that looks on in amused contempt and pity', and Frantz Fanon's conceptions of black psychological complexes, where split psyches result from experiencing ourselves through the projected fears, fantasies and desires of a white-dominated society.[26] Du Bois and Fanon do not pathologize black psyches, but render double-ness as constitutive of black people in white-led cultures rather than as a sign of madness. Fanon's argument that projected fantasies of fear and desire for the black 'other' disturbingly caused 'Shame . . . self contempt [. . . and] torment' is captured in the way that Leonora has come to associate blackness with negativity and attributes her failure to fulfil aspirations to be a ballerina to her black identity.[27] In the same way that Fanon writes, 'No exception was made for my refined manners, or my knowledge of literature, or my understanding of the quantum theory', Leonora's knowledge of eminent dancers such as Pavlova and Dame Margot Fonteyn was not enough to get her into the Royal Ballet and she received a three-year stream of rejection letters to her applications.[28]

Throughout the play Leonora is visited by Medusa, a spirit who represents the negative connotations that Leonora holds of her 'black' identity. Medusa fights with Leonora for control of the house and concomitant control of the audience's gaze, and tries to incite her to leave the house. She torments Leonora with racist ideas inferred from colonial notions, framing the rejection from ballet school by allusion to eugenicist notions of the difference between black and white people that are used to underscore notions of the type of dance that each is deemed capable of. As a black woman, Leonora is predisposed to modern dance, jazz dance, African dance or calypso, but her body is not thought to be shaped for ballet because her darker skin and broader size set her apart from the Western ideal for white, slim, ballerinas.

The political efficacy of Zindika's play rests in the juxtaposition of Leonora's story with the experiences of her lodgers, which engenders a meeting of old and new values about race and gender. Sarah Hemming of the *Independent* observes that the characters are 'caught awkwardly between their ancestry and their daily lives', and Ben Jancovich's review in *City Limits* suggests that they are all 'struggling to make sense of the discrepancy between roots and existence in a changing world'.[29] Institutional racism and sexism have undeniably affected Leonora's aspirations to become a professional ballet dancer, and the test of the extent to which things have changed lies in how these discourses affect Daphine and Melisa as young women in the 1990s.

Daphine is rebelliously Afro-centric, as Suzi Feay puts it in *Time Out*, she 'wields a copy of "Roots" and knows all about the "Black Athena" theory'.[30] Daphine's illiteracy is an impediment in a culture that privileges written academic knowledge, and she finds it difficult to learn in conventional educational institutions. Her lack of success at school is framed in terms of the lack of interest from teachers who thought that black girls would end up as welfare mothers, and she cynically reflects on how her difficulties as a black woman in Britain are compounded by the impact of Thatcherism's meritocracy. However, her inability to read makes her ideal for receiving the oral Obeah tradition knowledge from Leonora's mother Frieda, and the resolution rests in her memorizing orally imparted information, which signals both the importance of acknowledging different types of knowledge and a sense that what might be deemed ill in one cultural context is not necessarily so in another.

Daphine's ability to memorize the complex Latin names of healing plants provides a parallel for understanding Leonora's mental illness, in that she might be deemed mentally unstable, agoraphobic, or schizophrenic in Eurocentric terms, where in fact she could equally be seen as in touch with a spirit world that is simply misunderstood from such a vantage point. This is perhaps best seen in the way that Leonora uses a white-identified value system to separate herself off as superior to the other women. Leonora denigrates Daphine for being a single mother, calling her a prostitute, and criticizing her unemployment for bringing shame to the black race. She assumes that Melisa is from Hong Kong, and invokes an identification with Englishness to create an 'us' and 'them' divide that places Melisa as 'other': 'Still not use to our English weather yet I see. . . . I bet it never gets this cold in Hong Kong. . . . You soon get used to it like us English.'[31] Leonora's fear that Melisa's chanting and praying divinations to spirit Mioshan is drawing evil spirits to the house epitomizes how racist beliefs can stem from misunderstandings of another's cultural traditions.

Melisa rejects the culturally determined patriarchal demands that she should get married, and infers a woman-centred discourse as a site of resistance; her spiritual ancestors are women and she prays to a female spirit. Melisa is seemingly best able to function in Britain by combining conventional academic knowledge with spiritual wisdom, and, in many ways, she represents the ideal candidate for bringing together the old and the new in contemporary Britain. Melisa's rejection of the paternal value system contrasts with Leonora's internalization of the white patriarchal value system, a discourse in which she is deemed mad and pumped with anti-depression medicines that do not cure her. This system is one that can equally only conceive Medusa as evil, a belief that underscores her temperament as Leonora's nemesis in the play.[32]

The significance of the start of Leonora's recovery is such that it results from an encounter between spirit Medusa and Frieda's Obeah, neither of which falls within conventional British medical models for curing mental health difficulties. Frieda has come over from the

Caribbean to heal Leonora and take her back to safety, and the final confrontation sees Leonora goaded to leave the house by Medusa as Frieda tries to dampen what she sees an evil spirit. Leonora is saved from going under the truck's wheels, and her recovery is conceived as requiring movement from England, where she is deemed mentally unstable in Eurocentric psychiatric terms.

Benedict Nightingale of *The Times* felt that *Leonora's Dance* failed somewhat in its attempt to highlight racism:

> No doctors, no shrinks are on view; and it is hard to be sure that the agoraphobic woman at the evening's centre is quite the victim of racism she believes. . . . Her disappointment is sad – but have not a zillion white dancers been similarly afflicted? Nor are either of her tenants obviously the victims of racism.[33]

Feay's comment that the play is 'too oblique to be didactic' reflects on the effect of the magic realist style on the political impact of the play.[34] Nightingale's and Feay's interpretations are a reflection of the way 1990s black women's theatre moved away from explicitly didactic portrayals and inserted political beliefs into the characters' human stories. Melisa's flight from patriarchal expectations, and Daphine's single mothering, comment on the cultural expectations of women from different cultural backgrounds, for example. Leonora's struggles to become a dancer are clearly located as effects of racist discourses that affect black women differently from white women. As Aleks Sierz's commentary for the *Tribune* confirms, 'the Royal Ballet doesn't exactly welcome black dancers'.[35] Nightingale's suggestion that Leonora's mental vulnerability is questionable because the play does not depict conventional doctors or psychiatrists perpetuates a Eurocentric interpretation of mental illness that the play challenges. However, his reading is perhaps an indication of how political messages can be overlooked in plays that focus on individual stories.

afrocentrism and (in)sanity in bonnie greer's *munda negra*

Bonnie Greer's *Munda Negra* has never been produced, but is published in *Black Plays 3*, where Yvonne Brewster's introduction signals Greer's departure from the usual representations of black women: 'Bonnie could not be accused of sticking to tired conventions or hackneyed representations of reality . . . she produces work that is original.'[36]

Munda Negra is set in a multiracial inner- city community, where Anna Eastman, an 'African-American arts professor on sabbatical in Europe', is forced to confront unresolved issues of race and identity.[37] Anna is a successful career woman who was involved in the pro-black movement as an African-American student in the 1960s; her strong sense of an African/black ancestry forms the basis for revisionist lectures that deconstruct representations of African women in art. Her academic work on Eurocentrism and Western art history is based on being a fearless advocate of Afrocentrism and acknowledging how racist colonialist imagery has informed art production and affected how black people are represented.

Anna seems to function effectively in the public middle-class world of teachers, lecturers and art historians, where she rationally presents her arguments about race and representation and is in complete control in determining and explaining the effects of racism on notions of black women. In her private space, however, she experiences obsessive-compulsive phobias and alcohol-induced hallucinations that stem from unresolved childhood issues about her racial identity. Anna's split psyche comes from being 'a black girl who drew a self-portrait of herself as a white girl with blonde hair and was ridiculed for it', and throughout the play, she is tormented by voices of her younger inner self – Little Anna – who makes her confront unresolved anxieties about race.[38] Anna's double-consciousness is accentuated through a split between her Afrocentric adult world and Little Anna's world – a space where the inner child is in control and Anna verges on breakdown. Little Anna contradicts Anna's seeming Afrocentric perspective, visiting her in moments of racial turmoil and taunting her about the issues that she has yet to face up to, particularly an internalized desire to be the epitome of beauty in a neo-colonial context evoked by the painting of herself as a white girl with blue eyes and blonde hair.

Anna had a Catholic upbringing 'because that was the only school that wasn't segregated', during which she was made to pray to a white Jesus. However, she resisted the call to 'renounce Satan and all his works . . . if *you* renounce Satan, then I accept him. I accept the darkness' as a testimony to identification with blackness.[39] Her resistance is inferred through hallucinatory apparitions associated with icons of white Catholicism – the Pope and the Blessed Virgin Mary – with one visitation seeing Mary of Egypt (the black virgin) highlighting the religion's biases in suppressing her story (and by association black history) in favour of the dominant narrative of the birth of Jesus. Eurocentric understandings of Anna would undeniably deem her mentally unstable on the basis of these hallucinations; however, transcultural psychiatry might acknowledge them as part of her coping strategy as a black woman in a white-determined culture, where the visions embody her resistance to internalized racism and form the basis of her strong Afrocentric outlook.

Munda Negra shows the effects of changing politics of race from the community-based 1960s Black Nationalism to 1990s individualist principles. Anna's mental health difficulties stem from her adoption of a fierce 1960s Afrocentrism, which has no place in contemporary Britain. Anna's political stance on race, and her guilt about previously aborting her recently deceased ex-lover's baby to focus on her career, cause her to try to adopt his adopted mixed-race child (Nicole). She fears that Nicole's white mother's planned move from London to Shropshire will have a negative effect on a mixed-race child who will grow up in a predominately white-middle-class village. Anna obsesses about saving Nicole from relocation, while meeting her individual needs of becoming a mother to Neville's child. However, she does not have the support of her community, and both black and white friends and colleagues counter her militant Afro-American-centric views about race as manifestations of outmoded segregationist agendas that have no place in a tolerant multicultural Britain.

Anna's lectures on representations of black people in 'great art', her fears for the mixed-race child, and questions surrounding whether 1960s Civil Rights political activism have led to a changed world invite us to consider the politics of race in contemporary England, with particular comparisons drawn against the politics of race in the USA. Her individual story creates a frame in which to address a range of provocative questions, including: Who defines black people? Are all white people racist? What types of desire are interracial relationships founded on? What are the long- term effects of militant Afrocentrism? How does racism operate in urban and rural communities? Can a woman have an effective career and children? The visitations confront the sanctity of Catholicism, and parallels between art and religion are used to question how certain ideas about race and history have been created and sustained. The separatist black and white discourse that Anna invokes causes her mental health instabilities, and skipping off with Little Anna at the end of the play indicates that sanity might be assured if one makes the shifts to accommodate a changing world, though Greer does say, 'I like to think that, in giving in at the end of the play, Anna is really only biding her time.'[40]

middle-class miseries: resolving past traumas in bonnie greer's *dancing on blackwater*

Images of colonial discourse are at the centre of Greer's *Dancing on Blackwater*, which explores how two black British sisters (Carolyn and Lisette) reconcile their middle-class upbringing with their black heritages. Greer explains, 'I wanted to look at the experience of Black people who belonged to the so-called middle-class. That is my experience, and I have not seen that explored very much on the stage either here [in England] or in America.'[41] James Christopher's review for *Time Out* suggests that by

> [s]etting her play in the cherished heart of the stockbroking classes – a Green Belt country house – she brings an issue that theatre here seldom addresses into unsettling relief: the contradictions of being black, 'privileged' and English. To add insult to injury, she puts such exotic disparities as British public schools and the black African Diaspora into revealing and comical proximity.[42]

Carolyn is a successful PR agent who spends much of the play speaking to colleagues on her mobile phone. She has taken on Thatcherism's doctrine of individual success, and her achievements are premised on the ability to confidently assert herself as a black woman professional. Her younger sister, Lisette, has fared less well, working as a supply teacher at an inner-city multicultural London infant school. Lisette has a history of agoraphobia, anorexia, bulimia, self-harming and suicide attempts, and a nervous stutter is one of a number of symptomatic manifestations of her mental vulnerability. The sisters are clearing out a cottage in Kent that they have inherited from Lady Russell, a rich white woman whom their mother used to look after, and they are arguing about whether to keep it or sell it on. The old (heritage) Britain and the new (urban metropolis) are brought together by the contrast between the women's lives in the 1990s and the play's setting – 'a quaint room, locked in time, loved but unlived in. We can discern the shapes of Victorian and Edwardian antiques beneath the dust-covers.'[43] The setting underscores their debates about the past and the present, which are used to explore whether attitudes have changed with the passage of time. Kate Bassett's review in *The Times* describes how the play 'interestingly contemplates reincarnations of enslavement', reaching into the past as a way of understanding the present.[44] As Carolyn and Lisette sort through Lady Russell's ornaments, they discover symbols of Britain as it used to be in the days of Queen Victoria, Empire and slavery. Lisette wants to remember the past, and reminisce about their mother's suicide as part of the process of healing, but Carolyn is determined to live in the present and look to the future.

The remote cottage is familiar to them from regular childhood visits, and represents a place where they were exposed to middle- class pastimes, such as classical dancing, sonnet recitals, or learning French, and colonial imagery like Lady Russell's 'family portrait with a little black slave girl dressed in a silk dress with a turban on her head and a pearl earring dangling all the way to her shoulder'.[45] This period in their lives was also one rife with blatant racism, which they are still trying to come to terms with. They were sent to a public boarding school in Shropshire in the 1970s, where they were the only black girls and were subjected to racist treatment, such as visiting one of their posh school friends for a weekend in the country where they were served bananas for tea. Melissa Michaels's *What's On* review describes the sisters as a 'confusing oddity . . . unable to fit in with the white middle class, the black working class or the black Africans from whom they descended'. Lisette teaches in a predominantly black school, but her middle-class upbringing leaves her feeling culturally disconnected from the pupils.[46] Carolyn resents the middle- class education that they were given, and is generally cynical and outwardly angry at the assumptions of an institutionally racist society where they are disadvantaged as black women. At the same time, she resists attempts to understand her through certain assumptions of black cultural identity.[47]

The play hinges on an unexpected visit to the cottage by Mrs B and her self-elected mute daughter whose arrival shifts the dynamic between the sisters. The strangers stop at the cottage looking for food and shelter, as they pass by on a pilgrimage to take a black Madonna to the Archbishop of Canterbury. The sisters are trying to shake off the effects of old Empire on their psyches, and Carolyn has invested in the fast-paced modern life of selfish individualism. The visitors bring an alternative vision of the old that represents the past in terms of a simple and nostalgic Caribbean community life where women cook simple fresh, nourishing food and perform self-healing. The visit helps Lisette to gain confidence, embracing the alternative culture offered by the visitors as the start of her recovery process. Like Frieda in *Leonora's Dance*, Mrs B creates the conditions for Lisette to come to terms with the past traumas that have caused her neuroses and cures Lisette's stutter in an unconventional way (squashing her and almost squeezing the life out of her).

Lisette and Carolyn's anxieties about the circumstances surrounding their mother's suicide insinuate a 'Mother Country' that has done them a disservice, which is made explicit in Mrs B comment, 'A mother can kill you. And a mother country, too.'[48] The reasons for their mother's suicide are revealed as relating to the disappointment of coming to England in search of a better life and discovering the difficulties that black women migrants faced to establish the type of life they wanted. The two sisters continue to face issues of racist stereotyping as middle-class black women at the end of the twentieth century, and Carolyn implies that Lisette's 'madness' might be a useful form of resistance in a neo-colonial society: 'What's it mean to be well in a sick society, Mrs B? Sometimes I think she's better off the way she is. She doesn't have to deal with it. She just takes a kind of holiday from it with her numerous suicide attempts, her bursts of promiscuity, etc. sort of like a Benidorm of the mind.'[49]

maternal mind-doctors

The plays profiled in this chapter explore mental health difficulties that result from issues of race, class and gender, where the characters' mental troubles relate to their access or aspirations to a middle-class value system that is problematic for them as black women in Britain. The predominance of colonial imagery in all three plays is used to remind late-twentieth-century audiences of their potency, and continued long-term detrimental impact on black women's psyches. Significantly, what are deemed mental illnesses in Eurocentric terms are figured in these plays as a way of resisting the values of an institutionally racist and sexist society.

Tim Shields's discussion of healing madness in drama maps a tradition of 'mind-doctors' who are equipped with the professional education, power, training, expertise and language to make judgements about their clients' problems and identify ways of treating them.[50] Shields identifies 'the proliferation of gurus, counsellors, consultants, spiritual advisers – all equipped with appropriate credentials – ready to intervene in our lives' as a contemporary phenomenon, where the 'desire to offload, to devolve responsibility for our private selves on to suitably "qualified' others" is one manifestation of individualism in a culture where lifestyle gurus and makeover cultures predominate.[51] Shields argues that

[p]ortraits of mind-doctors as protagonists in contemporary plays are

not on the whole very flattering, which makes it significant that Leonora in *Leonora's Dance* and Lisette in *Dancing on Blackwater* are not healed within conventional psychiatric systems, but rather start their healing process in relation to first generation black maternal soothsayers that imply that steadfast communities of black women are sustainable in an individualistic context.[52]

The mind-doctors' quest to 'uncover hidden secrets . . . [and] engender transformations' is effectively enacted by black women as a way of avoiding the pitfalls of racist–patriarchal psychiatry.[53]

The individual traumas experienced by the characters in *Leonora's Dance, Munda Negra* and *Dancing on Blackwater* allude to broader issues of race, class and generation that remain unresolved. All three plays infer relationships between mothers and their children to imply a 'Mother Country' that has not quite lived up to its responsibilities. Mick Martin's review describes *Dancing on Blackwater* as 'carried by the precision and near poetic beauty of the writing, the gently expressed but complex insights it offers into the mother/daughter relationship, and by the author's ability to translate these into a wider consideration of second-generation black English women'.[54] Black women's theatre of the 1980s was severely criticized for being too explicitly angry and didactic, so using human stories to make political points engenders a contemporary aesthetic that continues to shape black women's playwriting in the twenty-first century. All three 1990s plays discussed here also trouble realist discourse, blending the past with the present and the 'real' world with spirit encounters to offer a commentary on black women's psyches that is intrinsically political.

notes

1. Black Theatre Co-operative, Clean Break Theatre Company, Temba Theatre Company and The Women's Playhouse Trust produced plays by these dramatists at venues including The Cockpit Theatre, Drill Hall, Soho Poly, Theatre Royal Stratford East and the Royal Court.
2. The new millennium has also witnessed what might be called a renaissance in black men's playwriting, with a number of significant productions at key London venues. Kwame Kwei-Armah's *Elmina's Kitchen* (2003) and *Fix Up* (2004) were produced to critical acclaim, with the former becoming the first non-musical black British play to be produced in the West End. Roy Williams's illustrious career includes millennial productions of *Fallout* (2003), *Sing Yer Heart Out for the Lads* (2002), *Clubland* (2001), *The Gift* (2000) and *Little Sweet Thing* (2005). Other 2000s plays by black playwrights include

Kofi Agyemang and Patricia Elcock's *Urban Afro Saxons* (2003), Lennie James's *The Sons of Charlie Paora* (2004) and Mark Norfolk's *Wrong Place* (2003).

3. See, for example, Jackie Kay's *Chiaroscuro* (1986), Winsome Pinnock's *Leave Taking* (1987) and *A Hero's Welcome* (1989), and Jacqueline Rudet's *Money to Live* (1984) and *Basin* (1985).

4. W. Pinnock, 'Breaking Down the Door', in V. Gottlieb and C. Chambers (eds), *Theatre in a Cool Climate* (Oxford: Amber Lane Press, 1999), pp. 27–38 (p. 31).

5. G. Griffin, *Contemporary Black and Asian Women Playwrights in Britain* (Cambridge: Cambridge University Press, 2003), p. 25.

6. E. Aston, *Feminist Views on the English Stage: Women Playwrights 1990–2000* (Cambridge: Cambridge University Press, 2003), p. 6.

7. Ibid., p. 60.

8. See Aston, *Feminist Views*, Griffin, *Contemporary Black and Asian Women Playwrights*; L. Goddard, 'West Indies *vs* England in Winsome Pinnock's Migration Narratives', *Contemporary Theatre Review*, vol. 14, no. 4 (2004), 23–33, and L. Goddard, *Staging Black Feminisms: Identity, Politics, Performance* (Basingstoke: Palgrave Macmillan, 2007) for further analysis of *Talking in Tongues*.

9. See D. Godiwala (ed.), *Alternatives Within the Mainstream: British Black and Asian Theatres* (Newcastle: Cambridge Scholars Press, 2006); S. Hensman, 'Presentation of Self as Performance: The Birth of Queenie aka Valerie Mason-John', in N. Rapi and M. Chowdhry (eds), *Acts of Passion: Sexuality, Gender and Performance* (London: The Haworth Press, 1998), pp. 209–19; and Goddard, *Staging Black Feminisms* for further analysis of Mason-John's *Brown Girl in the Ring*.

10. See also Jenny McLeod's *Raising Fires* (1994), Kara Miller's *Hyacinth Blue* (1999) and Yazmine Judd's *Unfinished Business* (1999) for explorations of themes of depression, dementia, spirituality and witchcraft that raise questions about notions of black women's mental health.

11. *Leonora's Dance* programme.

12. http://www.bbc.co.uk/radio4/science/allinthemind_20031118.shtml. Accessed 12 January 2006.

13. See, for example, A. W. Burke and J. Bierer (eds), *Transcultural Psychiatry* and *Racism & Mental Illness. The International Journal of Social Psychiatry*, vol. 30, nos 1 & 2 (1984); P. Rack, *Race, Culture and Mental Disorder* (London: Tavistock Publications, 1982), and K. Bhui, *Racism & Mental Health* (London: Jessica Kingsley Publishers, 2002).

14. See Rack, *Race, Culture and Mental Disorder*.

15. H. B. Lewis, 'Madness in Women', in E. Howell and M. Bayes (eds), *Women and Mental Health* (New York: Basic Books, 1981), pp. 207–27 (p. 223).

16. J. Ussher, *Women's Madness: Misogyny or Mental Illness* (London: Harvester Wheatsheaf, 1991), p. 75.

17. Wayne Buchanan's *Under Their Influence* (2000) and Joe Penhall's *Blue/Orange* (2000) explore black men, mental illness and psychiatric care.
18. See A. Mama, *Beyond the Masks: Race, Gender and Subjectivity* (London: Routledge, 1995) for a sustained interrogation of how black women are constructed within psychiatric discourses.
19. P. Marmion, 'Busting Loose', *What's On*, 10 February 1993.
20. Griffin, *Contemporary Black and Asian Women Playwrights*, pp. 110–11.
21. See L. M. Anderson, *Mammies No More: The Changing Image of Black Women on Stage and Screen* (New York: Rowman and Littlefield, 1997) for detailed discussion of the tragic mulatto archetype.
22. B. Tizard and A. Phoenix, *Black, White or Mixed Race?: Race and Racism in the Lives of Young People of Mixed Parentage*, rev. edn (London: Routledge, 2002), p. 102.
23. Tizard and Phoenix, *Black, White or Mixed Race?*, p. 11.
24. A. Wilson, *Mixed Race Children: A Study of Identity* (London: Allen and Unwin, 1987), p. vi.
25. Ibid., p. 1.
26. W. E. B. Du Bois, 'The Souls of Black Folk', in H. L. Gates, Jr and T. H. Oliver (eds), *A Norton Critical Edition* (London: W. W. Norton and Company, 1999), p. 11.
27. F. Fanon, *Black Skin, White Masks*, trans. C. L. Markmann (London: Pluto Press, 1986) pp. 116–17.
28. Fanon, *Black Skin, White Masks*, p. 117.
29. S. Hemming, '*Leonora's Dance* Review', *Theatre Record*, vol. 12, no. 3 (1993), 133; B. Jancovich, '*Leonora's Dance* Review', ibid.
30. S. Feay, '*Leonora's Dance* Review', ibid.
31. Zindika, *Leonora's Dance*, in K. George (ed.), *Six Plays by Black and Asian Women Writers* (London: Aurora Metro Press, 1993), p. 78.
32. See L. Goodman, *Mythic Women/Real Women: Plays and Performance Pieces by Women* (London: Faber, 2000), p. xv for further discussion of the historical construction of Medusa as evil. Dorothea Smartt's 'Medusa' performance poems revisit this myth as it pertains to notions of black womanhood. See D. Smartt, *Connecting Medium* (Leeds: Peepal Tree Press, 2001) and L. Goodman, 'Who's Looking at Who(m)?: Re-viewing Medusa', *Modern Drama*, vol. 39, no. 1 (1996), 190–210.
33. B. Nightingale, '*Leonora's Dance* Review', *Theatre Record*, vol. 12, no. 3 (1993), 133.
34. Feay, '*Leonora's Dance* Review', ibid.
35. A. Sierz, '*Leonora's Dance* Review', *Theatre Record*, vol. 13, no. 4 (1993), 213.
36. Y. Brewster (ed.), *Black Plays 3* (London: Methuen, 1995), viii.
37. B. Greer, *Munda Negra* in ibid., p. 42.
38. Ibid., p. 98.
39. Ibid., p. 74.
40. Ibid., p. 98.

41. *Dancing on Blackwater* programme.
42. J. Christopher, '*Dancing on Blackwater* Review', *Theatre Record*, vol. 14, no. 20 (1994), p. 1193.
43. B. Greer, *Dancing on Blackwater*, unpublished draft (courtesy Nitro, 1994), p. 1.
44. K. Bassett, '*Dancing on Blackwater* Review', *Theatre Record*, vol. 14, no. 20 (1994), p. 1193.
45. Greer, *Dancing on Blackwater*, p. 24.
46. M. Michaels, '*Dancing on Blackwater* Review', *Theatre Record*, vol. 14, no. 20 (1994), p. 1193.
47. The contrast between Carolyn and Lisette shows a typical intragenerational split between black women that occurs in several other black women's plays, such as Pinnock's *Leave Taking*, which compares a studious and a rebellious sister, or Rudet's *Money to Live*, where one sister is an ardent feminist and the other takes a job as a stripper. Carolyn and Lisette directly parallel the two central characters in Pinnock's *Talking in Tongues*, where Claudette is outwardly angry and recalcitrant towards white people, whereas Leela has tried her utmost to assimilate and has lost her identity in the process. Lisette's psychosomatic illnesses are comparable with Leela's and also with Leonora's in *Leonora's Dance*.
48. Greer, *Dancing on Blackwater*, p. 30.
49. Ibid., p. 73.
50. T. Shields, 'Theatricality and Madness: Minding the Mind-doctors', in D. Meyer-Dinkgräfe (ed.), *The Professions in Contemporary Drama* (Bristol: Intellect Books, 2003), pp. 37–45 (p. 37).
51. Ibid., p. 37.
52. Ibid.
53. Ibid., p. 38.
54. M. Martin, '*Dancing on Blackwater* Review', *Theatre Record*, vol. 14, no. 20 (1994), p. 1506.

6
a good night out, for the girls
elaine aston

Based on a series of talks given to a Cambridge elite in 1979, the late John McGrath's *A Good Night Out* was seminal to challenging an idea of theatre as overwhelmingly, if not exclusively, for middle-class audiences.[1] For McGrath politics were allied to the popular, and as director of the 7:84 Theatre Company he practised and promoted forms of working-class entertainment that offered a broad audience appeal. Similarly, against a backdrop of 1970s second-wave feminism, women's theatre companies and feminist practitioners were also concerned to challenge dominant theatre culture on grounds that were in part class-related, but were more particularly concerned with gender. Policy statements issued by the Women's Theatre Group (WTG), our longest-running women's theatre company, for instance, stated the intention 'to provide a good night out', and 'to make the name of the Women's Theatre Group synonymous with accessible, entertaining and stimulating theatre, which is by, for and about women'.[2] In brief, socialist and feminist companies such as 7:84 and WTG shared a commitment to an idea of theatre that could both entertain and politicize.

The 1970s have typically been viewed as the high point of British political drama. It was a decade in which socialism and/or feminism influenced form, content and context of theatrical production: provided (feminist) subject matter; shaped composition, aesthetics and style of performance (often agit-prop, or issue-based drama), and motivated the desire to reach non-theatre going audiences (of women). While this 'alternative' model of political theatre-making obtained in the 1970s, a decade when the political climate and funding policies enabled socially progressive theatre, it was not one that was readily able or equipped to survive the Thatcherite 1980s. As this decade privatized

114

rather than democratized, and introduced drastic cuts to public subsidy for the arts, all of this changed – eroded might be a better description – the means of alternative, subsidized, artistic production. [3]

As socialist ideas were weakened by the collapse of communism in the former Eastern bloc and feminism's public profile diminished, both as a consequence of the anti-feminist backlash and its own fragmentation into localized identity politics, by the 1990s it meant that there were serious questions to be asked about viable alternatives to a right-wing political agenda.[4] As the communist Mihail asks in Timberlake Wertenbaker's state-of-the-nation play *The Break of Day* (1995), as his former East European country descends from communist ideals into the chaos of capitalism, how is it possible to 'go into the next century with no ideal but selfishness?'.[5]

In Britain socialist and feminist 'ideals' in the 1990s transformed into a 'new' politics: *New* Labour's victory in 1997 and a '*new* feminism' promoted, among others, by journalist Natasha Walter.[6] Despite assertions to the contrary, Walter's style of 'new feminism' has most in common with second-wave bourgeois feminism: all for one, rather than a feminism for all. Further, while 'new feminism' focused on empowerment for women, it was less concerned with a socialist democratization of power and wealth, and concentrated instead on self- and sexual empowerment, as evidenced by the 'girl-power' phenomenon of the 1990s. In the academy, meanwhile, feminist scholarship became more preoccupied with what Angela McRobbie terms the 'Es and anti-Es': the essentialist and anti-essentialist debates that arose as feminists struggled with the issues fuelled by trying to move beyond identity-based politics into a more deconstructive postmodern feminist mode of theorizing. One of the curious side effects of this, however, has been to create what McRobbie describes as 'a resistance to looking outside theory and asking some practical questions about the world we live in'.[7]

In theatre, these kinds of political and cultural changes meant that 'some practical questions' needed to be asked about the survival of feminist work in the 1990s. Early on in the decade many of the alternative feminist companies that were launched in the 1970s or early 1980s ceased touring as their funding was cut and the networks of women-friendly venues and contacts were eroded.[8] Exceptionally, WTG survived, but only by rebranding and reorganizing the company. In 1991 it became the Sphinx Theatre Company, and the collective feminist organization of former years was replaced by a much smaller core management team of five posts, under the directorship of Sue Parrish.[9] As Parrish explained, the relaunch was designed to take the company in 'a new direction' and to achieve 'a wider appeal to its work' through productions and theatre events such as the 'Glass Ceiling' symposia.[10] The company's repertoire in the 1990s twins a more mainstream appeal, an all-women's Hamlet, for example (*The Roaring Girl's Hamlet*, Claire Luckham, 1992), with a continuing commitment to 'feminist ideas' plays, such as *Sweet Dreams* (Diane Esquerra, 1999), based on Ida Bauer, the 'Dora' of Freud's famous case, and to feminist icons, such as Virginia Woolf (*Vita & Virginia*, Eileen Atkins, 1999) or black blues singer Bessie Smith (*Every Bit of It*, Jackie Kay, 1992–3). Dramatists the company commissioned in the 1990s also included Pam Gems (*The Snow Palace*, 1999), whose professional writing career has been consistently more mainstream than many other feminist playwrights from the 1970s. While the rebranding of WTG reflects a 1990s flavour of 'new feminism' (company statements claim 'strong roles for actresses', opportunities for women directors and productions that offer 'inspirational women taking centre stage, striving to realise their ambitions and desires'), it also, given the repertoire, connects with a feminist past and to the orig-inating idea of 'a good night out' that is 'by, for and about women'.[11]

By and large, feminist theatre scholarship has always been suspicious of the mainstream for two often very good (justified) reasons: either because there is a likelihood that the work that the mainstream adopts will tend to be the most anodyne in political terms, or because it may consume and dilute the radical as it moves out of an alternative politi-cal and into a more mainstream reception context.[12] While this suspi-cion has been a consequence of the need to pay attention to ideas about and in feminist theatre work, it may nevertheless have contributed, as John Deeney observes, to an oversimplified binarism of alternative and mainstream when the realities of theatrical production are, Deeney argues, far more complex than this.[13] Deeney's point has particular rele-vance for the 1990s, a decade in which, as the Sphinx's mainstreaming woman-centred repertoire demonstrates, an idea of the 'alternative' no longer 'fits' dominant modes of theatrical production. Moreover, when companies and touring circuits decline and diminish, this increases the pressures on the 'individual' writer or production as the key to success.[14]

In turn this begs the question of where feminism directs its gaze in the 1990s. In other research contexts I have argued the need for and the value in paying feminist attention to the work of emergent and estab-lished women playwrights on the English stage in the 1990s that might otherwise get written out by theatre histories that document the 1990s as a 'shock-fest' of angry young men.[15] Here, however, like the Sphinx

Theatre Company, I am interested in a 'new direction': extending my gaze to examples of (mostly) commercial theatre. Rather like WTG's relaunch, this requires a simultaneous holding on to and letting go of the 'alternative' paradigm. In undertaking this, I note, on the one hand, McGrath's recognition, despite his personal investment in working-class theatre and audiences, that all theatre is a 'politicizing medium': a 'public act of recognition' that politicizes by making public sets of ideas, values, or attitudes even in the most conservative and 'trivial' of West End shows.[16] While, on the other hand, useful to my critical endeavours is the case that Maggie Gale makes in *West End Women* for examining 'commercially orientated theatre' that from a 1970s feminist viewpoint is considered not to 'warrant serious examination'.[17] Gale was concerned with an earlier, pre-1970s period of twentieth-century British theatre, but her argument has relevance to the 1990s that moves out of and beyond the 1970s paradigm.

In brief, in a more expansive idea of theatre than the 'drama' in the title of this essay collection suggests, I propose to take four examples of 'West End Women' shows from the 1990s: Eve Ensler's *The Vagina Monologues*, Jenny Eclair's *Prozac and Tantrums*, and Catherine Johnson's *Shang-a-Lang* and *Mamma Mia!*. While each of these makes different feminist connections – to violence against women (Ensler), to the 'beauty myth' (Eclair) and to cultures of romance (Johnson) – what brings them together in my contribution to *Cool Britannia?* are the politicizing possibilities of the popular as the shows variously offer 'a good night out, for the girls'.

talking vaginas: eve ensler

With the exception of *Mamma Mia!*, the show examples I have selected start out in less financially attractive circumstances than their eventual mainstream rewards. Ensler's *The Vagina Monologues* started in downtown New York in the mid-1990s, an off-off-Broadway show that upgraded to off-Broadway and toured cities across the USA and countries all over the world. In Britain the *Monologues* were first performed in 1999 at the King's Head Theatre in Islington, a 115-seater fringe venue, before transferring into the West End to the New Ambassadors Theatre and the Arts Theatre (2001–2). The show continues to have regular West End seasons.

I saw the show after its transfer to the Ambassadors, and with Ensler performing solo, rather than the three-hander version that different star actresses have since played. Although the show had attracted a mixed audience, it was predominantly female, middle-aged and well heeled, with women attending in small women-only groups of friends. Foyer conversations and in the ladies' toilets (although this hardly counts as empirical research, I never fail to find it fascinating!), suggested an element of the risqué. One overheard conversation suggested that the women concerned considered themselves daring to be at the show, citing other girlfriends whom they had not been able to persuade to join them.

While middle-aged women primarily attended the West End performance I saw, the *Monologues* have attracted audiences of young (university-age) women through the V-Day campaign. This is a fund-raising initiative that began in 1998. Benefit performances of the *Monologues* are held around Valentine's Day to raise awareness and money in order to help stop violence against women. After the first V-Day event it was decided to target universities and colleges as a way of reaching and getting the support of young women.[18] Second-wave feminist theatre had its own tradition of playing to and politicizing audiences of young women, and in some ways V-Day could be argued as a continuation of this practice. A crucial difference, however, is the way in which the interlinking of entertainment and direct action operates out of a site of privilege, the college campus base, whereas previously political touring theatre operated at grassroots, activist levels. If, before, the second-wave emphasis was on building activist connections across local communities, Ensler's V-Day initiative suggests a more global approach that, in truth, has much greater commonality with the style of high-profile charity fundraising that has proved increasingly popular since the Live Aid charity concert for Ethiopia back in 1985.

As a show, *The Vagina Monologues* offers a curious mix of the pleasurable and the painful. Formally Ensler's performance is indebted to popular entertainment styles of stand-up comedy and character-sketch shows. It even has the kind of audience participation one might expect at a pantomime: spectators are invited to join a chorus of chanting (reclaiming) the word 'cunt'. As Ensler shares some of her own vagina thoughts and experiences along with those of women whom she interviewed in the making of the piece, the show is often darkly funny, while at others, given the violence and abuse, it is not funny at all. In brief, the show is a celebration of female sexuality that at the same time aims to raise awareness about the violence committed against women as rape, abuse, or ignorance about the 'down there' female-body parts.

What I find particularly intriguing about this show is the way in which it transforms a 1970s style of feminism into popular entertainment, primarily 'by, for and about' women in the 1990s. What Ensler does is to take a 1970s style of radical feminism and give it a 1990s makeover: it takes consciousness-raising and radical feminism as a basis for a more up-to-date style of self-sexual-empowerment politics. In the process of this makeover, a 1970s emphasis on the collective (*à la* WTG) is rejected in favour of the solo, the star performer, and Ensler's high-profile commercial success with the *Monologues* has put her firmly in the feminist celebrity spotlight.

From an academic feminist viewpoint this is highly problematic and goes some way to explaining why, despite the show's popularity, it also receives some very negative responses (although not just from feminists).[19] Feminist theatre scholarship has repeatedly rehearsed the difficulties of universalizing women's experiences as the experience of all women.[20] In spite of this, cultural feminism became the media-friendly version of feminism in the 1990s, especially in North America. As McRobbie argues, in this context 'E' feminism has succeeded in 'defining the terrain of feminism'.[21] Ensler's show is no exception. As a North American import, her 1970s cultural–feminist revival is curiously at odds with the materialist–feminist British theatre tradition of violence against women plays or one-woman solos.[22]

Even stranger, perhaps, is the way that commercial success should follow from a style of feminism that in its own (second- wave) day caused the most antagonism in the mainstream. Sarah Daniels's radical–feminist stance in *Masterpieces* (1983), her savage critique of pornography as violence against women, caused a furore among the (mostly male) critics. So how is it possible to have an 'E' revival in the 1990s that attracts West End (and international) success? This I would argue is dependent on how the show works formally through the popular (stand-up and sketch styles) and the confessional in a way that 'protects' the spectator from feminism and from the violence.

As the next show example (*Prozac and Tantrums*) will illustrate, contemporary female stand-ups have popularized 'vagina comedy', while the 'girl-power' 1990s gave young women the confidence to 'body talk' – even, given the rise of ladettism, to 'filthy body talk'. So there is an immediate popular cultural appeal to 'talking vaginas'. Moreover, the confessional style of the piece, the concept of a 'talking cure' that underpins the show (making public confessions of abuse, rape and sexual experiences), fits with the popularity of confessional television shows in a way that makes the *Monologues* culturally recognizable and popular with younger women.

Part of the show's appeal also lies, I would suggest, in the way that despite lots of sexual slang and vagina talk, it avoids the 'f' word. The anti-feminist backlash made feminism a 'dirty word' in the 1980s and by the 1990s young women tended not to identify with feminism, while older generations of feminist women went back into the feminist closet. I find it exceptional now to hear young women in the classroom calling themselves feminists. On the other hand, I very often hear them say 'I'm not a feminist, but . . .'. That 'but' does quite a lot of (albeit in another way limited) political work: 'I'm not a feminist, but I see all kinds of things that are unfair to women.' While Ensler declares herself to be an activist feminist and believes that art should be political, I would argue *The Vagina Monologues* as a show that has a cross-genera- tional appeal, not because it is received as a feminist show, but because it appeals to the 'I'm not a feminist, but I am able to recognize the violence against women' position.[23]

However, in arguing against the injustice of violence against women, the show in some ways comes dangerously close to taking advantage of this. To give an example: one particular monologue, 'my vagina was my village', is based on the crimes committed against women in the former Yugoslavia – the Bosnian rape camps in 1993. The atrocities in the former Yugoslavia similarly had an influence on the writing of Kane's *Blasted*, but whereas Kane's composition and aesthetics work to shock politically, to reawaken 'naturalized' responses to violence, Ensler, by contrast, sentimentalizes and de-politicizes the violence.[24] Watching the documentary-style performance that Ensler made for HBO in 2001 reaffirmed the trouble I had with this sequence in the live show. In the recorded version Ensler introduces news photos of Bosnian rape victims while she 'explains' the atrocities and observes, as the camera focuses on the press images, how these abused women cannot look at the camera. In 'recapturing' those experiences and 'performing' them in the show, Ensler does not politicize; rather she spectacularizes the suffering of others. Feminist sociologist Bev Skeggs has a term that I feel pinpoints what is happening here. Skeggs describes the process of 'affect strip- ping': 'a process whereby affects are detached from the body of produc- tion and re-made as an exchange-value when re-attached to the body that does not produce the same affect but can capitalise upon it'.[25] Ensler 'capitalises' on the rape victims by reproducing their pain into a poetic lament, emotionalized by musical accompaniment and acted out in split subject mode: happy and violated vaginas performed by looking to and away from the camera respectively. Equally, this monologue testifies to 'E' feminism's ability to affect-strip contemporary feminism*s*: the 'local' experiences and histories of violence of these Bosnian women is subsumed by the universalizing woman/vagina 'speak', just as feminism's potential to politicize gives way to emotionalist and sensationalist effect.

Students I teach tend to be surprised by, if not disbelieving of, my interrogation of *The Vagina Monologues* as conservative in style and content because, by and large, they have no sense of feminism's contemporary past: no sense that we have been here before. For younger generations of the 'I'm not a feminist, but . . .' culture, feminism is assumed, is taken as a given, but is not a point of identification in terms either of politics or performance. Hence, while *The Vagina Monologues* initially appears to be the most likely successor to a 1970s tradition of 'alternative' theatre (*à la* WTG), given its attachments to feminism, more detailed investigation argues the show's political and aesthetic failure to progress. By contrast, my further show examples make no direct claims to a feminist political and yet all of them, in very different ways, mobilize political possibilities that 'warrant serious [feminist] examination'.

in-yer-face stand-up: jenny eclair

One of the star actresses to appear in Ensler's *The Vagina Monologues* is British stand-up comedienne Jenny Eclair. Eclair works in a variety of commercial contexts that include television comedy, radio chat shows and West End theatre, though she is best known for her stand-up comedy. Like most other stand-ups, Eclair served a long apprenticeship on the comedy and club circuit before securing commercial success. When in 1995 she won the Perrier Award for her stand-up performance *Prozac and Tantrums*, Eclair had already spent thirteen years on the comedy fringe circuit, which, though it has a certain cachet, is hard to make a living from. Winning the Award revitalized a struggling career (and bank balance).

Unlike Ensler, Eclair is not a political campaigner. Politics are not what she considers to be an area of her 'expertise', though 'social politics' is something that she claims for her work, and feminism she identifies with on account of working in the male-dominated world of stand-up comedy.[26] Her acknowledgement of a second-wave feminist past is reflected in a theatre repertoire that, for example, includes the 1997 revival of Nell Dunn's proto-feminist play *Steaming*, and her view that feminism was something she was 'born' into. Asked, for example, in interview if she is a feminist, Eclair answers, 'Well I just am, by accident of birth more than anything else. I mean it was all done for us.'[27]

However, although second-wave feminism had 'done' a lot of work challenging the sexual politics of theatre and its oppressive representations of women and the underrepresentation of their work, stand-up comedy remained hard for women to access. Even today, despite the efforts to challenge the male domination of stand-up by a 1980s generation of women performers (Eclair included), there is no significant increase of women in the field in the 1990s.[28] As the first woman to win the Perrier Award (1995), Eclair was also the only woman to win it for the next ten years.[29] The relative absence of women in stand-up comedy means that Eclair represents a mix of 'old' and 'new' feminisms: her 1970s paradigm of feminist-woman-breaking-into-a-man's-world, but refigured through the 'bad girl' image of the 1990s.

Eclair has an opinion about the theatre that chimes with McGrath's view that 'middle-class theatre is not by definition the only, or even necessarily the best, kind of theatre'.[30] 'Most theatre is really boring', Eclair claims, and describes her work as 'theatre for people who don't like theatre'.[31] While her one-woman shows and stand-up comedy offer a 'good night out' that primarily appeals to the 'girls', what is also distinctive about her audience address is that it is class- as well as gender-based. Unlike either WTG's earlier touring feminism which played mostly to middle-class feminists, or Ensler's West End or campus-based 'vaginas', which both attract a more middle-class audience base (especially given the class make-up of higher education), Eclair's stand-up has a much broader class constituency that is inclusive of working-class women. When I recently hosted Jenny Eclair's 'forty-something' stand-up performance, *Jenny Eclair: Middle-Aged Bimbo*, in the Nuffield Theatre at Lancaster University (31 January 2004), for example, a venue that usually plays to a student audience and offers a programme of contemporary experimental performance, the show instead brought in a forty-plus women's audience from neighbouring working-class Morecambe.[32] I want to pursue the broad appeal of Eclair's stand-up by examining her presentation of a resistant feminine and then by thinking about this more specifically in class terms.

Prozac and Tantrums signals feminism's as yet unresolved issues in relation to cultures of femininity. As McRobbie observes, 1970s feminist cultural studies created a particular tension or contradiction in wanting to legitimize the study of femininity (looking at women's representation in advertising and magazines, for example), at the same time as endorsing 'the political aim . . . to pull women away from cultures of femininity (the nail polish) towards feminism'.[33] In 1990, Naomi Wolf's *The Beauty Myth* identified beauty specifically as an unresolved issue for feminism. She argued 'the ideology of beauty [as] the last one remaining of the old feminine ideologies', the underside of feminism's success: 'a secret "underlife" poisoning our freedom; infused with notions of beauty, it is a dark vein of self-hatred, physical obsessions, terror of aging, and dread of lost control'.[34] When Eclair won the Perrier Award for *Prozac and Tantrums* in 1995 she gave a speech in comic vein that declared the show's success a 'blow for womanhood, for cellulite, for bodies that are falling apart everywhere'.[35] The show savages an 'ideal' of 'womanhood' that is both biologically determined (*Prozac and Tantrums* is a play on PMT in which Eclair re-presents the biological uncontrollability of the female body as a controlled, premeditated occasion for raging against the male sex) and socially constructed through commercial cultures of femininity (female celebrities, teen and women's magazines and marketing of cars for the 'little lady' all come under comic attack). The terror of the beauty myth that Wolf identifies for women is debunked through jokes about the ageing female body that has 'arse room', 'labia like spaniels' ears', cellulite and poor stomach muscles.

Beyond ideologies of the 'beauty myth', however, Eclair also savages the domestic feminine. While 1970s feminism invited women to reject the patriarchal domestic: to refuse to mother, cook, clean, and 'service' husbands, the pressure of the 1980s 'superwoman' (that encouraged women into multitasking careers of work, children and kitchen) and an anti-feminist backlash, has generated a return to a 1950s-style domestic in the 1990s – at least for those (middle-class) women who believe they want, desire and can afford it. *Prozac and Tantrums* takes every opportunity, however, to tell women that this isn't 'what they want, what they really, really want'.

At several points in her performance, Eclair appeals directly to the 'girls' in the audience, inviting them variously to pleasure in the cathartic release of her Rabelaisian body that farts, vomits, shits and overindulges in sex, booze and cigarettes. The interpellation of women as 'girls' does not connote with the good-girl feminine, but with the 'kick-ass', bad-girl feminism of the 1990s. Eclair's 'kick-ass' feminine developed out of her early career as a punk performance poet ('I've got this problem with my figure, my tits just won't get any bigger').[36] Punk culture enabled an alternative, resistant play with dominant cultures of femininity. Eclair's appearance in *Prozac and Tantrums* is semiotically encoded as a mix of teddy-boy-punk-feminine. Dressed in a glittery, lapelled jacket and black shiny drainpipe trousers, thick-soled, creeper-style shoes, and wearing heavy make-up (red lips and nails; false black

eye lashes) and a big blonde hairdo, she indulges in an excess of swearing, drinking and comic stories of outrageously promiscuous behaviour.
In the context of the 1990s, this monstering or excess of the feminine
further connotes the 'white-trash' feminine that associates with working-class women. Skeggs identifies a shift from the condemnation that
was heaped on the single mother as 'the source of all national evil' in
the 1980s to the 'hen-partying woman' as 'the figure of the immoral
repellent woman'.[37] This is a figure that Skeggs argues disgusts and
outrages not just the politically conservative, but also those of New
Labour and feminist persuasions.[38] Hen-partying woman is a 'national
sin'; Eclair's performance 'sins' against the nation. Her unruly, badly
behaved, loud-mouthed, vulgar, oversexed, alcohol-loving, bottle-
blonde persona works resistantly against the 'pathologizing, disgust-
producing register attached to working-class women'.[39] Her stand-up
style is one that delights in 'trash' behaviour in the spirit of celebration,
not condemnation.

As a performance, *Prozac and Tantrums* has much in common with
the characteristics that Aleks Sierz singles out as defining the 'in-yer-
face' drama of the 1990s: emotional, experiential, close-up, invasive,
taking you by the scruff of the neck, using shock tactics, swearing,
powerful and visceral.[40] Given the show's 'trash' content and in-yer-
face stand-up style, it is not to everyone's 'taste'. Yet stripping commercial cultures of femininity of their 'beauty myth' glamour; taking them
by the scruff of the neck, spewing them up and spitting them out in a
shock-fest of cellulite-ridden comedy is what makes the show effective
and affective for feminism that has yet to resolve the 'underlife' of feminine ideologies.

reviving the 1970s: catherine johnson

Asked in an interview to 'describe the ultimate girls' night out', Eclair
replies that 'there's nothing more scary than a bunch of 40-year-old
women on the razz'.[41] Playwright Catherine Johnson takes this as a
concept for her drama *Shang-a-Lang*, which focuses on a trio of working-
class women, Lauren, Jackie and Pauline, who have known each other
since school days and who get together to celebrate Pauline's fortieth
birthday at a 1970s weekend at Butlins, Minehead. *Shang-a-Lang* opened
at London's Bush Theatre, which under the direction of Dominic Dromgoole and his successor Mike Bradwell created opportunities in the
1990s for new writers and new writing that included a wave of in-yer-
face drama. *Shang-a-Lang* was one of several Bush productions to attract

mainstream success: the production went on national tour in the autumn of 1999, the same year that Johnson achieved a huge commercial success (Dromgoole calls it 'the equivalent of winning the lottery') writing the book for the Abba-based musical *Mamma Mia!* (London, April 1999).[42] Productions of *Mamma Mia!* have since opened in Europe, North America, Asia and South Africa.

Mamma Mia! also has a trio of older women who were friends in the 1970s, Dona, Tanya and Rosie. Set on a Greek island, the musical focuses on single mum Dona and her daughter Sophie, who is about to get married. A paternal trio appears as Sophie has three possible fathers all of whom she has (without her mother's knowledge) invited to her wedding in order to find out which one is her real father. These senior trios are mirrored by younger sets of all-girl and all-boy threesomes.

Like Carole Woddis, who has reviewed different generations of women's theatre, I saw *Mamma Mia!* as one prepared to 'sneer', but had to confess to enjoying it as a 'good night out, for the girls'.[43] The woman-centredness of the Abba musical arises out of a combination of the show's 'great songs for women',[44] Johnson's mother–daughter narrative, and the show's all-women production trio (Johnson as writer, Phyllida Lloyd as director and Judy Craymer as producer). Although several critics alluded to Johnson's 'feminist position', more specifically I would stress the show's rather curious mix of a 1990s 'new feminist' twist to a familiar tale (the daughter calls her wedding off; the single mum finds married romance) and an evocation of what Woddis describes as a 'the happy-go-lucky hedonism and nascent feminism of the '70s'.[45]

Of particular feminist interest to resurrecting the 1970s for 'girls' in the 1990s is the feminine excess of the high-camp, 'glamming-up' style of the mid-1970s: the white and silver suits and platform boots of the Abba women (circa *Mamma Mia!* in 1975–6). With the 'excuse' that in the 1970s Dona, Tanya and Rosie made up the original 'girl-power band' the 'Dynamos', the musical creates opportunities for the older trio of women (by far the most interesting threesome in the show) to 'glam' up. Interestingly, this glamming up also extended to women in the audience who, when I saw the show, included several groups of Abba- styled forty-somethings, along with women out on hen-party celebrations and cross-generational family groupings of mothers and daughters (who would have been far too young for Abba the first time around). While some women may well be die-hard Abba fans, the show's tongue-in-cheek style (it opens with a voice-over warning that the performance contains platform boots and white lycra), the 1970s

'hedonism' and 1990s 'girl-power' mix also enable a parodic relationship to this feminine excess. As an alternative to Eclair's 'disgust-
making' of the feminine, *Mamma Mia!* indulges it, overplays it, but to
the point of ridiculous, pleasurable excess.

To confess to a liking for all of this is to face the arbiters of political
and feminist 'tastes' that might well 'sneer' at both (musical) form and
(feminine) content. In Skeggs's analysis of the 'hens', however, she
argues that 'one of the most effective ways to deflect devaluing is to
ignore it, to enjoy that for which you know you are being
condemned'.[46] Her point obtains both for the glam-loving female spectator on a 'good night out' and for my own feminist investment in
entertainment that trashes the feminine (Eclair) or delights in feminine
'trash' (Johnson).

As resistant strategies, however, both come up against the difficulty
of finding ways out of representational systems that 'lock' women into
the heterosexual regulation of the sexual and the familial, the dangers
of which were more forcefully rehearsed in Johnson's *Shang-a-Lang*. Like
Eclair's *Prozac and Tantrums*, Johnson's *Shang-a-Lang* stages plenty of
'white-trash' behaviour to often hilarious comic effect: a chaotic excess
of sex, alcohol, swearing, fighting and vomiting. The working-class
'hen-partying woman' resonates in the figuration of the three women
who, looking for that 'good night out', are variously loud and vulgar,
indulge in binge drinking, and enjoy lots of sex (Lauren), or would like
to (Pauline). Where the musical obscures class issues (blue-collar shirts
and overalls get a Mediterranean blue-skies make-over), *Shang-a-Lang*
foregrounds working-class entertainment and leisure cultures in a
grungier style of gritty Bush realism.

Shang-a-Lang works off but also problematizes 1970s pop culture as
the romance 'heritage' of Johnson's turning-forty women.[47] Where the
musical has Abba's 'great songs for women', *Shang-a-Lang* turns to
the boy-band culture for girls. The highlight of the Butlins 1970s weekend is meant to be the appearance of the Bay City Rollers, the tartan boy
band, (in)famous for driving young girls to distraction.[48] In the play, it
turns out that the band has not got back together; this is a tribute band
and not the 'real' thing, except that Johnson's drama is at pains to
point out that there is nothing 'real' about this boy romance fiction.
Teen culture dictates that you always have to pick the boy in the band
who is really the one for you, and guitarist Stuart Wood ('Woody')
became the boy of Rollerette Pauline's dreams when she managed to
'snog' him after one of the band's concerts.[49] The inside cover of *Rollin'*
lists all the Rollers' vital statistics and Woody, with his, black hair, green

eyes, and vital statistics 'chest 34", waist 28", collar size 14", shoe size 8', quotes his ambition in life as 'simply to make people happy'. Yet holding on to the promise of romance in this boy-band figure from her 1970s teens only makes for Pauline's unhappiness. At the end of the play, rather than hankering after being part of a couple or a family unit, Pauline effects a closure on romance culture and its 'happy ever after' narrative by deciding to be 'by meself. Alone.'[50]

Beyond the fiction of the stage, however, Johnson's play points to a contemporary 1990s reality: one that fails to offer women more socially progressive models for mapping their sexual and familial lives. None of Johnson's characters (male or female) are able to establish 'successful' heterosexual and familial relations, which is not something that Johnson holds against or condemns her characters for. Rather, it reflects the fact that the greater sense of sexual empowerment for women in the 1990s is out of step with, or is outstripping, otherwise outmoded notions of traditional family values that for all New Labour's apparent 'coolness' it was keen to preserve.[51] Despite the 'girl-power' rhetoric, it is the relative conservatism of the 1990s that makes the 'hedonism and nascent feminism' of the 1970s feel not only progressive but attractive and necessary.

In conclusion, all three of these shows have something to contribute to the political through recourse to mainstream, popular stages, but in very different ways. Of the three, Ensler's *The Vagina Monologues* is the most problematic given her tendency to take away from, rather than add to, the legacy of second-wave feminism. In brief, her revival of a 1970s-style feminism for the 1990s is neither politically nor theatrically effective. On the other hand, Johnson's revival of 1970s popular culture in *Mamma Mia!* and *Shang-a-Lang* encourages a performative play of the feminine that is woven into the articulation of a desire for women's sexual and familial lives to change. Eclair, meanwhile, combines 'bad-girl' comedy with the well-established feminist tradition of challenging male domination and uses this to 'trash' the ubiquitous ideologies of the feminine. The impulse of her stand-up is social rather than political; it stops short of proposing an 'alternative', but its 'pulling power' lies in its persuasive and filthy comic polemic that reminds 'girls' that this is not what they really want.

Previously it was the 'job' of 'alternative', issue-based theatre performed by companies like WTG to encourage and to enable women to think politically about their lives and to imagine them as lives lived differently. As 'West End Women', however, Ensler, Eclair and Johnson work the mainstream for 'alternative' ways of politicizing through monologue, stand-up, musical and comic play form. Talking, joking, singing and comic dialoguing, they provide a 'good night out' that asks rather than answers some political and 'practical questions about the world' 'for the girls' in the 1990s.

notes

1. J. McGrath, *A Good Night Out: Popular Theatre: Audience, Class and Form* (London: Methuen, 1981).
2. For full details of company policies, see E. Aston (ed.), *Feminist Theatre Voices* (Loughborough: Loughborough Theatre Texts, 1997), pp. 33–51, pp. 49–51.
3. For example, McGrath's English 7:84 company lost its funding in 1984, which McGrath claimed was on political grounds. See McGrath's protest, 'No Politics Please, We're British', *Guardian*, 5 October 1984. The Scottish 7:84 has survived until now, though is currently under threat of losing its funding.
4. See S. Faludi, *Backlash: The Undeclared War Against Women* (London: Vintage, 1992).
5. T. Wertenbaker, *The Break of Day* (London: Faber, 1995), p. 83.
6. N. Walter, *The New Feminism* (London: Virago, 1999).
7. A. McRobbie, *In the Culture Society: Art, Fashion and Popular Music* (London: Routledge, 1999), pp. 75–92, p. 75.
8. Monstrous Regiment, Spare Tyre, The Chuffinelles, and Women and Theatre were among those companies that closed around 1992–3. For details, see Aston, *Feminist Theatre Voices*.
9. Further details of the restructuring can be found in iIbid., p. 34.
10. S. Parrish, 'The Power of Tradition', *The Glass Ceiling* (London: pamphlet, n.d.), p. 3. The 'Glass Ceiling' symposia were designed as fora to discuss the position and representation of women in the theatre.
11. See the Sphinx Theatre Company website http://www.sphinxtheatre. co.uk/index.cfm. Accessed 24 March 2006.
12. See Jill Dolan's fuller discussion of this point with reference to the Split Britches show, *Dress Suits for Hire* negotiating an off-Broadway run, in *The Feminist Spectator as Critic* (Ann Arbor: University of Michigan Press, 1988), p. 120. It is also worth pointing out that while individual women playwrights and productions have had mainstream successes, for companies themselves, the idea of making it 'big time' was more a question of up-scaling from small- to middle-scale touring, which only two of the founding 1970s women's companies managed to achieve (WTG and Monstrous Regiment).
13. J. Deeney, 'Workshop to Mainstream: Women's Playwriting in the Contemporary British Theatre', in M. B. Gale and V. Gardner (eds), *Women, Theatre and Performance: New Histories, New Historiographies* (Manchester: Manchester University Press, 2000), pp. 142–62.

14. Deeney, 'Workshop to Mainstream', quotes statistics that attest to a sharp decline by the 1990s in the percentage of touring work by women (and indeed of building-based work), at the same time as observing a 1990s trend in women playwrights emerging and sustaining careers, pp. 144–5.

15. See E. Aston, *Feminist Views on the English Stage* (Cambridge: Cambridge University Press, 2003).

16. McGrath, *A Good Night Out*, p. 83.

17. M. B. Gale, *West End Women: Women and the London Stage 1918–1962* (London: Routledge, 1996), p. 2.

18. For details see 'The story of V-Day and the College Initiative' by Karen Obel, director, V-Day College Initiative, in E. Ensler, *The Vagina Monologues* (London: Virago, 2001), pp. 129–71.

19. For a fuller discussion of the show's popular appeal but also the many criticisms of it, see S. Coleman, 'The Vagina Monologues goes Global', http://www.worldpress.org/Americas/606.cfm. Accessed 28 March 2006.

20. See, for example, Dolan, *Feminist Spectator as Critic*, pp. 83–97.

21. McRobbie, *In the Culture Society*, p. 79.

22. For an overview of feminist stagework that treats violence against women and 'utopian alternatives for women', see S. E. Case, 'The Power of Sex: English Plays by Women, 1958–1988', *New Theatre Quarterly*, vol. 12, no. 27 (1991), 238–45.

23. See Ensler, 'Beyond the Vagina Monologues', http://www.hopedance.org/archive/issue30/articles/ensler.htm. Accessed 26 March 2006.

24. See G. Saunders, *'Love Me or Kill Me': Sarah Kane and the Theatre of Extremes* (Manchester: Manchester University Press, 2002), p. 53.

25. B. Skeggs, 'The Making of Class and Gender through Visualizing the Moral Subject Formation', *Sociology*, vol. 39, no. 5 (2005), 965–82 (971).

26. See R. Bloomberg, interview with Jenny Eclair, http://www.thebloomsbury.com/extras/jennyeclair.php. Accessed 31 March 2006; see 'The Big Interview: Jenny Eclair', http://www.officiallondontheatre.co.uk/news/biginterview/display/cm/contentId/73860. Accessed 31 March 2006.

27. 'The Big Interview: Jenny Eclair'.

28. Ibid.

29. Laura Solon was the next woman to win the award in 2005.

30. McGrath, *A Good Night Out*, p. 4.

31. Quoted in 'The Big Interview: Jenny Eclair'.

32. Attracting local working-class audiences to the Nuffield Theatre is otherwise achieved by outreach community projects such as Ursula Martinez's *OAP* (February 2004), which involved working with a community of Morecambe pensioners.

33. McRobbie, *In the Culture Society*, p. 80.

34. N. Wolf, *The Beauty Myth* (London: Vintage, 1990), p. 10.

35. Quoted in J. Rampton, 'Comedy Gig of the Week – Jenny Eclair', *Independent*, 20 October 2001, http://www.findarticles.com/p/articles/ mi_qn4158/is_20011020/ai_n14436418. Accessed 12 May 2006.

36. Sample of Eclair's early punk poetry quoted in 'The Big Interview'.

37. Skeggs, 'The Making of Class and Gender', 965–66.

38. Skeggs references observations by Labour minister Peter Mandelson and Germaine Greer; ibid., 967.

39. Ibid.

40. A. Sierz, *In-Yer-Face Theatre: British Drama Today* (London: Faber, 2000), pp. 3–35.

41. 'The World According To . . . Jenny Eclair', Interview, *Independent*, 19 January 2005, http://www.findarticles.com/p/articles/mi_qn4158/ is_20050119/ ai_n9692315. Accessed, 12 May 2006.

42. D. Dromgoole, *The Full Room: An A–Z of Contemporary Playwriting* (London: Methuen, 2002), p. 153.

43. C. Woddis, *Theatre Record*, 26 March–8 April 1999, vol. 19, 432–33, 432.

44. Discussed in the television documentary *Abba's All Time Greatest Hits*, ITV1, 2005. *Mamma Mia!* producer Judy Craymer made the point, and also described the sentiments of the songs as 'feminine', while rock star Bono discussed Abba music as 'girls' music', suggesting that this was one of the reasons why the band had often not been taken seriously.

45. Woddis, *Theatre Record*, 433.

46. Skeggs, 'The Making of Class and Gender', 976.

47. This was a heritage which I also felt was shared by the small gatherings of forty-something women who made up the rather sparse audience at the Saturday matinee of *Shang-a-Lang* that I attended at the Theatre Royal Nottingham in 1999.

48. As the BBC's music website states, this was the Scottish band that 'had such a powerful effect on young women that, like the Beatles, they were judged to be a mania', http://www.bbc.co.uk/music/profiles/baycityrollers.shtml. Accessed 6 April 2006. The 'mania' was a 1970s phenomenon and came to an end when the band broke up in 1978.

49. Eclair's *Prozac and Tantrums* makes several jokes about this relating to the 1990s band Take That and former lead singer, Robbie Williams.

50. C. Johnson, *Shang-a-Lang* (London: Faber, 1998), p. 89.

51. See McRobbie's discussion of this in *In the Culture Society*, pp. 122–31, pp. 130–31.

part iii
nation, devolution and globalization

introduction to part iii

In his account of British playwriting in the 1990s Aleks Sierz concentrates almost exclusively on the output of two London theatres – the Royal Court and the Bush: perhaps more significantly, Sierz contends that the plays that came out of these two institutions constituted nothing less than an ambitious bid at forming a loose sense of collective national identity.[1] While he notes that Scottish theatre during the period also experienced a revival through work by new writers such as David Greig and David Harrower, the inference is clear.[2] As Ken Urban unequivocally states, 'London became ground zero for a revitalization of British art and culture', whereby a group of largely white middle-class male writers in their twenties had now come to represent the entire geographical and cultural diversity of Britain.[3]

The relationship between individual notions of self-hood and those between the individual and national identity becomes the focus of three chapters in the volume. David Pattie's '"Mapping the territory": modern Scottish drama', locates a fracturing of identity away from the dramas of the 1970s: with their clear 'representations of working life centred around the heroic or otherwise mythical figure of the Scottish working man', plays such as Bill Bryden's *Willie Rough* (1972), Hector MacMillan's *The Sash* (1974), and Roddy McMillan's *The Bevellers* (1973) were illustrative of the period. However, Pattie argues that 'Thatcherism, and the fallout from the referendum debacle in 1979, changed the picture utterly', and the 1980s led to corresponding changes in theatre – notably the parallel development in English theatre at the time, which saw a significant number of new plays by women such as Rona Munro, Sue Glover, Marcella Evaristi and Anne Marie Di Mambro. Arguably, however, the key Scottish work of the 1990s is not a play, but Irvine Welsh's novel *Trainspotting* (1993): not only did it ask uncomfortable questions about Scottish identity, but it also left a significant mark on British culture throughout the remainder of the decade. Paradoxically, its subsequent adaptations for stage and film led to it becoming an influential catalyst in the London-based phenomena of 'Cool Britannia': certainly its cultural impact at the time cannot be overestimated, not least within playwriting circles. However, it did so at a cost, in that both Harry Gibson's 1994 stage adaptation and Danny Boyle's 1995 film leached away much of the novel's critique of Scottish politics. Gibson's adaptation, despite its Glasgow premiere, subsequently transferred to London's Bush Theatre, after which its subsequent move to the West End pre-empted the emergence of the in-yer-face dramatists, to the point where many became known for a short while as the 'Trainspotting generation'.[4] Welsh himself contributed to this association further by writing the play, *You'll Have Had Your Hole* (1998), which became almost an amalgamation of the clichés that *Trainspotting* had originally set down for the genre.

However, Pattie maintains that during this same period a group of young playwrights working in Scotland – David Greig, Chris Hannan and Stephen Greenhorn – looked towards a more nuanced understanding of modern Scotland. Despite the immense profile *Trainspotting* exerted in bringing Scotland to the attention of mass audiences during this period, Greenhorn, Greig and Hannan were never invited to the Cool Britannia party, and much of their work during the 1990s never commanded the same degree of attention accorded to their London counterparts.

Pattie identifies Chris Hannan's *The Evil Doers* (1990) as an early attempt at understanding how Thatcherism had impacted on Scotland. With its central Glasgow setting, Pattie describes the play as a 'city comedy'; like the earlier Jacobean work of English dramatists such as Ben Jonson and Thomas Middleton in plays such as *Volpone* (*c*.1605–6) and *A Chaste Maid in Cheapside* (1613), a moral comparison between the city of the present and that of its past is set up. In *The Evil Doers* the physical effacement of old Glasgow whereby 'the old signposts of identity no longer point to the old locations' leads to a corresponding moral and existential displacement in the characters.

However, unlike the in-yer-face dramatists at the time such as Butterworth, Grosso and Penhall, who tended to set their plays within a knowable and realistic London, the Scottish dramatists Pattie discusses utilize other dramatic forms to depict setting. Often these are shaped by the discourses of postmodernism and globalization, such as the 'road-movie' structure Greenhorn employs in *Passing Places* (1997) to explore modern Scotland, a form Scottish novelist Alan Warner used the same year for *Demented Lands* – his sequel to *Morvern Callar* (1995).

In David Greig's *Europe* (1994) and *The Cosmonaut's Last Message to the Woman He Loved in the Former Soviet Union* (1999), geographical boundaries and self-identity become increasingly displaced whereby the action shifts from Scotland to the forgotten cosmonauts floating in their capsule above the earth. Similarly in *Europe*, the location is set in a nameless cross-border town; here, as in Welsh's novel, Pattie observes that trains function in Europe as 'symbols of cultural escape – of the porousness of boundaries', and it could be argued that both the closed local factory in *Europe* and the abandoned Leith Central Station in *Trainspotting* are synonymous as sites 'of missed connections historically and socially, where the reality which engulfs the characters becomes increasingly difficult to map and understand'.[5]

The central motif in *Trainspotting* also shares similarities with Pattie's comment that the three playwrights in his chapter set out to provide rudimentary maps in attempting to assess shifting definitions of Scottish identity. Yet Welsh's novel also provides more literal and metaphorical escape routes from Edinburgh as a symbol of national identity than the plays Pattie discusses. Whereas Mark Renton, the central protagonist in *Trainspotting*, makes periodic English raiding forays to carry out housing benefit fraud and exploit the burgeoning property market of 1980s London, he finally escapes Edinburgh for Amsterdam. In contrast, the playwrights Pattie discusses are more mindful of Scotland as their central subject and offer their audiences a far more searching and disturbing topography in the 1990s than its twee depiction through the millennial decade in popular television series such as *Monarch of the Glen* (2000–2005) and *Two Thousand Acres of Sky* (2001), which in their treatments of Scotland and Scottishness 'owe[s] more to the discourses of tourism than of drama'.[6]

Roger Owen's chapter, '"The Net and the self": colliding views of individuality and nationhood in the pre-devolutionary plays of Mark Jenkins and Ed Thomas', offers a rather more pessimistic view of Welsh theatre in the 1990s, where both politically and culturally the decade saw contradictory impulses at work. On the one hand, the growth of Welsh-language teaching in schools since the 1950s and its dissemination through terrestrial television with the launch of BBC Wales in 1964 and Channel Four Wales (SC4) in 1982 made questions concerning definitions of Welsh identity less problematic than in Scotland. Arguably, this more established sense of national identity also made the question of devolution in 1997 a less divisive issue. Moreover, during the same time Wales also experienced its own version of 'Cool Britannia', with the emergence of popular new beat groups such as The Manic Street Preachers, Super Furry Animals and Catatonia. While its English counterpart Britpop made the condition of Englishness quintessential to its themes and imagery, much of this was refracted through the stylistic nostalgia of 1960s bands such as The Kinks and The Beatles. In contrast, their Welsh counterparts seemed to expound a far more modern sense of national identity (such as Catatonia's 1998 album and song of the same name, *International Velvet*, which opened with the lyrics, 'Everyday When I Wake Up I Thank the Lord I'm Welsh'), that were at times deliberately trenchant and uncompromising.

However, Owen's chapter, with its emphasis on playwriting from the late 1980s, to the early 1990s perhaps serves to illustrate that a renaissance was not enjoyed in all branches of Welsh culture, and for theatre in particular the decade was characterized as one of slow decline. Writing in 1997, Anne Marie Taylor made the following assessment:

> If one of the main features of postmodernity is being severed from a shared sense of tradition . . . unlike other cultural forms that shape a sense of continuity and have been seen to occupy an often privileged place in Wales' heritage, the drama of the contemporary period has frequently been cut adrift.[7]

Arguably the high point in Welsh theatre came in the early 1990s, when not only the work of Ed Thomas and Mark Owen seemed to indicate the embryonic stirrings of a playwriting tradition, but theatre companies such as Brith Goth and Volcano were making a name for themselves in the sphere of devised work. However, Nic Ross more pessimistically charts the period from 1979 to 1995 as 'little more than a footnote in dramatic history, primarily because work of worth that has been produced remains unpublished'.[8] Roger Owen makes the same observation in regard to Mark Owen's work: many of the plays finally produced in the 1990s were in fact written during the previous decade, and in terms of their engagement with Welsh identity the plays 'display a marked suspicion of political and personal idealism, particularly in the form of utopianism, and require their audience to reassess the balance between historical aspiration and responsibility'.

In contrast, Owen argues that Thomas's work displays a more overt sense of cultural fluidity; yet even here the outlook that the work depicts appears pessimistic. Anne Marie Taylor comments that Thomas's work articulates 'the dead-end situation of modern Wales, an overlooked country clinging to the edge of Europe, cut off from any kind of heroic past and communal present'.[9] In *House of America* (1988), for instance, brother and sister Sid and Gwenny seek escape from their Welsh heritage by recourse to fantasies derived from the America of Jack

Kerouac's *On the Road* (1957); and in *Song from a Forgotten City* (1995) we hear Carlyle's story of the silent Welsh pub after news of its defeat at an international rugby match. However, Owen argues that this strategy can also reveal Wales afresh.

'Irishness' in plays such as Martin McDonagh's *The Leenane Trilogy* (1996–97) and Conor McPherson's *The Weir* enjoyed immense popular success among English audiences during the 1990s. One might conjecture that part of the reason for this came out of the comfortable familiarity these plays reinforced by perpetuating an unchallenging series of stereotypes based around Irish rural life and national characteristics. However, Nadine Holdsworth and Wallace McDowell in their chapter, 'A legacy of violence: representing Loyalism in the plays of Gary Mitchell', provide a less comfortable or received view of Irishness through their discussion of Gary Mitchell's plays in the 1990s, which deal with the fiercely held sense of Englishness upheld by sections of its Loyalist communities in Northern Ireland.

From W. B Yeats's plays to O'Casey's *Dublin Trilogy*, for many Protestants modern Irish drama has always suspiciously appeared to represent and defend nationalist aspirations. As Holdsworth and McDowell point out, Mitchell's drama in the 1990s serves to expose 'the legacy of sectarian conflict and the impact of the changing political climate for working-class Protestant individuals, families, communities, institutions and cultural traditions in Northern Ireland'. During the mid- to late 1990s Mitchell as a Protestant playwright was seen to be redressing the balance somewhat by articulating Loyalist communities' sense of feeling beleaguered at home and prey to caricature as 'the blockers of progress' in contributing to a political solution for Northern Ireland's long-term future. David Dunswith, presenter of the BBC radio programme *Talkback*, usefully summarizes the fears and alienation that motivate acts of sectarianism in the Loyalist community:

> Protestants are an embattled minority. They see that Britain was willing to send a task force to defend the concept of Britishness in the Falkland Islands away off near Argentina. They see the way Britain fights to keep Gibraltar from Spain. And when they listen to the British political leadership saying that Britain has no selfish or strategic interest in remaining in Northern Ireland they ask, 'what do they care about their kith and kin here a few miles from them?' They fear the imperial power of Rome. They dread the Republic. They feel they are losing everything. It almost reaches the level of hysteria. The sense of identify amongst Catholics is much stronger.[10]

For a short period Mitchell's work enjoyed a high profile in Britain, with plays such as *The Force of Change* (2000) and *Loyal Women* (2003) being staged at London's Royal Court and *As the Beast Sleeps* (1998) adapted for television. Mitchell was also seen as providing an authentic voice for working-class Loyalist concerns, as at the time he was still living in the Protestant Rathcoole district of North Belfast, which was frequently used as the setting for several of his plays.

Despite Holdsworth's and McDowell's belief that Mitchell's treatment of Loyalism 'offers more complex and nuanced readings of the factors contributing to a crisis in Loyalist identity that are often overlooked in cultural representations and media treatments', old suspicions over Irish drama's nationalist sympathies spilled over into reality when in December 2005 Mitchell and his family were forced out their home by Loyalist paramilitaries, who presumably objected to their representation on stage. As Holdsworth and McDowell observe, the Northern Ireland depicted in Mitchell's plays, with its 'ongoing sectarian violence, barbaric intra-communal punishment beatings and people being forced from their homes by tactics such as petrol bombs and threats to personal safety', all too clearly demonstrates the precarious boundaries between Mitchell's 'fictional' representation of his community and its harsh everyday realities.

Feelings of the individual's powerlessness against political systems also inform Dan Rebellato's '"Because it feels fucking amazing": recent british drama and bodily mutilation'. Rebellato draws attention to the motif of bodily mutilation as a dominant theme in several key plays from the period. On one level this could be interpreted as demonstrating another feature of what Vera Gottlieb and others call the 'privatized dissent', and retreat from direct political engagement by the in-yer-face generation into a solecism based around the subject's dysmorphia.[11] However, Rebellato argues that these acts of self-mutilation and dismemberment are symptomatic of a wider politics – namely a culture of globalization and consumerism in which the subjects in these plays have become enmeshed. Incidents, such as Gary in *Shopping and Fucking* craving the 'good hurt' (56), obtained from sexual violence inflicted on his own body, or one of the speakers in Sarah Kane's *4.48 Psychosis* describing self-mutilation as feeling 'fucking great . . . fucking amazing', perhaps point to a desire within these characters to experience something genuinely *real* that is not in some form or another commodified.[12]

The volume closes with playwright David Greig's chapter 'Rough Theatre'. Taken from his closing keynote paper at the 2002 conference, this contribution does much to both summarize and assess the impact not only of notions relating to 'political theatre' in the 1990s, but does so in the light of world events in the new millennium, causing us to re-evaluate our defintions of what constitutes political theatre now.

The chapter takes as its starting point Greig's experiences in Palestine during 2001, where he collaborated on writing a play for the Al Kasabah Theatre in Ramallah. The ever-present danger that the company faced from shelling by Israeli tanks, as well as the primitive physical conditions under which the performances took place, led him on returning home to question the degree to which British theatre ever really engages in political discourse.

To illustrate this, Greig compares the physical environment of the Royal Court building in London: from its bullet-ridden logo to the 'distressed or unfinished features such as bare brickwork and exposed plaster', Greig argues that a self-consciously uneven look has been created architecturally in order to act as an 'explicit statement of the theatre's political history and intent'. Greig's analysis is interesting in the light of an interview from its former Artistic Director Stephen Daldry in 1995, before major refurbishment courtesy of a generous allocation of lottery grant money:

> This crumbling ramshackle building has the status of myth. It holds the fingerprints of the greatest writers and actors of our age. One said to me that if you squeeze the bricks, blood would come out.[13]

Daldry's musings go to show just how easy it is to become immured in self-belief derived simply from what Greig terms 'the semiotics of . . . design details'. While the Royal Court claims to represent the political, its 'unfinished features such as bare brickwork and exposed plaster' are actually predetermined features created by architects, whereas the Palestinian Kasabah theatre's 'distressed' interiors and exteriors are created directly out of political conflict.

Greig's differentiation between 'the politics of creating self-conscious theatre amongst real bullet holes and the creation of self-consciously political theatre amongst a "bullet-hole" look' goes towards providing an outline or manifesto for what he calls 'Rough Theatre'. In 1997 Greig argued that political theatre defined itself by putting forward an advocacy for change, but by the time of the Bristol conference in 2002 (shaped by his experiences in Palestine and the events of 11 September 2001), Greig was 'no longer satisfied with letting [his] work simply exist and not questioning whether it was helping or hindering the powers shaping our lives'.[14] He goes on to pose the question, 'how can I, as a theatre- maker, explore, map and advance a progressive agenda?'

The outline for 'Rough Theatre' arises out of Greig's earlier definition: namely the purpose of political theatre is to question received ideology, although here he calls it by another term – 'the management of the imagination by power' – and he provides examples taken during his stay in Palestine, where events directly witnessed by day underwent manipulation that very evening on the CNN news broadcasts. Of course, the term is a familiar one to readers of George Orwell's *Nineteen Eighty-four* (1949) as we become privy to Winston Smith's growing realization that everything from the chocolate ration to who Oceania is currently at war with has simply been 'managed' by Big Brother.

Greig focuses on of the 2001 attacks on the Twin Towers in New York and the Pentagon in Washington as a key moment when such methods of control temporarily failed and 'the unimaginable . . . suddenly erupted into the realm of the real'. Of course this was achieved at a terrible cost, both on the day and in ongoing events associated with the 'War on Terror'. However, Greig believes 'that if the battlefield is the imagination, then the theatre is a very appropriate weapon in the armoury of resistance', for live performance also has at least the potential to briefly disrupt and reveal the normally seamless reality of what we take to be unquestioned 'common sense'.

Greig cites from Adorno the idea of 'normality' simply being a *trompe l'oeil* image painted on a cloth underneath which the truth exists; similarly it is hoped that the contributions to this volume go some way to revealing a wider and more complex map – both geographical and imaginative – for British political drama during the 1990s.

notes

1. See A. Sierz, 'In-Yer-Face Theatre: New British Drama Today', *Anglo Files; Journal of English Teaching*, no. 126 (2002), 8–14 (10); A. Sierz, *In-Yer-Face Theatre: British Drama Today* (London: Faber, 2000, repr. 2001), p. xiii.
2. Sierz, *In-Yer-Face Theatre*, pp. 39–40.
3. K. Urban, 'Towards a Theory of Cruel Britannia: Coolness, Cruelty, and the 'Nineties', *New Theatre Quarterly*, vol. 20, no. 4 (2004), 354–72 (355).
4. J. Romney, 'The Acid House-Bleak House', *Guardian*, 1 January 1999.
5. A. Kelly, *Irvine Welsh* (Manchester: Manchester University Press, 2005), p. 48.
6. S. Blandford, 'BBC Drama at the Margins: the Contrasting Fortunes of

Northern Irish, Scottish and Welsh Television Drama in the 1990s', in J. Bignall and S. Lacey (eds), *Popular Television Drama: Critical Perspectives* (Manchester: Manchester University Press, 2005), pp. 166–82 (p. 173).

7. A. M. Taylor, 'Introduction', in A. M. Taylor (ed.), *Staging Wales: Welsh Theatre 1979–1997* (Cardiff: University of Wales, 1997), pp. 1–7 (p. 1).

8. N. Ross, 'Leaving the Twentieth Century: New Writing on the Welsh Language Mainstage 1979–1995', in A. M. Taylor (ed.), *Staging Wales: Welsh Theatre 1979–1997*, (Cardiff: University of Wales, 1997), pp. 18–32 (p. 31).

9. A. M. Taylor, 'Welsh Theatre and the World', in *Staging Wales*, pp. 111–19 (p. 116).

10. Cited in S. McKay, *Northern Protestants: an Unsettled People* (Belfast: Blackstaff Press, 2005), p. 26.

11. Sierz, *In-Yer-Face Theatre*, p. 39.

12. S. Kane, *Complete Plays* (London: Methuen), p. 217.

13. S. Daldry, 'Omnibus: Royal Court Diaries', BBC1, 25 October 1998. Cited in P. Roberts, *The Royal Court and the Modern Stage* (Cambridge: Cambridge University Press, 1999), p. 219.

14. Cited in D. Edgar, *State of Play, Issue 1: Playwrights on Playwriting* (London: Faber, 1999), p. 66.

7
'mapping the territory': modern scottish drama
david pattie

In an article on recent Scottish women's writing, Adrienne Scullion commented on the changing nature of Scottish identity:

As a . . . consequence of these legislative and constitutional changes, the 'imagined' nature of Scotland also shifts: Scottish culture, and within that issues of representation and identity, has been preoccupied with ideas of colonialism, marginalism, and parochialism. But, in a context where a significant degree of political independence has been achieved, the dynamic must shift from aspiration and desire to definition and responsibility. The fact of the Holyrood government will result in shifts in how we understand and participate in the dynamic processes of Scottish identity.[1]

If there is one thing that Scullion's article makes clear, it is that, post devolution, Scottish culture operates in different territory. The threats and promises of the devolution debate – a debate, which Andrew Marr's *The Battle for Scotland* makes clear, lasted for most of the twentieth century – are no longer enough; we need new maps to help us negotiate the difficult terrain ahead. Previously existing versions of Scottishness – discourses now very familiar to any student of the country's political and cultural development – are far too narrow and confining to do justice to our experience of an expanded world; the old stories (tartanry, the kailyard, Clydesideism, et al.) no longer tell us much that is useful about ourselves.

For Scullion, Scottish theatre provides a natural home for debates on

143

the nature of Scotland at the turn of the century (as indeed it did in the 1970s and 1980s):

> [Much] of contemporary Scottish theatre has the ambition to be a site of both political *and* social debate, and aesthetic and dramaturgical innovation and experiment. It is certainly the case that the writers and directors of new theatre in Scotland have set themselves an agenda very different from the fashion-victim, violent chic introspection of contemporary London theatre, perhaps from a fuller awareness of the significance of representation within a culture in political flux and of limited financial resources. In a wider context of change and adaptation, contemporary Scottish dramatists are increasingly able to experiment with historical and geographical settings and with character and narrative conventions, as well as to challenge the orthodoxies of what it might mean to write a 'Scottish play', what it might mean to make theatre in and of Scotland.[2]

On first reading (at least, a Scot's first reading) one is tempted to ignore the side-swipe at current English drama; even post devolution, the temptation to contrast good Scottish practice with the mistakes made by the English (especially the Southern English) is still strong, and even the best of us succumb. However, in this context, the opposition is interesting, because behind it is the unspoken assumption that there is such a thing as a habitual Scottish practice that reflects a specific Scottish identity (at least when contrasted to the activities of our nearest neighbour). One might choose to argue with Scullion's implicit argument on a case-by-case basis (Martin Crimp's *Attempts on her Life*, 1997, for example; all of Kane's work; and so on, and so on). More interestingly, one could argue that it is now difficult to assign any specific territory – any specific idea of Scotland or the nature of Scottish identity – to the work that many Scottish dramatists produce.

This chapter will pursue the implications of this argument, with reference to work by five contemporary Scottish dramatists – Chris Hannan, Stephen Greenhorn, David Harrower, Gregory Burke and David Greig. These writers create a composite image, not only of Scotland but of the contemporary nation-state, that does not trade in the idea that a country's essential qualities can be revealed through the study of its people and the societies they create. Rather, their work tends to suggest that national and cultural identity is always in the process of formation, that it is always up for grabs, and that any attempt to arrive at a final definition of identity (whether Scottish identity or that of any other country) will be doomed to failure. In other words, and to return to a metaphor used above, it might seem that we need new maps to orient ourselves as Scots in the modern world; but there are no guarantees that such maps will become generally available – or that they will identify the terrain that we actually encounter.

a brief history lesson

I have argued elsewhere that Scottish drama in the 1970s was in part governed by two impulses: first, the desire to represent, fix and (most commonly) to celebrate a type of existence and a particular location that had not previously featured consistently in any dramatic representation of Scotland; and second to create a heroic myth of contemporary Scottishness based on a firm understanding of the firmly rooted lives of the Scottish people.[3] The Scottish urban working classes had been largely ignored by those working in a Scottish playwriting tradition (such as it was: David Hutcheson's 1977 book, *Modern Scottish Theatre*, remains a good, if chastening, documentation of the uneven history of playwriting in Scotland). In the 1970s, in a climate more conducive to creative work, this began to change. As has been well documented, the early work of 7:84 Scotland helped not only to establish a touring network in the country, but also to provide a useful model of a working-class theatre, able to represent the country in both its rural and its urban aspects; elsewhere in the theatre, representations of working life centred around the heroic or otherwise mythical figure of the Scottish working man, in plays such as Bill Bryden's *Willie Rough,* Hector MacMillan's *The Sash* and Roddy McMillan's *The Bevellers.* Such work was, arguably, necessary; at a time of resurgent nationalism, Scottish self-identity was an alarmingly evanescent thing, described in Tom Nairn's influential work as a combination of tartan mysticism and kailyard sentiment (when Scullion talks of marginalism, colonialism and parochialism, she raises the spectre of Nairn's double-headed monster of false consciousness). Nairn's argument was adopted almost as a badge of shame by those writing and thinking about Scottish culture; a healthy interest in working-class realities seemed to provide an antidote for a country that displayed something more akin to a national pathology than a national identity.

Thatcherism, and the fallout from the referendum debacle in 1979, changed the picture utterly, but not in the ways that one might expect – and, at a guess, not in the ways that the then Prime Minister intended. Her impact on the working classes in Scotland was as devastating as it was elsewhere; however, her attacks on the welfare state and the other legacies of socialism sounded markedly different north of the border:

[After] the 1987 election results were out, the term 'Bloody English' was on a lot of lips in Scotland, and I found myself falling into this, probably to the concern of my English friends. Thatcher seemed to be hated so intensely north of the border because she personified every quality we had always disliked about the English; snobbery, boorishness, selfishness, and, by our lights, stupidity.[4]

This is undoubtedly true, if not exactly admirable: Scots have their stereotyped picture of Englishness, and Margaret Thatcher did seem to fit the stereotype alarmingly snugly. Paradoxically, though, Thatcherism's assault on both the real and imagined Scotland served two purposes. First of all, it provided most Scots with a convenient hate figure, against whom they could find common cause (the Conservatives share of the Scottish popular vote nose-dived during the 1980s, and has yet to recover; the Scottish Constitutional Convention attracted wide support, with the obvious exception of the Conservatives, and the less obvious exception of the SNP, who were worried at the thought of another 1979). Second, cultural representations of Scotland began to change. Thatcherism, even though it was profoundly contradictory and *ad hoc* in practice, always sought to give the impression that it was monolithic, and that the Prime Minister enshrined the eternal verities of human, and more specifically, English behaviour. Rather than opposing Thatcherism with a monolithic version of Scottish identity, Scottish writers and artists began to explore versions of Scottishness that had the kind of flexibility and openness that Thatcherism notably lacked. This change was reflected in the theatre; 7:84 and Wildcat pursued a path laid down in 1970s, but other groups explored the cultural politics of Scotland itself (the theatre group Communicado, for example, took on the central myths of Scottishness in *Mary Queen of Scots Got Her Head Chopped Off* (1987) and *Jock Tamson's Bairns* (1990). For the first time, also, women playwrights such as Rona Munro, Sue Glover, Marcella Evaristi and Anne Marie Di Mambro, and gay writers (John Binnie) established a significant presence on the Scottish stage; their work necessarily contained other images of Scottishness that helped to counter and enrich the work done before the events of 1979.

Writing at the end of the decade, Cairns Craig provided an apt summary of the oddly healthy state of Scottish culture:

The appropriate comparison is perhaps with Ireland in the 1890s after the death of Parnell. The energies which had been built up in the political sphere suddenly had nowhere to go, and transferred themselves into cultural activity. Instead of political defeat leading to quiescence, it led directly into an explosion of cultural creativity, a creativity coming to terms with the origin of the political defeat and redefining the nation's conception of itself. The 80s have been one of the most significant decades of Scottish cultural self-definition in the past two centuries.[5]

In part this is because the events leading up to and resulting in the 1979 referendum, whatever their political outcome, focused their attention on the fact that Scotland was profoundly different in social texture and values from England. The Thatcher years, years of aggressive English nationalism, only emphasized this difference. The effort to capture and explore the texture of difference that constituted this enduringly Scottish experience proved an enormous impulse to artistic endeavour. The issue was self-definition and self-discovery: the challenge was to be met by an originality and intensity which, perhaps, had been lacking in Scotland since the period immediately following the First World War.[6] A fine irony: an all-encompassing political philosophy that claims to speak to the soul of Britain speeds the cultural disintegration of the British state. In a sense, almost all the art produced in Scotland during the 1980s was an art of dissent; it engaged with Thatcherism from a peculiarly Scottish perspective; at the same time, it opposed a dynamic, complex and fluid Scottish culture to the monolithic Englishness of 1980s Conservatism.

lost in scotland: chris hannan and stephen greenhorn

What happened, then, in the 1990s, after Thatcherism finally passed into history? One route, at least, was closed off to us: there was no way to reconstruct the monumental, essential portraits of strong, authentic Scottishness that had governed the stage in the 1970s; dramas that dealt with the world of work (Mike Cullen's *The Cut* in 1993 and Gregory Burke's recent success, *Gagarin Way* in 2001) dealt rather with the fallout from the death of heavy industry. Rather, in the 1990s, Scottish dramatists found themselves in a world where identity was a great deal more fluid than it had been, where there were no ready-made versions of Scottishness with which to ally their characters, and where the question of identity – and the sense that the relation of identity to nationality – is itself a profoundly complex matter.

A play produced at the beginning of the decade can stand as a useful introduction to this world. Chris Hannan's *The Evil Doers* (1990) is a city comedy; and the city is Glasgow – the bastion of the old industrial Scotland, and the cradle of the strong, Scottish working-class male. In *The Evil Doers*, the characters exist in a Glasgow where the old signposts of identity no longer point to the old locations:

> SAMMMY . . . So here we are in the East End of the city – and can I just interject with the information that fifteen or so years back this was one of the most depressed areas of the city . . . 'Parkhead Forge' – this pyramid structure in glass and steel-tubing – is the £40 million pound jewel in the East End crown.[7]

The shopping centre has replaced the Forge: an industrial city has turned into a prime shopping location. In this new version of West Coast Scotland, the working-class man is lost in an entirely familiar place. Sammy, who describes the new Parkhead Forge in such glowing terms, has rechristened himself Danny Glasgow, and offers tours of his native city to interested tourists; but the city itself is no longer the location he is familiar with, and his position within it is at best marginal. In a telling comment, Sammy's daughter Tracky sums up her father's profoundly dislocated state; she tells another character 'He's all over the place.'[8]

However, as the decade progressed, the positive implications of this sense of displacement began to reveal themselves. Stephen Greenhorn's *Passing Places* begins in a location not too far away from Hannan's Glasgow. The central characters, Alex and Brian, are employed in a sports shop in post-industrial Motherwell, the 'surfing capital of Scotland' (which has earned this unlikely name because their psychotic boss Binks keeps a surfboard in his window). Sacked after the place is robbed, they steal the surfboard in a quixotic act of revenge and flee in a Lada Riva up to the far North of Scotland, pursued by Binks.

The play is a road movie for the stage, or, more precisely, it is two road movies, each one using a different map of the country. One of the movies stars Binks as he travels up the tourist route to the North, taking in Fort William, heading up the Great Glen to Inverness, then via the A9 to Thurso, where the play ends. His journey can be thought of as a route march through tourist Scotland; he reacts to each new location with a mingled incomprehension – 'Drumna-fuckin-Drochit? What Kind of Place is that?' – and the kind of innately superior paternalism the Lowlander adopts in the wilds of the North.[9] Even though he travels from the Central belt to the far North, Binks never actually moves; he simply replaces one stereotyped image of Scotland with another.

On the other hand, Brian and Alex meander up the West Coast, taking the road less travelled; through Ardnamurchan, across to Skye, around the coast to Assynt, Tongue and then to Thurso where Binks catches up with them. Their Scotland is populated by a multinational mix of travellers, incomers and locals; it is a place where the accent is as likely to be French or Ukrainian as it is Scottish, a place where they feel like strangers in their own country. As they travel, they come to see Scotland as a location that is huge, complex and (for the Lowland Scot) largely unexplored. However, it is a land that can only be described in a vocabulary denied to them; Alex, for example, can't bring himself to use the word 'beautiful'. Fittingly, when the word beautiful finally becomes part of their vocabulary, it comes in both English and Ukrainian. For Alex and Brian, the over-familiar territory of Scotland gives way to a country that cannot be described in one language, or by reference to one, unvarying set of cultural notions or maps. Alex and Brian's journey is, then, both a psychological and a political/social remapping of their country. Scotland comes to seem to them a location both uniquely personal and at the same time alive, various, vibrant and multifaceted. Scotland is not the small, narrow country that Binks traverses – it is far too big to be simply described in any one language, or through any one set of experiences.

lost in europe: david greig's *one way street* and *europe*

The central, indeed the only, character in David Greig's *One Way Street* (1995) (developed with Graham Eatough for the company Suspect Culture) is Flannery. An Englishman abroad, he has been commissioned to write a book that will guide the tourist around Berlin; the play follows his movements around the city. However, even though his journey seems to be fixed by Berlin's geography, he soon finds himself lost in a space that is unmappable. This is because Flannery, despite his name, is no *flâneur*; he is not a detached observer of the city scene. On the contrary, he is lost in a uniquely personal version of Berlin, a version of the city created by three interacting forces: Flannery's own history; his troubled relationship with a German woman; and the uncontainable life of the city. The play is formally a monologue, but the actor playing Flannery also incarnates the characters that he meets, and his relationship to them. In performance, it seems as though the character of Flannery is being formed at each moment by these encounters.

As the play develops, we move from the idea of a geography that can be contained in a guidebook to a geography that is mapped out by the experience of the individual interacting with other individuals; from the idea of a linear progression through time and space to the interaction of self and the environment, the influence of environment on the self, of other selves on the self, in a series of ever-widening circles of influence. The play finishes, appropriately, in a revolving restaurant high above the city, a location both firmly placed in Berlin and separate from it, and with Flannery similarly poised between versions of himself:

> *The restaurant spins a mile up above the city. Round and round at a steady one revolution an hour. Only slightly more revolutions than the city's had. The carpet of lights stretches to the horizon and we look out over the east, slowly turning to the west . . . and back again . . . Somewhere in the puddle of light below us Tony is moving, trying to pull me down to Earth. Up here, Greta touches my face. We don't speak. Silently she draws me into her orbit.*[10]

Europe takes place in a nameless middle European town, close to a border that has been contested for much of its history.[11] The town's inhabitants have lost any secure sense of their national or cultural identity; the local factory has shut down, and trains no longer stop at the station. Of all the changes through which they have lived, this last is arguably the most important. Trains cross borders; they are symbols of cultural escape – of the porousness of boundaries.

Europe describes a struggle between those who have nothing to hold on to but a fixed idea of identity and those who want to escape, who want to get the chance to discover and interpret the outside world for themselves. On one side, Berlin (a profoundly ironic name in the circumstances) says he is drawn towards the town's neo-fascists because their beliefs are 'dumb and blunt'.[12] Fret the stationmaster is furious at inter-railers ('Inter-railers – travelling about without a bloody destination . . . expecting nothing . . . letting it happen . . . getting on and off trains with complete disregard for the principle of the thing . . .').[13] In other words, he wants the stability of a fixed system in which boundaries are respected, as against the freedom to pass across frontiers as and when the mood dictates.

To Berlin, the neo-fascists, and Fret, Greig opposes a pair of female characters whose relation to their location is rather less fixed. Adele, Fret's daughter, is fascinated by trains; by their power, their energy and their ability to move quickly across different territories. In more general terms, she is fascinated by the idea of leaving, and of defying borders (in a telling and rather beautiful metaphor, she likens a train to 'a chain of Amsterdam diamonds'[14]. On the other hand, Katia, an émigrée forced out of her homeland, cannot share Adele's romanticized idea of the self in transit. Katia doesn't possess what Salman Rushdie has called the 'hopefulness' of the migrant[15] ('Whatever you can imagine for yourself, Adele, this continent can come up with much worse. You'll soon learn the best way is to stay where you are, keep quiet and lie low'[16]). However, she finds that there is no safe haven in this town; her father Sava and the traveller Morocco are both assaulted by the local right-wingers. She might have fled her homeland, but in a sense she has not yet escaped: the same forces that drove her out also operate in the new location.

Europe finishes with the train station in flames, and Adele's and Katia's fathers dying in the blaze. Both women escape, naming all the places that are now open to them, and as they do so, Berlin provides a grim coda to the burning of the station – this grotesque act has, at least, put the town on the map: it has served to remind the rest of Europe that the town exists. The play ends by posing a pair of stark alternatives: those who stick to and defend the idea of boundaries die or kill, because the claims of territory are inherently a violent response to political changes that are out of the individual's hands; and those that attempt to evade or escape boundaries are better placed to survive in the new Europe.

A more recent play – the magnificently titled *The Cosmonaut's Last Message to the Woman He Once Loved in the Former Soviet Union* – traverses the same borders as *Europe*; this time Scottish characters are added to the mixture. The play interweaves the stories of a group of characters, using as a loose link the presence of a forgotten Soviet space capsule, wheeling above the world, carrying two cosmonauts who have no chance of escape, and no secure way of contacting the world below them. Their attempts to communicate with the world are mirrored by the failures in communication that bedevil the play's earthbound char-acters. It is not, however, that this failure is a sign of affectless post-modernity; rather, if there is something that the play stages, it is the need to establish some kind of shared language, and, alongside it, some kind of commonality:

KEITH: . . . If only you could sit down with everybody over a whisky. If only every single encounter was just two people, and a wooden table and a whisky . . . It's tearing me apart to be honest with you. It really is. I'm shaken up . . .[17]

There is a neat ambiguity in that last line: the phrase 'to be honest with you' is a piece of conversational static, a relatively meaningless honorarium to the addressee. However, it is also, in this context, rather more troubling – as though Keith's honesty is itself tearing him apart. This reading is supported by what we know of Keith's character up to this point: we have seen how difficult it is for him to be honest both with Vivienne (his wife) and Natasja (his mistress). Indeed, after this conversation, he will remove himself from communication altogether, disappearing only to reappear in the play's final scene. In *Cosmonaut*, therefore, communication is both promise and threat. On one side is the promise held out by Keith, and confirmed by the man with whom he is speaking: Eric, a World Bank official, whose job it is to broker difficult negotiations between countries in conflict:

> We bring these men together in a room with a wooden table. We bring them whisky and we talk it over until . . . they realise that the chaos of their lives can simply be left behind.[18]

On the other hand, when two characters are together on stage, they are as apt to misunderstand each other, to evade contact, and to use language to differentiate rather than to connect: Keith's attempts to speak Gaelic to the proprietor of a Highland hotel is instantly rebuffed, because the gesture is read not as communication, but as a profoundly patronizing usurpation of Gaelic culture. [19]

Cosmonaut extends and develops the argument over language and identity posed in *Europe*: as in the previous play, there is a struggle between forces that seek to fix meaning and identity, and those who try to communicate across boundaries. For example, one of the characters in the later play, Bernard, is comically paranoid about the encroaching effects of American culture, and equally doctrinaire about the innate superiority of Europe. However, as in the previous play, the world is too porous to support the existence of fixed boundaries. To pass on the message contained in the play's title, the last surviving cosmonaut dynamites the capsule in which he has travelled; as he intends it, the message is carefully directed, to be interpreted by just one person: the woman of the play's title – a woman who is no longer alive.[20] It is worth noting, also, that the message that Oleg sends is not only directed to a person who no longer exists, but also toward a country that no longer exists – Oleg has been in space for twelve years, and does not know about the break up of the Soviet bloc. His message, though, is meaningful, although the meanings it generates are traumatic: Natasja sees the death of her father (or she thinks she does: Oleg's fellow cosmo-naut, Casmir, is her father – but Casmir dies long before the spacecraft explodes), and Bernard sees an echo of a traumatic event in his own life (the destruction of the Arianne rocket, Europe's belated attempt to get into space) and suffers a debilitating stroke which destroys his powers of speech.

Before his stroke, Bernard comes as close as any of the play's charac-ters to a definition of the satellite's import:

> Someone's up there watching us. Waiting for us to . . . generate the right answer . . . Like a teacher who comes into a roomful of noisy fighting children and doesn't shout but stands quietly. A still point. Drawing the kids' attention one by one. Until they're all ready to learn . . .[21]

As with every other element in a richly ambiguous play, this image is not without its ironies; we have witnessed the capsule's inhabitants tearing into each other, verbally and physically, like the noisy fighting children that Bernard describes. We have also seen Bernard intercept the capsule's last attempt at communication (he misinterprets it as an alien attempt to speak to Earth); we've also heard his response to the 'still point' he eulogizes – 'Why won't you talk to me, you motherfuck-ers?'[22] However, the promise of the still point – of the moment when communication can begin – is never entirely forgotten: during the play, the characters do manage to find such points, over a shared drink, while working in the garden, or climbing up to a hotel roof to see the stars. These points can be reached in any location; no part of the continent is privileged over any of the others. The play finishes on the exchange, 'What do you want?/Only to talk', spoken in a bar in the Western Highlands; even such an apparently insignificant, unmarked corner of Europe is a place that can be cleared for communication.[23]

fighting over scotland: david harrower and gregory burke

So far, the plays analysed seem to point out a clear message: identity, as envisaged by Scottish dramatists, is fluid rather than fixed, and explores new territory rather than remaining rooted, either in one location or in one view of the world. However, this is not the whole picture: even in the plays discussed above (most notably in *The Evil Doers*, but also in *Europe* and *Cosmonaut*), there is something profoundly unsettling, even profoundly painful, in the experience of losing your place on the map. The experience of devolution, from 1999 onwards, served to sharpen the debate over Scottish identity that had been rekindled in the 1970s; now, Scottish identity had a new focus – the parliament in Edinburgh. We had finally said 'yes' to a measure of self-determination; and yet the very fact that we were now a (partly) self-determining geographical and cultural entity itself prompted questions about the nature of the country – and in particular about the status of those who found themselves marginalized and under attack. This debate is reflected in two post-devolution plays: David Harrower's *Dark Earth* (2003) and Gregory Burke's massively successful *Gagarin Way* 2001). Both plays, as in Greenhorn and Hannan, present sharply conflicting images of Scottishness; in these plays, however, characters do not have to travel through versions of their city and their country. The contradictions in the new map of Scotland run right through the places where they live – and these contradictions have only been sharpened by the new political dispensation.

In *Dark Earth*, an urban couple, out for a drive along the Antonine Wall, are forced to spend the night in a farmhouse when their car breaks down. The farmhouse is not remote: no part of Central Scotland is particularly far from any other part, and the remains of the Roman wall stretch across the most populous part of the country. However, in terms of the characters' experience of Scotland, the farmhouse exists in a different time and place. As Christine (the daughter of the couple who own the farmhouse) notes, her home stands on historically significant ground: at one time or another, it has been traversed by the Romans, the Votadini, the Selgovae, the Young Pretender and his supporters, and generation after generation of farmers.[24] However, the farm is no longer viable: an apparently rooted sense of identity has in fact already been disrupted. The family are poised to move to Falkirk, and their history will go with them. There are no visible signs of the Romans, of the Jacobites, or of any of the waves of historical change that have passed over it; the history (the dark earth of the play's title: the term means both the soil found in archaeological excavation, and the silted soil of farming land) is hidden in the ground – its only visible manifestation the memories the family will take away with them.

It is not that urban and rural images of Scotland are simply opposed to each other. There are faultlines in the relationships on both sides, and there are moments where allegiances on both sides shift: by the end of the play, characters are forced into sharp opposition because the versions of Scotland they inhabit cannot be reconciled. The main dividing factors – the elements that split one Scotland from the other – is not history or culture, so much as class and income: a furious exchange between Petey (the owner of the farm) and Euan (one half of the urban couple) finishes on Petey's telling assertion – 'You're livin in another country, son . . . .'[25] As indeed they are: the characters traverse the same territory, but their experience of that territory is so different as to convert Petey's answer from a cliché into an uncomfortable truth.

In Gregory Burke's *Gagarin Way*, two factory workers kidnap one of their managers; they confidently expect to find that the manager is Japanese, or at the least Dutch – this will mean that the planned end of the kidnap, the execution of a multinational's executive, will be comfortably distanced from their own lives. However, when the man they have captured revives, they find that he is disturbingly local: he is from the same territory as they are, he knows the same place-names, and he knows the political and cultural history of the area as well as do his kidnappers. Their act is intended as an assertion of local control over international capital; however, the man they kidnap wearily informs them that, for capitalism if for nothing else, there are no differences worth the assertion: 'You want arrogance? Greed? Stupidity? Look around. There's no need for defences when something's everywhere.'[26]

As in *Dark Earth*, characters who nominally share the same location inhabit different versions of Scotland: in this case, even a shared history does not create a communal identity. As the play notes, even the creation of a Scottish parliament cannot forge a unified identity that Scots can comfortably share. From the factory workers' point of view, the parliament is little more than a joke:

EDDIE: (*to Frank*) . . . Ken, . . . the new parliament. The one they're building. The one that's gonnae give us (*shouting in Braveheart style*) freedom.[27]

The brief, satirical reference to *Braveheart* is telling: for a short period around the release of Mel Gibson's film, the figure of Wallace was a totem of political defiance in Scottish cultural life. In typical Hollywood style, the film showed the formation of a national community at a point of crisis; *Gagarin Way* suggests that, in the face of the eternal crisis generated by global capitalism, not even Wallace, as imagined by a Hollywood superstar, would be enough to form a single Scotland from the various versions of the country that house the rich and the poor.

conclusion

In the introduction to a recent series of essays on modern Europe, Brian Graham comments:

> Identity is not a discrete social construction that is territorially defined in different spatial entities. . . . Perhaps best visualised as a multiplicity of superimposed layerings, identity has potentially conflicting supranational, national, regional and local expressions, in turn fractured by other manifestations of sameness – religion, language, high culture – that are not necessarily defined in terms of these same spatial divisions. . . .[28]

Scottish dramatists – at least some of them – seem drawn to an image of the world and their own country that might not provide a central, defining map of a Scottishness that requires exploration; they seem to be creating a sense of identity in general that is fluid and constantly transforming itself – while at the same time showing themselves fully aware of how divisive and fragmented the experience of identity in the modern world might be. In some of the work, there is a sense of hopefulness; there is no one identity to which Scots should conform, and, indeed, that lack of definition is itself a strength, because it allows flexible communities to establish themselves across seemingly inflexible boundaries. However, there is also something profoundly disturbing about the sense that stable identities have become unfixed. In *The Evil Doers, Dark Earth* and *Gagarin Way*, characters frantically try to re-establish a cultural centre – a sense of a peculiarly Scottish identity (or at least a version of it) – in the midst of uncontrollable flux. However it is imagined, Scottish playwrights perceive contemporary Scottish identity as comprising the multiple layerings described above; and nowhere in the work I have discussed is there the sense that a final map of contemporary Scotland – one that will take account of a contradictory, porous, unfixed and frequently destabilizing reality – is in any way possible.

notes

1. A. Scullion, 'Self and Nation: Issues of Identity in Modern Scottish Drama', *New Theatre Quarterly*, vol. 17, no. 4 (2001), 373–90 (373).
2. Ibid., p. 376.
3. D. Pattie, 'The Decentring of *Docherty*: The Scotsman in Modern Scottish Drama', *International Journal of Scottish Theatre*, vol. 1, no. 2 (2000). E. Journal. http:// www.artsqmuc.ac.uk/ijost/Volume1_no2

4. C. Harvie, 'Scottish Journey', *Cencrastus*, 1989, 4–9 (5).
5. C. Craig, 'Scotland Ten Years On: The Changes that Took Place While RipMacWinkle Slept', *Radical Scotland*, Feb–March 1989, 8–10 (5).
6. Ibid.
7. C. Hannan, *The Evil Doers* (London: Nick Hern, 1990), p. 15.
8. Ibid.
9. S. Greenhorn, *Passing Places*, in P. Howard (ed.), *Scotland Plays* (London: Nick Hern, 1998), p. 181.
10. D. Greig, *One Way Street*, in P. Howard (ed.), *Scotland Plays*, p. 259.
11. D. Greig, *Plays: 1* (London: Methuen, 2002), p. 6.
12. Ibid., p. 60.
13. Ibid., p. 17.
14. Ibid., p. 39.
15. S. Rushdie, *Shame* (London: Jonathan Cape, 1983), p. 86.
16. Greig, *Plays: 1*, p. 5.
17. Ibid., p. 235.
18. Ibid., p. 239.
19. Ibid., p. 298.
20. Ibid., p. 295.
21. Ibid., p. 288.
22. Ibid., p. 256.
23. Ibid., p. 301.
24. D. Harrower, *Dark Earth* (London: Faber, 2002), p. 45.
25. Ibid., pp. 92–3.
26. Ibid., p. 86.
27. Ibid., p. 65.
28. B. Graham (ed.), *Modern Europe: Place, Culture and Identity* (London: Arnold, 1998), p. 2.

8

'the net and the self': colliding views of individuality and nationhood in the pre-devolutionary plays of mark jenkins and ed thomas

roger owen

In his three-volume analysis of pre-millennial society, *The Information Age: Economy, Society and Culture*, the Catalan sociologist Manuel Castells notes how the rapid technological and social changes of modernity have facilitated the rise of what he terms 'the network society'. In this new society, he argues, the primacy of many long-established structures of cultural authority and continuity – including institutionalized religion, patriarchalism and the nation-state – have been undermined by networks of influence and interest which are not tied to the traditional agencies of power. Castells asserts that, as a result of this change, 'the search for identity, collective or individual, ascribed or constructed', has become in itself 'the fundamental source of social meaning'; however, faced by 'global flows of wealth, power, and images', many people's daily lives now involve complicated negotiation between what he describes as conflicting forces of 'abstract, universal instrumentalism' and 'historically rooted, particularistic identities'. He concludes that '[o]ur societies are increasingly structured around a bipolar opposition between the Net and the self.'[1]

In this chapter, I will attempt to relate Castells's notion of the Net and the self to a study of political drama in Wales, noting how his terminology provides a valuable means of examining the way in which, and the extent to which, contemporary dramatists locate the Welsh experience in a rapidly changing wider world. I will do so with reference to some of the work and ideas of Mark Jenkins and Ed Thomas, two dramatists whose views on Welsh identity have been fundamentally different, and whose plays have exemplified a deep-rooted conflict concerning this issue within Welsh culture at the end of the millennium. I will describe Mark Jenkins's work as a materialistic and 'interpersonal' drama which depicts the Welsh experience as merely one of any number of possible variations on a broadly international, historically coherent theme of civic relationships and responsibilities. In relation to Castells's terms, I will argue that Jenkins's work suggests a view of the world in which the Net and the self coexist but remain essentially *divergent*, so that the self can always retain its integrity as a site of interface within the Net. Conversely, Ed Thomas's work will be described as an idealistic, 'self-inventive' drama in which the Welsh experience is defined as a unique form of resistance to the broader social and historical values of contemporary realism: in Castells's terms, it suggests a view of the Net and the self as *convergent*, where the self is redefined – and, significantly, dissipated in time and space – by its encounter with the Net as an active structure.

castells's 'network society' and welsh identity politics

Before examining Jenkins's and Thomas's work in greater detail, the implications and context of some of Castells's ideas need to be explored further. Castells's conception of the network society argues that contemporary social change is related to, and consistent with, the information technology revolution.[2] The Internet is one of the prime exemplars and vehicles of that change, and the network society is thus presented as an essentially anti-hierarchical realm, 'shaping life and being shaped by life at the same time', and 'characterized by widespread destructuring of organizations, delegitimation of institutions, fading away of major social movements, and ephemeral cultural expressions'.[3] Crucially, the idea of the Net creates a continuum between spheres of individual and social action and militates against the 'structural schizophrenia between function and meaning' which polarizes the presupposedly 'instrumentalist' Net and 'particularist' self.[4]

One of the prime institutions to be 'delegitimated' by the network society is the nation-state, and it is here that Castells's idea becomes most directly applicable to the context in which we may view the work of Mark Jenkins and Ed Thomas. Castells defines nations in the network society as 'cultural communes constructed in people's minds and collective memory by the sharing of history and political projects'.[5] These cultural communes 'have a life of their own, independent from statehood, albeit embedded in cultural constructs and political projects'.[6] They do not equate to the traditional model of the independent nation-state, which, Castells argues, is largely meaningless given the forces of globalization, digitally disseminated culture, international trading blocs 'and . . . the widespread (re)construction of identity on the basis of nationality'.[7] When discussing contemporary nations, therefore, Castells outlines a series of different models, some of which include the integration of a nation with a state, others which do not. The one that most closely approximates to Wales's position is the 'national quasi-state', a category of nations 'that stop at the threshold of statehood, but force their parent state to adapt, and cede sovereignty'; they are so called 'because they are not fully-fledged states, but win a share of political autonomy on the basis of their national identity'.[8]

The Welsh experience – though Castells makes very little direct reference to it in his work – thus emerges as part of a complex international tendency away from ingrained hierarchical structures towards more fragmented, dynamic – and potentially less stable – arrangements. It also demonstrates another favoured Castellian trope, the resurgent power of identity, by which the influence of these broader international movements may be regarded (only) through the optic of the social actor's preferred peer grouping. However, it is important to note that, even here, within the Welsh context itself, there is potential conflict between instrumentalism and particularism; in this case between increasingly manufactured and saleable visions of one-nation Welshness and particularistic, historical differences of identity between communities within Wales. Evidence of this conflict was increasingly apparent during the 1990s and was the subject of fierce debate between various parties, of which Mark Jenkins and Ed Thomas may be taken as representatives. Jenkins attacked the instrumentalist tendency amongst cultural nationalists by decrying their vision of a 'virtual reality Wales', in which Wales itself was seen as a collective identity project: '"collective visions" and artistic expression are inevitably destructive of each other', he argued, adding that '[t]he history of Europe this century should have warned us that where collective visions prevail, art dies and life becomes nasty, brutish and long for audiences who have to suffer it.'[9] Thomas, meanwhile, regarded the project of national reinvention as a cultural necessity and a redress to historical degeneration: 'Wales desperately needs to be re-invented,' he noted, 'its out-moded stereotypes need to be crushed and a new self-image created . . . The arts, and those who work in the arts in Wales, must realise the role they have to play in this invention.'[10]

This dispute about the redefinition of Wales as an identity project was resolved, in one sense, by the devolution referendum of 1997, in which a tiny majority was secured for the creation of a National Assembly, thus transforming the notion of Welsh self-determination from the level of cultural aspiration to political reality. The debate concerning the precise form of that self-determination has continued postdevolution, of course, and in many ways has become more urgent with the increasing aggrandizement of Cardiff as a seat of national government during the early twenty-first century. However, as regards Jenkins's and Thomas's work for the stage, the terms of the debate about the relative instrumentalism or particularism of Welsh identity – the degree to which it could be identified in relation to views of the Net and the self – were fully articulated long before 1997,; and it is for this reason (as well as the constraints of space) that I have chosen to concentrate here on plays written by these two dramatists before the advent of devolution.

net/self divergence: mark jenkins

Mark Jenkins was born and brought up in London, the son of a Welsh father. However, he has spent a good deal of his adult life in Wales, working as an academic, and his reputation as a playwright was built while resident in Cardiff. This reputation was due at first to the international success of *Playing Burton* (1987), his monologue concerning the career and transformed identity of the actor Richard Burton. This was among Jenkins's earliest works for the stage, and was preceded only by *Birthmarks* (1985), a frank assessment of the life of Karl Marx, and *Mr Owen's Millennium* (1985–6), another monologue, relating the life and career of the industrialist and social reformer Robert Owen, both of which will be considered here. Other plays by Jenkins in the 1990s include the love story, *Nora's Bloke* (1994), and *Downtown Paradise* (1995), which concerns the relationship between an idealistic lawyer and a charismatic inmate of Death Row. A more recent monologue, *Rosebud* (2004), discussing the creative life of Orson Welles, has also been well received.

In dealing with Jenkins's plays as examples of political drama, a key factor is the way in which his enquiry into the personal domain (through the lives of his characters) is manifested through a broadly 'interpersonal' drama as outlined by the German critic Peter Szondi in his classic *Theory of the Modern Drama*.[11] In basic terms, Szondi's notion of the interpersonal proposes that it is through communication with and interrogation of others that the individual's experience of life is given substance; and that reality is thus constituted primarily in the public domain. This play of interpersonal conflict, he argues, has been the epitome and mainstay of European drama from the time of the Renaissance, as well as one of the most enduring artistic manifestations of the great historical project of liberal humanism. Following Szondi, Mark Jenkins's politics as a dramatist may be understood in relation to long-standing discourses around the social and civic rights and responsibilities of the individual, manifested through a broadly materialist and anti-utopian realism (in which, as noted above, the self remains intact and separable throughout its engagement with the Net).

Birthmarks, first staged in 1987, concerns the hidden personal history of Karl Marx, and contrasts two quite different visions of Marx in the public domain. First, he is seen as a social being within his own milieu, a view which, while it humanizes him to a degree, also proposes deep flaws in his physical being and his moral character, such as unreconstructed opinions and behaviour towards women, Jews and his contemporaries, and a ceaseless pursuit of his own interests. Second, he is seen as a political and philosophical icon, and crucially is represented as complicit in his own sanctification. Jenkins brings these two aspects together in the central action of his play, which contrasts the birth of Marx's legitimate daughter (who dies) with the birth both of an illegitimate son by his housekeeper, Lenchen, and of his own masterwork, *Das Kapital*. Whereas his grief for the former is presented as genuine but short-lived, his attempt to suppress all knowledge of the latter child for the sake of his political reputation is presented as the moment most genuinely indicative of his philosophy. Marx encourages his colleague Engels to take public responsibility for Lenchen's pregnancy, thus consciously creating the space necessary to convince his followers of his ideological infallibility. Ironically, then, we see the great philosopher of dialectical materialism furnishing his own epoch with the lie that will allow him to transcend history and become a myth. Jenkins reflects this transformation into a materialist deity in a final nightmarish *tableau vivant* in which Marx, on a magisterial plinth, dictates sections of *Das Kapital* to his wife Jenny, while Lenchen, her child now removed for adoption, scrubs the floor. As Marx dictates an analysis of commodity, the women toil, unacknowledged, before breaking off from their tasks to let out an prolonged (pre-recorded) scream. In the meantime, Marx's countenance acquires an iconic (Jenkins's staging notes bluntly state 'godlike') character, resembling its depiction on his gravestone in Highgate Cemetery.[12]

Birthmarks is a piece rooted firmly within the interpersonal dramatic tradition. Located in a coherent and comprehensible social world, it employs its characters' various interactions as a means of revealing their underlying motives and moral natures. However, Jenkins's desire to explode the authoritarian, utopian narrative of Marxism in the final *tableau vivant* leads to a drastic disruption of the play's cohesion. There, the action is set in an abstract, symbolic location quite unlike any other in the play, 'out of time and space'.[13] Though it contains dialogue, the scene ceases to constitute an interpersonal exchange; rather, the world of the play is reappropriated by the playwright and rendered entirely rhetorical. This is an indication of Jenkins's disgust and personal anger at Marx's tacit aspiration to iconic status, and his technique of representation here parallels Marx's own wilful abandonment of his historical self to the force of the mythical Net.

This merging of the worlds of the self and the Net, by which a character encounters their own mythology, is a device seen in a number of Jenkins's plays after *Birthmarks*; however, increasingly, Jenkins finds ways of reintegrating these moments of theatrical singularity into the dramatic action. His play *Mr Owen's Millennium*, for example, concerns the career of another great social reformer – in this case, the Welsh industrialist Robert Owen – and reveals the tensions within a life lived across a series of moral 'sites': the greater good of humanity, social advancement, individual morality and personal happiness. Again, we see a theatrical examination of utopianism, based on the presentation of a strong, charismatic – and historically real – individual; and, as in Marx's new world, Owen's utopian settlement at 'New Harmony', Indiana is corrupted when frail humanity's self-motivation seeps into the fabric of the dream. Here again, what happens when utopia is betrayed seems to be the acid test of the value of political action.

Mr Owen's Millennium is a monologue, but can still be seen as an interpersonal drama as a result of its binding historicism. Set in 1858 (the year of Owen's death), it shows the speaker reflecting upon his long life and achievements from his room at the Bear Hotel, Newtown. In that sense, the play is tied to a real historical process, and, though it is narrated by a highly idealistic individual, the meaning of Owen's life is expressed through the public relationships negotiated and neglected by him over the years. Having said that, Jenkins derives much dramatic and theatrical interest here (as in *Birthmarks*) from putting this inter-personal technique under stress.[14] Owen is a figure as authoritative and lucid as one would expect of a great rationalist, but there are elements in his behaviour that defy the tenets of that rationality. For example, when discussing his long-dead adversaries, including the Duke of Wellington, he freely confesses to conversing with them daily, noting that they all now, to a man, acknowledge the folly of their former disputes: 'They all admit that I am right, all the spirits. Wisdom after the event, see.'[15] Similarly, the theatrical presentation of the play occasion-ally troubles its underlying sense of rational causality. Unlike that in *Birthmarks*, the action here does not establish a strong sense of dramatic location at the outset, but is instead located in a single spotlight, a limi-nal 'place' which strengthens the play's invocation of past events from Owen's life.

Significantly, Jenkins checks this manipulation of liminality by steer-ing the work away from a reliance on the fantastical or delusional and back towards the interpersonal. It is Owen's old age that has rendered him liminal (he has outlived the vast majority of his contemporaries), and not the dramatist's will to present him as overtly authored. The characteristics of the theatrical presentation are thus folded back into the service of the dramatic action – a device that, as we shall see, is diametrically opposed to Ed Thomas's practice of unfolding the dramatic out into the theatrical.

Owen's social liminality is interestingly associated with the most telling image of himself as a Welshman. Having confessed to the collapse of his grand schemes to 'Remake the world anew. That's all! Remake the world anew!', Owen is presented as a man outside his time, and removed from public space.[16] Tellingly, it is at this point that he remarks upon the image of himself as Welsh – and degenerated: 'I've failed, you know! I've nothing now to show. A crank! An old Welsh wizard weaving legends from the wings of bats and night-jars, concoct-ing elixirs to wash away the warts from the fingers of vagabonds and beggars.'[17] Though Owen occasionally speaks Welsh during the play (when recalling his youth), Jenkins draws relatively little attention to this aspect of his identity, and thus presents the Welsh experience as one that, though it certainly exists in the wider world, does not provide an optic on that world. Owen is not seen to bring his Welshness to bear on his social project. It is worth stressing that this does not necessarily indicate a view of Welsh identity as subordinate or marginal on Jenkins's part; however, it does reinforce the notion that features of identity such as Welshness are seen by Jenkins as discrete categories, existing in the social Net, and largely removed from the integral self.

Playing Burton further develops a number of Jenkins's main themes. Again, the play is a monologue, in which the great Welsh actor returns to face his public and to review his life. As with Owen and Marx, *Playing Burton* concerns the encounter between a man and his own mythology, and like Owen, Burton is another embodiment of social liminality. Although undoubtedly in some senses an 'instrumentalist' theatrical construct (addressing his audience from beyond the grave), Burton's primary characteristic – that of transformation – is strongly related back to his historical persona as an actor, his cultural condition as an exile, and his alcoholism. The play shows his vocal and physical transformation, at an accelerated rate, from Richie Jenkins of Pont-Rhyd-y-Fen, to high-living Hollywood icon during the 1960s and 1970s, to the ravaged figure in his last film, *1984*. His biography is thus manifested as an interpersonal conflict within a single body, a fact that exploits (not always unproblematically) the persona of the actor in order to reintegrate that transformational process into a recognizable social and historical context.

Like *Mr Owen's Millennium*, *Playing Burton* involves the migration of its central character – one who could be classed as a glorious failure – to America to test the mettle of his dream. Burton's removal from the world of his youth, far from being a tragic severance, was in many ways a consummation devoutly to be wished; after all, his prospects in Wales 'were . . . lower than the horizon'.[18] The Welsh Burton is a boy, an inept role-player hopelessly unaware of his own underlying urge for empowerment, whilst the American Burton is a man, making his own decisions and his own mistakes. He is obviously invigorated by his arrival and success in America, and *Playing Burton* indulges its audience with the sense of excitement about the elevation of his life history from mere biography to epic in the great imperial playground. Significantly, then, the landscape of fantasy in this play is – once again – historically and geographically real.

Towards the end of the play, his commentary on his roles becomes less articulate (he can barely recall the events surrounding the filming of *Wagner*, for example, for shame at his drunken vindictiveness). His – and our – grasp of the meaning in the interplay between his various personae begins to loosen, and his performance – increasingly distorted by alcohol – begins to lapse into incoherence: it is significant that the words he speaks at the end of the play are largely not his own. His world, as so often in Jenkins's plays, dissolves into a singularity, in which his historical project is subsumed into an amorphous mass of contradictions in a space rendered liminal both by the fact of theatrical presentation and by the character's vacation of the world that he himself created. But, once again, this dissolution is saved from chaos by contingent factors in the character's own life; and this serves to fold the potential chaos of the theatrical presentation back into the realm of the dramatic action. For the spectator, at least, if not for the character, the notion of the self is always held in suspension from the Net.

net/self convergence: ed thomas

Ed Thomas was born in Ystradgynlais, Powys, and spent his early working life as an actor. His career as a playwright began in 1988, with the production of his play *House of America*, which, over the 1998 (itself a rare thing in Welsh theatre), created strong interest in his work both inside and outside Wales. It was followed by the next two elements in his 'New Wales Trilogy', *Flowers of the Dead Red Sea* (1991) and *East from the Gantry* (1992); and then his Welsh-language play *Adar Heb Adenydd* (1989: translated into English and expanded as *The Myth of Michael Roderick*, 1991), *Song from a Forgotten City* (1995) and *Gas Station Angel* (1998). After a significant hiatus, Thomas's most recent play, *Stone City Blue*, was produced in 2004.

Following the success of *House of America*, Thomas quickly established a political programme for his work as a 'theatre of invention'.[19] This took as its starting point the postmodern idea that all views of reality are fundamentally unstable and ephemeral, because the terms by which one might understand reality are in constant flux (as noted above, because the self is constantly redefined and reconstituted in its encounter with the Net). Thomas's 'theatre of invention' was also based on a dynamic reappraisal of the nature of Welsh identity, with both the individual and the nation defined as almost infinitely malleable and constantly reshaped by suggestion and intervention – in other words, as essentially theatrical. This view was supported by Thomas's reading of the work of historian Gwyn A. Williams, who, in his seminal *When Was Wales?* (1985), argued that the Welsh experience had been characterized throughout its history by crisis and discontinuity, and that, in the contemporary world, it had acquired a quasi-theatrical character.[20]

In relation to Welsh identity, Thomas's plays counterbalanced two extreme and exclusive views: that Wales was, to all traditional intents and purposes, dead; but that it was also a viable and necessary expression of social, cultural and political identity. This view closely echoes

Castells's notion of a 'project identity', in which a society undertakes a process of transformation as a form of cultural resistance to assimilation, but that in doing so, it radically shifts its internal cultural consensus. In Thomas's case, this shift was allied to a sense of play, and gave his drama a positive dynamism in terms of its discussion of Welsh identity which countered the generally pessimistic national discourses of decline and suppression.

House of America concerns the calamitous collapse of the Lewis family, Mam (who is never named), Sid, Boyo and Gwenny. Depressed about a lack of employment and the seeming inevitability of reduced aspirations, Sid dreams about escaping to America to find his absent father, Clem. Short of the necessary funds and moral courage to fulfil this objective, he retreats into a fantasy world based around Jack Kerouac's *On the Road*, and eventually draws Gwenny in with him as Kerouac's girlfriend, Joyce Johnson. In the meantime, as an open-cast-mining project eats into the hillside behind the Lewises' house, and Mam's sanity fails, Clem's murdered body is found by the coal diggers. Consequently, Sid and Gwenny retreat ever further from reality until their game subsides into an incestuous affair, whereupon, after discovering that Gwenny is pregnant with Sid's child, Boyo murders his brother.

The action of *House of America* has affinities with Homi K. Bhabha's notion of 'mimicry', in which a pathological need for acknowledgement and confirmation by the dominant 'other' engenders a passionate self-loathing in the subaltern, who then, more or less involuntarily, reasserts his/her identity through the servility of self-deceit.[21] It is also, to apply Castells's terms again, consistent with the idea of the self's convergence with the Net. Sid Lewis's decision to abandon his given social identity – even his own name – by immersing himself in the persona of Kerouac is an obvious example of a disastrous self-deceit; but the play expands upon this process by actively creating the terms by which the audience may become implicated in the same deceit. It plays upon the allure of the American 1950s beatnik culture, and valorizes Kerouac's elemental life and work, portraying him as a pioneer, navigating the contours of a dream. Kerouac's words are intoned reverentially by both Sid and Gwenny during the play, and are used to seduce her and the theatre audience itself; and though Boyo belittles Sid's fixation with *On the Road*, the play itself trenchantly defends its appeal. References to other classic pieces of American popular culture also pervade the play, such as the prescribed interval music (by Dionne Warwick, Lou Reed, Frank Sinatra and The Doors, among others), or film references (an early scene in the play takes place as the family watch *The Godfather* on television). Again, although there are elements of comedy associated with some of these moments, American culture remains unmocked throughout.

By comparison, traditional icons of Welsh culture and identity do not fare well. The Lewises present themselves as a fragmented yet totemic Welsh family, impoverished but held together by the determination of a widowed mother to do her best for her adult sons. This echo of many classic stories of Welsh industrial life is given a cruelly ironic twist here, as the absence of the father is entirely Mam's doing, and her urge to sustain the family's unity is a doomed attempt to postpone the discovery of her homicidal past. Similarly, the coal industry is seen not as a harsh but ultimately heroic enterprise uniting the men of the village in song and chthonic mystique; rather it is a meaningless indignity, performed on the surface by machines (described as 'dinosaurs' by Gwenny) or pitiful, solitary automata such as the workman, Clint, who she and Sid find searching for his lost head among the coal debris. Later, Mam, in her feigned insanity, dresses in a stovepipe hat and daffodil for Boyo's hospital visit, and sups invisible *cawl* from a wooden bowl. This treatment of Welsh identity is typical of much of Thomas's *oeuvre*, in that it asserts the possibility of Welshness as a structure for identity in spite of its scorn for many traditional icons and practices which have been defined as central to that identity.

In *House of America*, the line between empowering self-invention and the self-deceit of mimicry is thin indeed. Invention certainly comes at a price for Sid Lewis: when used to displace the shame of his failure as a man, his essentially benign dream of freedom, 'chasing the sun' across America, costs him his grasp on reality, and ultimately his life.[22] The play also leaves its audience with another painful image of invention, in the drug- and alcohol-crazed Gwenny's final involuntary monologue of invasion and occupation by a monstrous, physical 'other'. Thomas is not ignorant of the potential pitfalls which may be encountered in the course of the identity project to which his 'theatre of invention' is dedicated, then; but it is significant that his general dramatic technique constantly allows the characters' world to be unfolded out into the theatrical event, thus ensuring that the predominant feature of his work is its theatrical energy rather than the self-deceit and loss which afflicts some of his characters.

This process of unfolding the action is strongly evident in Thomas's *Song from a Forgotten City*, in which the action is occasionally unfolded to the point where this device becomes in itself the *subject* of the action.

The action begins with the discovery in a room at the Angel (a city centre hotel in Cardiff) of Austin Carlyle's dead body. This is followed by a scene loosely depicting his arrival at the hotel foyer, on the day of an international rugby match (which Wales has lost 16–14), during which Carlyle declares himself to be 'the writer of this fiction'.[23] The action then reconstructs an ultimately violent and possibly imaginary episode between Carlyle and a television executive, Jackson, before reverting to the foyer. Carlyle's arrival at his designated room heralds the second act, in which his assertion of authorship, and the very existence of the hotel, is questioned by his two querulous associates, Benny and Jojo. They believe Carlyle to be a delusional depressive, whose erratic visions are a by-product of his poetic nature, heroin abuse and grief at the loss of his lover, Yvonne. Carlyle shoots Benny, whereupon the action reverts to the hotel, in which Carlyle is attempting to write his narrative of the Welsh metropolis. After being chastised by the hotel's Night Porter for discharging a gun in his room, Carlyle plays the tape recording of his voice, heard previously during the discovery of his corpse at the very beginning of the play. At the end of a taped statement, '*CARLYLE brings the gun to his head and laughs. He pulls the trigger. He stands there smiling.*'[24]

Song from a Forgotten City reiterates the concerns with identity and invention established in Thomas's previous works. Like Sid Lewis, Carlyle is involved in a project of the imagination which displaces his immediate reality, writing a script set in an imaginary Welsh metropolis within a Wales that he also identifies as imaginary. Carlyle's assertion that 'the only country you've got is the country in your head . . . it's just an idea . . .' directly aligns him with Ed Thomas's own views on national self-invention.[25] This view is angrily rejected by Jackson, a television producer; but his essentialist retort – that he has been to the 'real' country in person, while fishing – is undermined by the fact that his manner of speech implies both obsession (the fact that he 'saw fish' is reiterated rhythmically until it acquires the sense of a litany) and a constriction of social context which disqualifies him from passing reasonable judgement (he describes his fellow television executives as 'the finest men and women you could meet in your life').[26] Added to this, Thomas further undermines Jackson through a memorable visual rejoinder:

> *CARLYLE pulls a dead, poisoned, plastic fish and a hand holding a sword out of a bucket.*
> CARLYLE: I don't think so, Mr Jackson.[27]

In spite of the comic effect of this visual intervention into the fabric of his drama, there are insidious implications to such interference. Thomas's characters are divested of their status as arbiters of their own experiences, and the dramatist himself threatens to become an oppressive instrumental force as a result of the serial contortions of the narrative and the play's general dramatic style. In this particular drama of self-invention, the characters seem to have to be content with having their 'selves' invented for them. The Night Porter, for example, comically succumbs to the notion that he is a product of Carlyle's authorship, and a minor character at that (Well fuck me, there was me thinking I was real')[28]. While this discovery of external prescription has, after Pirandello, become a relative commonplace in modernist drama, its implications here are highly charged, both emotionally and politically. Carlyle, the creator of a vibrant and emancipated urban Welsh world, is not a credible author. Like Jackson, he is delusional as a result of drug use ('things can get fuzzy man . . . like blurred . . . My memory gets blurred Jojo on account of . . . my head . . . my smack') – a fact that is confirmed when his capacity to discern his own location within the 'fucking hotel' is called into question in Act Two by his colleague Jojo:

> JOJO: It ain't a hotel, Carlyle.
> CARLYLE: Uh?
> JOJO: This ain't no hotel.[29]

In production, the dramatic action is here unfolded into the theatrical presentation by the fact that the actor who plays the Night Porter also plays the role of Jojo. In effect, therefore, the figure over whom Carlyle claims authorship tacitly succeeds in dislocating his creator. This overthrowing of the dramatist's authority is entirely consistent with the idea of the self as dissipated across the cultural Net, and as possessing different – even contradictory – components of identity at different 'sites' on the Net. It is also consistent with the nature of myth, in which the author is made absent, and communication is reiterative and cyclical, rather than rational and linear. *Song from a Forgotten City* frequently operates in this way, through repetitive dialogue, thematic reference and stage imagery, and the presentation of highly analogous material by different means. The Bellboy's encounter with a fisherman on the banks of the Taff early in the play, for example, has resonances throughout: Carlyle was discovered in infancy by a fisherman called Michael Butts, the existence of fish in upland rivers (as noted earlier) is

regarded by Jackson as an index of the reality of the nation; the fisherman himself possesses a beloved Sindy doll and a maligned Ken (who,
he claims, 'will shag anyone'), just as Carlyle yearns to repossess the
dead Yvonne, with whom he performed sex acts for money, though he
rails against Amos's suggestion that he and Yvonne were, consequently,
'slags'.[30]

The notion of myth is vital in Thomas's work because it is the prime
factor uniting theatre and the act of self-invention. From works such as
Flowers of the Dead Red Sea and the appropriately entitled *Myth of Michael
Roderick*, his plays have operated with a largely chaotic plot line over-
laying a deeper, coherent but partially hidden narrative structure. It is
this approximation to the form of myth that gives his work power without revealing it as a prescription for a new identity of any particular
kind. All is up for grabs in Thomas's vaudevillean national powerplay.

conclusion

It is with this question of myth that we may briefly contrast Thomas's
and Jenkins's work, and discuss the way in which their plays reflect
notions of Welsh society that counterbalance instrumentalism and
particularism. Returning to Castells's notion of the relationship
between the Net and the self, myth would seem to represent, for
Jenkins, an attempt to deny the idea that other sites on the Net must,
like the integral 'home site', be inhabited equally by selves. No matter
how populous the Net, the selves within it remain whole and recipro-
cal. For Thomas, the Net necessarily invades and subverts the self, and
myth is merely the inevitable expression of a multi-site individuality. In
relation to theatre, this difference – however arbitrary and nice the
distinction may seem – is an important one, because these dramatists'
plays are only as good as an audience's willingness to accept their
fundamental premises. In that respect, Castells's remarks on the role of
language in the process of national identity construction and retention
in the information age are particularly significant:

> language, and particularly a fully developed language, is a fundamental
> attribute of self-recognition, and of the establishment of an invisible
> national boundary less arbitrary than territoriality, and less exclusive than
> ethnicity. This is, in a historical perspective, because language
> provides the linkage between the private and the public sphere, and
> between the past and the present, regardless of the actual acknowl-
> edgement of a cultural community by the institutions of the state.[31]

This idea is already, of course, apposite to the Welsh experience of bilingualism (and is not uncontroversial in this respect); but in relation to the theatre, it has an added dimension, in that theatre – whether in Welsh or English – may also operate as a kind of spontaneous language. The crucial question is whether the construction of this '*fully developed language*' of theatre requires Jenkins's historical interpersonalism as its basis or Thomas's mythical self-invention in order to '[provide] the linkage' between the private sphere of theatrical presentation and the public sphere of social politics. It is a question whose answer lies far beyond the scope of this chapter, but its very nature as a question gives rise to a number of considerations that are in themselves significant in assessing the 'reality value' of Welsh politics and identity.

Whatever the writers' own personal political views, the techniques adopted by Jenkins and Thomas as dramatists suggest an ideological collision between a materialistic and an idealistic politics. For Jenkins, the politically 'real' is located in the action that people take in their own lives, regardless of the wider discourses of meaning which they may be serving. Reality, in this sense, is historical; and the substance of one's life may be traced through one's biography – hence Jenkins's interest in the lives of Robert Owen, Richard Burton and, more recently, Orson Welles. From this perspective, his work is in line with Barthes's fundamental contention against myth as a form of propaganda, as an anonymous and pervasive authoritarian discourse.[32] For Jenkins, myth – utopianism being only one example – is to be rejected because it engenders belief by making the historical inaccessible, invisible and unreal, and subsequently is predisposed to destroy the real lives of those people who believe in it: one needs only to consider those anonymous figures in *Mr Owen's Millennium* who valorize the great reformer as a deity to appreciate this point. In contemporary political terms, it could be argued that Jenkins's anti-mythical, realistic technique finds its equivalent in the work of figures such as John Pilger and Noam Chomsky, whose passionate denouncement of centralized American power and the persuasiveness of 'The Great Game' of international strategy has served to explode that 'new world order' mythology which constituted the early 1990s zeitgeist.[33]

Conversely, political reality for Ed Thomas is essentially related to performance, in that the aspiration for freedom, in terms both of the imagination and social action, can only be realized once one begins to act as if essentially unconstrained. David Ian Rabey's description of *The Myth of Michael Roderick* as 'a rampage through spurious notions of imaginative circumscription, determinism and integration into the fictitious cult of normality [which] exposes them all as essentially fears of freedom', rings true for a great deal of Thomas's work, and gets very close to the heart of his theatrical vision.[34] His dramatic politics thus determinedly conceive and expresses questions of identity and collectivity in terms of play rather than historical orthodoxies, and that, in the end, is what makes them pervasive, potent – and fragile. In that sense, they might find their equivalent in the ideas of Manuel Castells himself, who, in outlining his vision of the 1990s 'Network Society', argues that the new networking logic 'induces a social determination at a higher level than that of the specific social interests expressed through the networks', in which 'the power of flows takes precedence over the flows of power' and which demonstrates 'the pre-eminence of social morphology over social action'.[35]

The fact that Welsh drama may give us a clear view of such an ideological conflict in the 1990s suggests, at least, that the politics of representation in Wales – even before devolution – was expressive of issues that were also being reflected in some of the most pointed historical and political debates of the age. In that sense and to that extent, they were undoubtedly 'real'. And, as the novelist and cultural historian Emyr Humphreys noted in his momentous historical study of Welsh culture, *The Taliesin Tradition*, Wales's (marginal and endangered) position in relation to the great powers of the age has meant that those questions that most deeply affect the Welsh – such as the expression and significance of identity – have a habit of prefiguring the major debates on such issues elsewhere.[36]

notes

1. M. Castells, *The Rise of the Network Society* (Oxford: Blackwell, 1997), p. 3.
2. It is worth noting, however, that Castells argues that this social change is neither directly caused by, nor directly responsible for, technological development: 'technology does not determine society. Neither does society script the course of technological change, since . . . the final outcome depends on a complex pattern of interaction.' Ibid., p. 5.
3. Ibid., p. 2; p. 3.
4. Ibid.
5. M. Castells, *The Power of Identity* (Oxford: Blackwell, 1997), p. 51 (The italics are Castells's own).
6. Ibid., p. 29.
7. Ibid., p. 27.
8. Ibid., p. 52.

9. M. Jenkins, 'Virtual Reality Wales', *New Welsh Review*, no. 30 (1995), 74–7 (74).

10. E. Thomas, 'Wales and a Theatre of Invention', in N. Wallace (ed.), *Thoughts and Fragments about Theatres and Nations* (Glasgow: Guardian Publications, 1991), pp. 15–16 (p. 15).

11. P. Szondi, *The Theory of the Modern Drama* (Cambridge: Polity, 1987).

12. M. Jenkins, *More Lives Than One [Selected Works]* (Cardigan: Parthian, 2004), p. 118.

13. Ibid.

14. There, we see deep fractures in the way that the characters – largely members of the Marx coterie – interpret the nature of social reality (they could hardly be a revolutionary faction otherwise); these fractures ultimately dispel the proto-Marxists' utopian fantasy of revolution; but crucially this element of the dramatic action does not disrupt the play's construction of reality itself.

15. Jenkins, *More Lives Than One*, p. 184.

16. Ibid., p. 190.

17. Ibid., p. 200.

18. Ibid., p. 6.

19. See Thomas, 'Wales and a Theatre of Invention'.

20. See G. A. Williams, *When Was Wales?* (London: Black Raven, 1985), p. 304; also R. Owen, 'Powerful Simplification: Theatre in Wales in the 1990s and Beyond', in B. Kershaw (ed.), *The Cambridge History of British Theatre vol. 4* (Cambridge: Cambridge University Press, 2004), pp. 485–97; also R. Owen, 'The Play of History: The Performance of Identity in Welsh Historiography and Theater', in *The North American Journal of Welsh Studies*, vol.1, no.2 (2001) at http://spruce.flint.umich.edu/ ~ellisjs/VolOne.html.

21. See H. K. Bhabha, *The Location of Culture* (London: Routledge, 1994), pp. 85–92.

22. E. Thomas, *Three Plays*, B. Mitchell, ed. (Bridgend: Seren, 1994), p. 44.

23. E. Thomas, *[Selected] Work '95–'98* (Cardigan: Parthian, 2002), p. 40.

24. Ibid., p. 122.

25. Ibid., p. 48. See also Thomas, 'Wales and a Theatre of Invention', p. 15: 'It is not geography that makes a country but the people within it. A people invent a country because they desire its invention. Wales was invented by the Welsh because they desired a Wales.'

26. Ibid., p. 48.

27. Ibid., p. 49.

28. Ibid., p. 42.

29. Ibid., p. 98; p. 101.

30. Ibid., p. 17; p. 38.

31. Castells, *The Power of Identity*, p. 52 (the italics are Castells's own).

32. See R. Barthes, 'Myth Today', in *Mythologies*, trans. A. Lavers (London: Jonathan Cape, 1972), pp. 109–59.

33. See J. Pilger, *The New Rulers of the World* (London: Verso, 2002).

34. D. Rabey, cited in C. Savill, 'Wales is Dead!', *Planet* (February/March 1991), 86–91 (88).
35. Castells, *Rise of the Network Society*, p. 500.
36. See E. Humphreys, *The Taliesin Tradition* (London: Black Raven, 1983).

9
a legacy of violence: representing loyalism in the plays of gary mitchell
nadine holdsworth and wallace mcdowell

Despite the existence of the 'peace process', in many working-class Protestant, Unionist and Loyalist communities in Northern Ireland, ongoing sectarian violence, barbaric intra-communal punishment beatings and people being forced from their homes by intimidating tactics such as petrol bombs and threats to personal safety, occur on a regular basis.[1] This culture of violence and intimidation recently directly impinged on the Protestant playwright, Gary Mitchell, who forms the focus of this chapter. Mitchell has made a career of creating plays that explore the legacy of sectarian conflict and the impact of the changing political climate for working-class Protestant individuals, families, communities, institutions and cultural traditions in Northern Ireland. Media reports implicated Mitchell's portrayal of Loyalism when, in December 2005, 'rogue' Loyalist paramilitaries petrol-bombed Mitchell's car and forced him, his wife, seven-year-old son and father out of their home.[2] Whether Loyalist paramilitaries reacted to Mitchell's unflattering dramatic portrayal of them or domestic incidents closer to home, it is impossible to say, but these dramatic events certainly turned the spotlight on his depiction of Loyalist culture. This chapter will examine three of his plays from the late 1990s: *In a Little World of Our Own* (1997), *As the Beast Sleeps* and *Trust* (1999). In these plays, produced immediately before, during and after the announcement of the Good Friday Agreement in Northern Ireland, Mitchell tries to provide explanatory texts for the contemporary state of Loyalism and offers more complex and nuanced readings of the factors contributing to a crisis in Loyalist identity, factors often overlooked in cultural representations and media treatments.

In *Ulster Loyalism and the British Media* (1998), Alan Parkinson considers the reasons behind the relatively negative portrayal of Ulster's Protestants and Unionists on the UK mainland, highlighting the tendency to focus on 'the negative images of Loyalism – bigotry, intolerance, intransigence, the "blockers" of progress'.[3] This singular image of the Ulster Protestant tends to dominate outside Northern Ireland, yet it masks a considerable heterogeneity. The wide variety of Protestant churches on offer in Northern Ireland and the political divisions within political Unionism exemplify this situation. Loyalism, as it is manifest in paramilitary organizations, is also a fractured beast, with the primary split between two main groupings, the Ulster Volunteer force (UVF) and the Ulster Defence Association (UDA).[4]

In broad terms, Loyalism refers to a position that supports the union between Northern Ireland and Great Britain and is against the Irish state. It refers to loyalty to and defence of the crown and British state, the Protestant faith, value-systems, communities and heritage. Peter Shirlow and Mark McGovern stress how this loyalty has created a sense of a 'collective self', which is tied up with the notion of a mythic, 'imagined' homogeneous community fighting against the sociopolitical and cultural dissipation threatened by the long fight of Irish Nationalists for a united Ireland and, more recently, by the 'peace process'.

The 'loyalty' which is so substantial in the construction of the collective self can be given to institutions or groups such as the Ulster Unionist Party (UUP), the British state or paramilitary organizations, ideals or principles or to a range of communal and interpersonal relationships (neighbours, family, fellow-workers). What is important too is that through the enunciation of allegiance these miscellaneous loci of self-identity can be fused: loyalty to the state, to the Union, to the local community and the family blend to mean one and the same thing, the 'British/Protestant way of life'.[5]

The sense of the 'collective self' coming under attack from the 'collective other' has created a 'siege mentality' according to commentators such as Steve Bruce, Sarah Nelson and Peter Taylor.[6] In the early 1970s, these aspects of the Protestant psyche lead many Protestant men to take on the self-appointed mantle of Ulster's 'frontier defenders'. The UDA began life as an umbrella organization that housed a number of highly localized 'defence associations' which emerged in Northern Ireland in response to sectarian rioting that engulfed the province between 1968 and 1970. Initially the UDA attracted tens of thousands of volunteers onto the streets, but the day-to-day active membership was much smaller. This 'permanent cadre of foot soldiers' became virtually 'full-time paramilitaries' and centred their operations on a network of pubs and illegal drinking dens in Loyalist areas.[7] Throughout the 1970s and 1980s there was a shift of UDA focus away from the defence of communities towards an increased campaign of indiscriminate murder of Catholics. In addition, there was a rise in other criminal activity, which at first took the form of post office and bank robberies, ostensibly to raise funds for the organization. However, criminality soon became more about the private gain of individuals involving extortion, protection rackets and drug dealing. This situation ultimately led to the British government proscribing the organization in 1991. This, then, was the condition of the UDA when the IRA declared its ceasefire in August 1994, forcing the Combined Loyalist Military Command to announce its ceasefire in October of the same year.

The ensuing 'peace talks', under the chairmanship of George Mitchell and constantly cajoled, prodded and prompted by the governments of the UK, Ireland and the USA, led to the Good Friday Agreement of April 1998. This put in train a set of interlocking structures intended to take account of the variety of relationships within Northern Ireland, between Northern Ireland and the Republic and between Britain and Ireland. It enshrined the principle of consent in terms of whether the people of Northern Ireland stayed with Britain or joined the Republic. It advocated the removal of Articles Two and Three of the Irish Constitution which made a territorial claim over the North; it offered a new elected assembly with full powers over a range of portfolios such as agriculture, health and education (though not, unsurprisingly, law and order or defence). At its core, the Agreement endeavoured to provide Unionism and Nationalism equal legitimacy and equal respect within an entirely new constitutional arrangement. Referenda to endorse the Agreement took place both north and south of the Irish border in May 1998. Support was overwhelming in the Irish Republic and among Nationalist voters in the North; whereas the Unionist vote split virtually fifty-fifty between the pro- and anti-Agreement camps.

These developments saw the UDA develop two clearly discernible approaches. One, represented by the organization's 'politicians', wore sharp suits, gave press conferences, debated openly with members of Sinn Fein and ran for political office. The other was a combination of those who opposed the agreement, those who were concerned that their lucrative criminal lifestyle was under threat, and those who simply still hated Catholics – it was this wing that carried on its murderous campaign despite being nominally on ceasefire. Bruce describes the world of post-ceasefire paramilitarism as being occupied by 'young unemployed and marginally employed young men [who] have few opportunities for political and social expression other than violence, and see little chance of making a better life for themselves and their families'.[8] It is the two wings of the UDA and the tensions between them that Mitchell stages, alongside concerns with the interrelationship between joblessness, poor socioeconomic conditions, structures of working-class masculinity and continuing lawlessness.

Mitchell is renowned for maintaining a close association with his birthplace. Rathcoole is a working-class, Protestant housing estate in North Belfast replete with symbolic manifestations of Loyalist identity: red, white and blue kerbstones, murals, Union Jacks and Ulster flags. Suffering from poor socioeconomic conditions, high unemployment, racketeering and feuds between factions within the UDA over territory and control, Rathcoole is a site familiar with violence. By remaining in the heart of Rathcoole and setting the majority of his plays there, Mitchell claims he writes from a position of authority. His treatment of the subtle nuances of a turbulent and evolving set of social, political, economic, gender-based and community relations has earned him a reputation for providing reports from the 'front line'. Or, in Liam Fay's words, 'As the most talented and prominent dramatist to write about the unionist community from within, Mitchell is frequently patronized by Irish and English critics as though he were some kind of idiot savant bringing us eyewitness news from inside the asylum'.[9] This reputation is strengthened by Mitchell's self-confessed involvement in paramilitary activity during the 'murky' years of his teens and early twenties.[10]

Whilst many critics have overplayed the representation of Mitchell as the 'lone dramatic voice' writing about Ulster unionism, Mitchell has undoubtedly made a significant impact on English and Irish stages.[11] He became the first Protestant and first person from Northern Ireland to win the Stewart Parker Award for his play *Independent Voice* (1994), about freedom of speech in Northern Ireland, originally produced by Tinderbox Theatre Company. Staged at the Lyric Theatre, Belfast, *Tearing the Loom* (1998) uses the period of the 1798 United Irishmen's Uprising to consider 'the often neglected dissenting tradition and divided loyalties of Ulster Protestantism in the face of the United Irishmen's non-sectarian ethos'.[12] Another Lyric Theatre production, *Marching On* (2000), explores the cultural and political significance of the annual Protestant marching season. However, the critical success of

In a Little World of Our Own secured Mitchell's reputation. First performed at the Peacock Theatre in Dublin, the play toured all over Ireland, and the Abbey Theatre performed it at its first ever visit to the Lyric, Belfast. At the first Irish Theatre Awards, it won Best Director, Best Supporting Actor and Best Play of 1997. In 1998, the play opened at the Donmar Warehouse in London as part of the Four Corners season, where it had a rapturous critical reception that earned Mitchell high-profile commissions from the Royal Court and Royal National Theatre, where he became Resident Playwright in 1998. Mitchell's next play, *As the Beast Sleeps* (1998), premiered at the Peacock Theatre, Dublin, but also toured to London and received a much larger audience after being adapted for television.

More recently, Mitchell has developed a strong relationship with the Royal Court Theatre, which staged *Trust*, which subsequently won the Pearson Best New Play prize, *The Force of Change* and *Loyal Women*. *The Force of Change* provides a powerful account of the Royal Ulster Constabulary as it struggles to come to terms with the implications of the Patten Report into policing and the difficulties Protestant men face negotiating their place within a force actively promoting women and Catholics as part of its professional image makeover as the Police Service of Northern Ireland. In *Loyal Women*, Mitchell explores the complex internal politics of the Rathcoole Women's branch of the UDA through the eyes of Brenda as she struggles to reconcile her past and present in the WUDA with her domestic responsibilities.

By representing characters caught up in political processes and, specifically, the close-knit, hermetically sealed world of the UDA, Mitchell provides a unique voice in contemporary Northern Irish theatre. Other playwrights currently producing work in Northern Ireland include Tim Loane, Daragh Carville, Owen McCafferty and Marie Jones, but none addresses the impact of the peace process in such a direct or localized way as Mitchell. Carville tends to avoid directly referencing the Northern Ireland political situation in his plays, such as *Language Roulette* (1996), which explores the role of language to evade truth among a group of young adults. Loane, however, has confronted the political situation within Ulster Unionism in the farce *Caught Red-Handed* (2002), and Jones looks at Protestant identity in *A Night in November* (1994). This play charts the journey, both physically and metaphorically, of a Protestant social security clerk from sectarianism to an embracing of his 'Irishness' via a trip to the football world cup in the USA. Jones, like Mitchell and McCafferty, has achieved considerable success outside Northern Ireland. Most notably, *Stones in his Pockets*

(1999), a whimsical two-handed comedy about the filming of a Hollywood epic in rural Ireland, explores the global commodity that is 'Oirishness', yet has ironically played all around the world. McCafferty deals with the fact of living in contemporary Northern Ireland, but in an elliptical way, largely eschewing direct political reference. *Closing Time* (2002) presents characters in a run-down hotel, lost in a sea of alcohol, and, although we never discover which side of the sectarian divide they come from, it is difficult, as Michael Billington writes 'not to see the play as a metaphor for Northern Ireland's own political stasis'.[13] In *Scenes from the Big Picture* (2003) McCafferty leaves the background of his characters unclear, concentrating instead on what Kate Bassett called 'a picture of an ordinary day's damage and pain, with Ulster's political troubles seeping in too'.[14] The play charts characters, among them a drug-dealer, a shopkeeper, two estranged brothers, and parents whose son was shot dead, as their stories interweave through a series of urban environments. Whereas Mitchell exposes in vivid and explosive detail the effect of living in a community dominated by paramilitaries, McCafferty's writing focuses on, as Benedict Nightingale recognizes, 'a strong overall feeling that ordinary people were wanting, trying and failing to escape the town, the Province and themselves'.[15]

For many, the 'peace process' initiated a space for identities to be renegotiated and redrawn, a shift evident in some quarters of the UDA as several former paramilitaries tried to transform into legitimate politicians who stressed a new order based on compromise, dialogue, and political rather than violent solutions. However, Mitchell is concerned with the other side of the coin. Rather than exhibiting faith in political processes and cultural renewal, Mitchell's characters present a vision of intransigence and festering resentment. As opposed to communities redrawing the boundaries of behaviour and cultural exchange, Mitchell exposes the segregated, claustrophobic grass-roots Loyalist communities that spawn and conceal paramilitary violence, reject official law and order in favour of internal policing and normalize the legacy of violence as it is handed down from generation to generation.

Billy Mitchell, a Loyalist paramilitary convicted of two sectarian murders, is quoted as saying in the context of the peace process, 'When you incite people to form armies and then walk away, you create a monster and the monster does what it wants . . . Basically, I think Mary Shelley could have written *Frankenstein* about us.'[16] This notion of a monster generating its own logic and wreaking havoc is similarly evoked by Allen Feldman's assertions that violence has become a 'self-legitimating sphere of social discourse' in Northern Ireland, a potent cultural language operating independently from ideology and played out through an ensemble of performed practices that achieve legitimacy through their perpetual re-enactment.[17] Interestingly, Mitchell's work also interrogates how violent solutions, once rationalized on ideological grounds against the IRA and the Catholic 'Other', have increasingly imploded within Protestant communities. In his plays, characters issue continual threats of reprisal as a way of gaining control within their own community, and violence becomes the only solution – whether fighting petty criminals, school bullies, Loyalist renegades or women who have sex with Catholics. As Margaret Llewellyn-Jones remarks, 'the writer's anger about the corrosive effect of this kind of tribal violence, which turns sour essentially good qualities such as loyalty, community, solidarity, religious morality and support' forms the backbone of Mitchell's work.[18]

Significantly, the vast majority of Mitchell's plays are set solely, or predominantly, in domestic interiors through which UDA officers and enforcers come and go like family members amidst seemingly innocuous scenes of tea-drinking and ironing – contexts that signify Mitchell's preoccupation with how the quotidian and the familial inculcate a culture of paramilitarism. In particular, Mitchell utilizes close-knit family structures and relationships between brothers, parents and children, husbands and wives to explore the hierarchies, divisions and complex relations that underscore Loyalist communities – a preoccupation that functions in line with Alan Finlayson's observation that 'the family is the microcosm of the greater family of the nation of Ulster' in cultural discourse.[19] In Mitchell's plays there are continual tensions between family and political loyalties in which the family generally loses out as they become sites of turmoil: divided, defiled and neglected, with their eventual collapse serving as a metaphor for the implosion evident in Loyalist culture. This factor is further represented through Mitchell's employment of the renegade, the singular figure whose personal agenda fractures the strict adherence to clearly demarcated hierarchies and the ideological framework of loyalty to the collective self. A dual concern with how the patriarchal structures, ideologies and macho culture central to Loyalism pose an obstacle to the peace process and how the peace process has affected structures of working-class masculinity also resides at the heart of Mitchell's work.

Set in Rathcoole, *In a Little World of Our Own* centres on three brothers: Ray, an aggressive UDA enforcer of the old school; Gordon, a respectable insurance broker struggling to come to terms with his loss of faith; and the adolescent Richard who has learning difficulties.

Fiercely protective of each other, the brothers are all trying to assert their independence from the family unit while remaining inextricably tied to it. Gordon has plans to marry his fiancée Deborah and to move out. Ray prioritizes and romanticizes his role as a UDA hard man over and above his family responsibilities and constructs himself as a hero protecting his community by diverting young petty criminals from a life of crime. While idolizing Ray and making every effort to emulate him, Richard is making the transition to adulthood through his interest in girls and growing self-assurance.

Mitchell establishes an ingrained culture of violence at the beginning of the play when Ray is seen pocketing money and receiving a box of chocolates as a thank-you for retrieving stolen property with menaces. The acceptance of violent internal policing remains integral to the ethos of community relations in working-class Protestant estates such as Rathcoole. As Ivy, a local resident testifies:

> Only for the UDA, you couldn't have lived on this estate. You have youngsters growing up here never knew anything but strife. If someone is giving a lot of hassle to their neighbours, people call the paramilitaries in. No one gets a beating without forewarning.[20]

Yet Ray is aware that this kind of warped community ethic is rapidly losing credibility as the UDA seeks respectability and a place at the political table. Mitchell signals this new order through the off-stage presence of Monroe. Like the media-savvy Alec in *As the Beast Sleeps*, he represents the powerful former paramilitaries turned politicians who support the ceasefire, attempt to breach separatism through dialogue, distance themselves from sectarian attitudes, stress the need for media-friendly tactics and use the UDA to fund their entry into legitimate political processes. However, as James McAuley notes and Mitchell portrays, 'the transition from 'soldiers' to political representatives has been open to widespread suspicion [particularly] within the very Protestant working-class communities they claim to represent'.[21] Ray deeply resents the new order compromising his methods and remains suspicious of politics or peaceful means brokering effective community relations:

> RAY: The world's gone fucking mad. Pricks like Monroe are just shit. What people don't understand is this. The world is a violent place. We know that better than anybody. Whether it's dealing with the IRA or dealing with petty theft or glue-sniffing. Whatever. Namby-pamby ways don't get results.[22]

Mitchell also highlights the fragility of Monroe's position and, as an extension, the peace process as the narrative unfolds. When his fifteen-year-old daughter, Susan, and the object of Richard's adolescent crush, takes up with a Catholic, in Monroe's eyes this is worse than if she had started seeing a 'retard'. When Ray brutally rapes and beats Susan to death in a savage renegade reprisal for spurning his brother in favour of a 'taig', Monroe refuses to cooperate with the police and insists on street justice. As suspicion falls on Richard, Mitchell launches a complex lament for the innocent and highlights the harrowing consequences of a culture steeped in sectarianism and perverted interpretations of religion, loyalty and revenge. Initially the audience suspect Ray will claim a second innocent victim by forcing a confession from Susan's Catholic boyfriend in a dual act of deflection and sectarianism. However, as the real assailant becomes clear, Walter, the UDA's grim arbiter, demands sacrifice and martyrdom closer to home after warning Gordon that 'an eye for an eye' implicates his devout mother and fiancée. Invoking God's command that Abraham kill his own son to demonstrate his loyalty, Walter urges Gordon to shoot Richard in the knee to avoid an internal feud between Monroe and Ray, and a public relations disaster. Walter is insistent that Gordon demonstrate his loyalty to the UDA over his family, stressing 'it's not about the wound, it's about the act, that's remorse and that's respect'.[23] The stress on the 'act' is important as it is about being seen to do the 'right' thing, to even the score and, as such, the 'act' is performatively staged to carry the most impact. Walter urges Gordon, the non-violent brother who has distanced himself from Ray's criminal activities, to come back into the fold, to obey the law of the UDA and to demonstrate his remorse by shooting his innocent brother.

The use of religious discourse to justify violence is a dominant feature of the play. As Mitchell states, 'God is a character in the play . . . he plays himself, jealous and terrible.'[24] Ray, when explaining Susan's death to Richard says, 'that's because of her and the taig fella. God seen all that, and God told me that he would have to take Susan away to make her better'.[25] Deborah similarly interprets her faith in a way that tells her what she wants to hear, and she ends up corroborating Ray's version of events to Richard. Deborah is the only female character seen in *In a Little World of Our Own*, and her pathetic compliance is indicative of the play's problematic gender representations. The only other women referred to are the voiceless, infirm matriarch banished upstairs and the off-stage Susan whose objectified, violated body becomes the site on which Ray enacts his violent sectarian misogyny.

Initially there is an indication that Richard will break the mould as, when facing a real-life trauma, he is unable to utilize the art of bluff, deception and distraction Ray tries to teach him when playing poker. His gradual revelations implicate his brother, but the spotlight turns on Richard and the final blow for peace comes with a vicious twist at the end of the play when he shoots Ray before the UDA can kill him. As Billington stresses, 'Ray's ultimate triumph is to pass on to Richard his belief in violent solutions'.[26] Richard's actions and the sacrifice of his innocence alongside his brother is the ultimate act of loyalty in a world warped by misplaced allegiances and immoral justifications. Richard's actions are also evidence of a particular concern of Mitchell's with the way younger generations become embroiled in a self-contained and self-perpetuating moral code that leads them to implement the legacy of violence bequeathed to them.

The divisions between the old and new orders, the challenge posed by the renegade, the crisis in masculinity instigated by the peace process and the implosion of violence are the core concerns of *As the Beast Sleeps*. Kyle and Freddie are best friends and soldiers within Kyle's UDA unit: low down in the command hierarchy, they have been trained to loyally take orders to torture and murder Catholics and to hijack lorries of alcohol and cigarettes to stock their local UDA club to raise money for 'the cause'. Now, the club has gone legitimate with proper accounts and Larry, their commander, runs it to raise money to bankroll Alec's political career and has designs on getting in on the political act himself. Alec represents the new face of a publicly articulate Loyalism that uses money to fund respectability through sharp suits and fancy hotels. In contrast, Kyle and Freddie embody the generations of men of action – ingrained in traditions of violence – cast adrift from their previous role, livelihood and status. As McKay asserts, 'they hate peace because it has brought them nothing and has taken away their livelihood'.[27] As the play deals with attempts to wean Kyle and Freddie from habitual behaviour, it becomes clear that they are the Frankenstein's monsters Billy Mitchell referred too. They are caught in a period of transition, a no-man's land – once respected as soldiers and defenders of the community and now that same community's greatest embarrassment as their inarticulacy and immediate recourse to violence is incompatible with the new culture of protracted dialogue perpetrated by people like Alec. Even Larry, their UDA unit commander, recognizes that power is only accessible through acceptance of political processes, although he too finds himself at odds with the new operational methods as Alec infers that his past makes him unsuitable for a political career.

Clearly economic factors play a significant role in Kyle and Freddie's

predicament. Over the last two decades, the shift towards a post-industrial economy favouring the service and public sector has seen an
increase in low-paid work and underemployment among an increasingly marginalized and alienated Protestant working class in Northern
Ireland. No wonder the promise of status and an income from paramilitary activity remains a popular option in hard-line areas. As Feldman
writes, 'to the extent that the Protestant working class has lost a secure
economic base in industrial production, the involvement of factions of
this group in paramilitary violence can also be understood as a staged
re-entry into the public arenas of social production'.[28] Kyle and Freddie
have previously earned a living robbing banks and hijacking goods
vehicles to help fund the UDA, but in the post-peace-process era they
are now unemployed and unemployable as their aptitudes and skills are
not easily transferable. Mitchell highlights their lack of money, showing that they can no longer fund nights out at their local club, and
Kyle's wife Sandra borrows from her mother to redecorate the family
home. Domestic scenes focusing on Freddie, Kyle and Sandra's attempts
to decorate their house provide a metaphor for the ambivalence shown
towards the peace process. There is a sense of renewal and the possibility of change through the physical transformations under way, and
Kyle's refusal to countenance stolen wallpaper. He wants it to be
'proper', even if sectarian overtones remain in the Glasgow Rangers
Football Club wallpaper they have chosen, but their economic situation
means they cannot afford legitimate merchandise – just as they cannot
afford to buy the official line of the UDA command to step down from
the activities that have sustained them. Mitchell aptly illustrates the
significance of their economic position by having the major crisis of the
play unfold after Freddie and Sandra attempt to regain some power by
robbing the very club that their criminal activity once bankrolled.

In *As the Beast Sleeps*, the UDA club is the primary site for the struggle over meaning in the new climate of peace. Freddie remembers how
'We used to walk into that club and every fucker in the place would be
patting us on the back and yelling our names out – the drink would just
flow all night.'[29] In the contemporary climate, there are no longer any
free drinks and no money to buy any, and before the play begins Jack
has banned two of Kyle's unit from the club. Kyle and Freddie's fight to
brush off these humiliations and to maintain the status they once held
is manifest through their aggressive assertions of presence within the
club, with their increasing lack of power signified by Norman's attempts
to silence them and their segregation and physical ostracism to the
margins. This internalized struggle over territory provides an inverted

image of the sectarian battles over the right to command terrain that preoccupied men like Kyle and Freddie in the pre-peace- process era. When Freddie's increasingly erratic behaviour culminates in him taking a pool cue and smashing up the club, he attempts symbolically to destroy what it represents: a new order in which the cause he has dedicated his life to has been abandoned by men he trusted, who he believes have placed him closer to the Nationalist goal of a United Ireland. None the less, Mitchell makes it clear that Freddie's romantic affiliation of the club with a steadfast anti-Nationalist/Catholic stance is a myth when Larry admits that he only used its punishment room and his well-rehearsed intimidation tactics to bring renegade Loyalists to heel. A concern with internal policing and the capacity for violent implosion is also explored through Larry's request that Kyle form a punishment squad to track down and tackle renegades who jeopardize the peace process.

Kyle's loyalty to his friend, wife and the UDA command structure is put to the ultimate test when he has to bring in Freddie for robbing the club with an unknown accomplice – in turn starving the UDA of the funds that sustain their place in political dialogue. For both characters, loyalty is core to their dilemma. For Freddie, the peace process constitutes the ultimate act of betrayal – disloyalty to fellow Loyalists, the community and Ulster. Refusing to confess the identity of his accomplice or the location of the stolen money, Freddie takes the brutal punishment inflicted on him – a demonstration of his loyalty to the collective self/unionist cause. By interrogating and assaulting his friend, Kyle also hopes to demonstrate his loyalty to the collective self/unionist cause. However, the revelation that Sandra was Freddie's accomplice places Kyle in the family versus UDA dilemma faced by many characters in Mitchell's plays. To conceal Sandra's identity Kyle would have to be disloyal to his UDA command, but handing over his wife would have devastating consequences for his family. The fact that Mitchell leaves Kyle's predicament unresolved highlights the complexity of his dilemma.

Mitchell has written that *Trust* 'has a universal theme: parenting'.[30] This is explored through the character of Jake and his relationship with his father, Geordie, a UDA 'fixer', and his mother, Margaret, one of Mitchell's more complex female characters. At fifteen, Jake is a transitional figure caught between childhood and adulthood, his mother's protective wings and his father's wish for him to assert his independence. The narrative revolves around the fact that the sons of a local RUC officer are bullying Jake at school. Geordie fails to accept his son's predicament because it disturbs his own construction of himself as the local mafia-style 'don', to whom people come for money, jobs, deals and solutions to their problems. Margaret, angered by Geordie's reticence, takes on the role of the renegade by undermining the hierarchies implicit within the patriarchal structure of the Protestant family, gender relations and the UDA command. Without Geordie's knowledge, Margaret sets in motion a disastrous chain of events when she instructs Trevor, a known UDA killer, to involve Jake in a reprisal attack, to get him 'blooded' so he will gain respect. However, Margaret becomes 'the Rathcoole Mother Courage who destroys what she wants to protect' after Trevor viciously assaults a child following Jake's refusal to get involved.[31] Fearing a reprisal attack, Trevor gives Jake a knife, which he ends up using to stab his tormentor, and it is inferred that Margaret will resort to sacrificing her husband to the police to save her son from prison.

Trust investigates how organizations such as the UDA, RUC and British Army are reliant on a hyper-masculine culture that seeks power through physical threat (an extension of the playground bullies Jake has to contend with) and cultural expression through gambling, football, drinking, sexist behaviour and rampant anti-intellectualism. Jake's unwillingness to embrace these public signifiers of working-class masculinity and his preference for staying alone in the domestic arena completing homework, watching cartoons and playing computer games disappoints Geordie, as he wants a son created in his own image. Through this father/son relationship, Mitchell explores how the ongoing presence of violent paramilitarism is tied to a culture of machismo handed down from generation to generation. During an initiation ceremony into a 'Real Men's Night' at the local UDA club, Geordie forces Jake to drink a pint, takes satisfaction watching him exhibit heterosexual desire and, with his sidekick Artty, teaches him the art of self-possession. Reviewing the play, Jeremy Kingston dismissed the scene as 'a comic interlude in the gathering menace', but arguably it is *part* of the gathering menace as Jake watches: inwardly digesting the bodily and verbal signification acceptable for him in this aggressively macho culture and the modes of response appropriate to the culture of secrecy, deceit and interrogation he inhabits.[32]

As the title ironically suggests, *Trust* presents a world in which everybody is a potential enemy or informant and treated with the utmost distrust. The characters converse in a strictly coded verbal and physical language, and even the most private relationships are laced with suspicion. Mitchell explores this through Julie and Vincent, who enact the play's sub-plot about a bungled attempt to sell stolen arms from the British Army to the UDA. Planning their escape from Northern Ireland, Julie asks Vincent whether he is using her to set a trap for the UDA, just as Geordie and his sidekick, Artty, have to ascertain whether Julie and Vincent are setting them up. Nobody can be trusted, and Mitchell makes it clear that this equally extends to the RUC and the British Army, who are more than willing to do a deal to secure the safe return of the missing arms and to conceal evidence of collusion between army personnel and the UDA. However, as Ian Shuttleworth recognizes:

> the most significant feature of the play is easy to miss. In this story of Loyalists, police and the army, *nowhere* in the play – whether directly or even by the merest implication – is *any* mention made of sectarianism, Republicanism, the 'enemy' or any such dimension. The mechanisms of funding, arming and local codes of respect have entirely obscured the supposed reason for the UDA's existence; they are here, we infer, because they are here.[33]

Through an examination of Mitchell's plays, it is easy to conclude that he has reached the disturbing conclusion that the largest threat to the Loyalist community is itself and the masculine culture of allegiance, confrontation, intimidation, interrogation and violent reprisal it perpetuates. The plays offer a documentation of a community in flux, faced with challenges provoked by accelerated political and historical processes. Indeed, it is arguable that Mitchell's ultimate significance lies in his explicit exposure of these processes, as the plays are written without the benefit of reflective hindsight, about a community for whom nothing is guaranteed and where a wide range of eventual outcomes is possible.

notes

1. There is a tendency to use these terms interchangeably, so the following definitions may be helpful. Protestant: although the Anglican Church is well represented in Northern Ireland, the predominant sect is that of Nonconformist Presbyterianism. Unionist: politically dedicated to the maintenance of Northern Ireland's position as an integral part of the United Kingdom. Loyalist: a branch of Unionism, overwhelmingly working class in composition, which adopts an 'Ulster first' approach that has brought it into conflict with the British government as well as Irish Nationalism and Republicanism.
2. The same night, Mitchell's uncle experienced a similar attack when masked

men ordered him to leave Rathcoole. Threats of violence drove Mitchell's parents from their home in Rathcoole seven months earlier.

3. A. Parkinson, *Ulster Loyalism and the British Media* (Dublin: Four Courts Press, 1998), p. 162.

4. C. Coulter (ed.), *Contemporary Northern Irish Society – An Introduction* (London: Pluto Press, 1999) provides useful further information on the heterogeneity of forms found in Ulster Protestantism, Unionism and Loyalism.

5. P. Shirlow and M. McGovern (eds), *Who are 'The People'?: Unionism, Protestantism and Loyalism in Northern Ireland* (London: Pluto Press, 1997), p. 179.

6. See S. Bruce, *The Edge of the Union: The Ulster Loyalist Political Vision* (Oxford: Oxford University Press, 1994); S. Nelson, *Ulster's Uncertain Defenders* (Belfast: The Appletree Press, 1984) and P. Taylor, *Loyalists* (London: Bloomsbury, 1999).

7. H. McDonald and J. Cusack, *UDA – Inside the Heart of Loyalist Terror* (Dublin: Penguin Ireland, 2004), p. 25.

8. S. Bruce, 'Turf War and Peace: Loyalist Paramilitaries Since 1994', *Terrorism and Political Violence*, vol. 16, no. 3 (2004), 501–21 (507).

9. L. Fay, 'Perfectly Beastly', *The Sunday Times*, 10 February 2002.

10. See S. McKay, *Northern Protestants: An Unsettled People* (Belfast: The Blackstaff Press, 2000), pp. 112–18.

11. C. Spencer, 'Memorable Trip to the Other Side of the Troubled Divide', *Daily Telegraph*, 25 September 2001.

12. M. Heaney, 'Paying Dues to the Union, *The Sunday Times*, 17 February 2002.

13. M. Billington, 'Closing Time', *Guardian*, 11 September 2002.

14. K. Bassett, 'Theatre: Seasick but Ship-Shape', *Independent*, 20 April 2003.

15. B. Nightingale, 'Playing Belfast and Furious', *The Times*, 12 April 2003.

16. McKay, *Northern Protestants*, p. 52.

17. A. Feldman, *Formations of Violence: The Narrative of the Body and Political Terror in Northern Ireland* (Chicago: The University of Chicago Press, 1991), p. 5.

18. M. Llewellyn-Jones, *Contemporary Irish Drama and Cultural Identity* (Bristol: Intellect, 2002), p. 110.

19. Alan Finlayson, 'Discourse and Contemporary Loyalist Identity', in Shirlow and McGovern (eds), *Who are 'The People'?*, pp. 72–94 (p. 83).

20. McKay, *Northern Protestants*, pp. 106–7.

21. J. McAuley, '"Flying the One-Winged Bird": Ulster Unionism and the Peace Process', in Shirlow and McGovern (eds), *Who are 'The People'?*, pp. 158–75 (p. 169).

22. G. Mitchell, *Tearing the Loom and In a Little World of Our Own* (London: Nick Hern, 1998), pp. 3–4.

23. Ibid., p. 51.

24. Cited in McKay, *Northern Protestants*, p. 118.

25. Mitchell, *Tearing the Loom and In a little World of Our Own*, p. 59.
26. Michael Billington, 'Closed World of Loyalist Hard Men', *Guardian*, 5 March 1998.
27. McKay, *Northern Protestants*, p. 113.
28. Feldman, *Formations of Violence*, p. 5.
29. G. Mitchell, *As the Beast Sleeps* (London: Nick Hern, 2001), p. 55.
30. G. Mitchell, 'Balancing Act', *Guardian*, 5 April 2003.
31. M. Billington, 'Trust', *Guardian*, 18 March 1999.
32. J. Kingston, 'Loyalist's Loyalty Ends at Home', *The Times*, 17 March 1999.
33. I. Shuttleworth, 'The Horrifying Minutiae of Life in Ulster', *The Financial Times*, 18 March 1999.

10
'because it feels fucking amazing': recent british drama and bodily mutilation

dan rebellato

A young man and his girlfriend approach a street vendor with a sharpened fork which they both plunge into one of the man's eyes, twisting the fork each time to ensure maximum damage.[1] The supervisor of an institution wrestles an inmate to the ground and hacks off his feet, which are then carried away by rats.[2] A bureaucrat performs a specialist surgical procedure on a student, known simply as The Cut. It is unclear from the student's gasps whether this is horrifying or sublime.[3] In themselves, these moments from Martin Crimp's *The Treatment* (1992), Sarah Kane's *Cleansed* (1998) and Mark Ravenhill's *The Cut* are nothing new. There is a history of spectacular violence in British theatre that stretches back at least to the images of the crucifixion in medieval pageant plays, and no doubt beyond. None the less, over the last fifteen years, there has been an intensification of these images and, in particular, a proliferation of images involving bodily mutilation and dismemberment.

Violence is central to Aleks Sierz's definition of in-yer-face theatre. His book accurately demonstrates the extraordinary series of staged atrocities in the plays of the 1990s. Even more importantly, perhaps, violence characterizes the relations between stage and audience in these plays. Sierz says that this kind of theatre 'takes the audience by the scruff of the neck and shakes it ... smashing taboos ... creating discomfort', these plays 'hit' the audience with 'intense emotional material'.[4] For this reason, Sierz refers to in-yer-face theatre as 'experiential'. Of course, all theatre is experiential, but he means that this theatre offers an experience of discomfort that, in a sense, draws attention to experience itself. These are plays and performances that draw attention to the body, the performer's and the audience's, through enacting grotesque acts of physical cruelty.

Sierz does not seem to think that this attention encourages the audience to reflect on their own body, contemplate the limits of the flesh, and so on. For Sierz the aggression is all about shock, sudden visceral reactions: nausea, revulsion, fear, anger, emotions that are generally associated with instinctual reactions. And this, for Sierz, is part of the value of these shows; after a decade or two of ideologically driven plays (the socialist dramas of the 1970s, the feminist plays of the 1980s), not thinking, reconnecting the audience with its primal feelings, was a valuable thing to do.

I want to put to one side the question of whether Sierz is right about the mode in which these plays work, and first consider why playwrights and other theatre-makers should have felt the need to create images and experiences of bodily mutilation *in the 1990s*. Sierz is right, perhaps, in attributing some of it to generational shift, not wanting to do what previous generations had done (though it's worth remarking that writers like Brenton, Griffiths, Churchill and Daniels sometimes used aggressive effects in their work). But why did the tide of fashion turn in this particular direction? Why was violence, particularly this series of bodily dismemberments, the way in which the new generation chose to establish its distinctiveness?

Sierz is somewhat inconsistent in his answer; he mentions a series of violent episodes in the history of the 1990s – the atavistic resurgence of genocide in Bosnia, Rwanda and elsewhere, the discovery of Fred and Rosemary West's serial sex-murders, a number of terrorist attacks and high-school killings – but, dreadful though these events were, one might reasonably point to equally appalling acts in previous decades that did not prompt such a response, or indeed the more extreme terrorist and military atrocities of the current decade that have so far been reflected on the whole in rather sedate documentary theatre practices.[5] Elsewhere, Sierz suggests that the virtue of in-yer-face theatre is to force us to face the guilty secret of humanity: 'the power of the irrational and the fragility of our sense of the world'.[6] Such an analysis sees the horror evoked by this theatre as a permanent underside to human civilization and leaves unanswered the question, why did these images proliferate in the 1990s?

And proliferate they did. Not only in the theatre, but in the art world; in the work of the Young British Artists, bodies were distended, preserved, miniaturized, parodied, punctured and transplanted. In their sculptural work, *Zygotic acceleration, biogenetic, de-sublimated libidinal model (enlarged x 1000)*, Jake and Dinos Chapman produced plastic mannequins of children but with sexual organs instead of mouths and noses, a nightmarishly sexualized image of children that seemed to comment on and be complicit with a culture that was both terrified by paedophilia and fascinated with its images. Jenny Saville's paintings from the early 1990s engage with the body as corporeal mass, but these are not celebrations of carnality; for example, in a painting like *Branded* (1992), the palette is greys and blues, such that the flesh appears diseased or dead.

Both of these artists featured heavily in 'Sensation' (1997), an exhibition of Young British Artists from Charles Saatchi's collection that was responsible for accelerating a number of artistic careers and establishing British art as a centre for taboo-breaking and conceptual challenges. There were continuities between 'Sensation's' imagery and that unfolding on our stages. Kane's *Cleansed* seemed to pick up – perhaps unconsciously – on the show's images of bodily distortion and dismemberment, just as Jez Butterworth's *Mojo* seemed to tune into the mixture of brutality and comedy in Quentin Tarantino's films *Reservoir Dogs* (1992) and *Pulp Fiction* (1994). Throughout the culture, bodies were under attack: distorted, distended, dismembered.

postmodern culture, posthuman bodies

But what is it that needs explaining? One theoretical response to this would dispute the language I'm using. Postmodernist theories of the body offer an influential account of why culture stages the body in crisis. Some have suggested that to see the body as *distorted* in these images is to fall prey to a Romantic illusion: a nostalgic fantasy that imagines a golden age when our bodies were whole and healthily autonomous, when there were clear lines dividing human from animal or human from machine. In fact, this argument runs, the human body is always already permeated with technology. The birth of human sciences such as anatomy was simultaneous with the discovery of a continuity between humans and other animals; and the more rigorously science tried to explore what was unique to human beings, the more it turned to mechanical models to explain human behaviour. The human body is not separate from animals and machines, but already permeated by them. To see the body as *distorted* in these images is to imply some fixed point of bodily integrity against which distortion could be measured and condemned. In fact, some claim, these images may be a sign of our freedom from a profound misrecognition of the body.

Such a position, argue many postmodernists, offers a humanist view of the body which was never adequate and is thankfully in decline, giving way to a recognition of the posthuman body. This is a body whose overlap with technology is evident, and has abandoned any claim to humanist uniqueness. Donna Haraway's 1985 essay 'A Cyborg Manifesto' has been influential in this debate; this essay announced the advent of the cyborg: 'a cybernetic organism, a hybrid of machine and organism ... a creature in a post-gender world'.[7] Posthumanists like Haraway argue that these divisions of humans from animals have been cosy ways for patriarchy to universalize its own idealized self-image and to marginalize the messy and animalistic female body. Permeation by technology may indeed be a path to liberation; as Judith Halberstam and Ira Livingston write, in their book *Posthuman Bodies*, 'The posthuman body is a technology, a screen.'[8]

The same image and the same sentiments were proposed over ten years before by the doyen of postmodern thought, Jean Baudrillard, in his essay, *The Ecstasy of Communication*, where he claimed that 'the human body, our body, seems superfluous in its proper expanse, in the complexity and multiplicity of its organs' and that in the rootless proliferation of objects we become 'a pure screen, a pure absorption and resorption surface of the influent networks'.[9] A similar claim was made by Michel Foucault, who described the body as 'the inscribed surface of events (traced by language and dissolves by ideas), the locus of a disso-ciated self (adopting the illusion of a substantial unity), and a volume in perpetual disintegration'.[10] The body is a zero, a mere site on which society (and other 'influent networks') can inscribe itself. In Martin Crimp's *Attempts on Her Life*, the unknowable heroine is described as wishing to become a screen. Later, her fusion with technology becomes actualized as she seems to have become a car. [11]

In November 1994, two months before the premiere of Sarah Kane's *Blasted*, the replacement of bodies with screens was literally instantiated when the Visible Human Project went online. Joseph Paul Jernigan, of Waco, Texas, a convicted killer was executed by lethal injection at the age of 39. Jernigan had signed a donor consent form, and as a result he became the first Visible Human. After death, his body was photographed by the processes of computer tomography and magnetic resonance imaging, which enabled photographic slices to be taken of his body. After the first series of photographs he was dismembered and more photographs were taken. Finally he was frozen and then planed into 1 mm slices, each slice being digitally photographed and the whole collection placed on the Web. Jernigan's body was literally replaced by images on a screen; indeed, the 1 mm slices of his dead body dried out so quickly that as the screen images were captured Joseph Paul Jernigan's material body dissolved into the air.[12] The Visible Human was also, perhaps, the first posthuman.

In the background of these claims lie familiar postmodernist claims about the replacement of reality with the simulacrum. Arthur and Marilouise Kroker, two postmodernist popularizers, argue in *Body Invaders* (1988) that 'if, today, there can be such an intense fascination with the fate of the body, might this not be because the body no longer exists?'[13] The body is reduced in postmodern thought to an unknowable blank. In his early book, *Symbolic Exchange and Death* (1976), Baudrillard saw the body in contemporary society as dispersed into four images: the corpse, the animal, the robot and the mannequin. Yet even as he claimed that these functions were reducing and rewriting the body, he none the less affirmed that there was something about the body, some residual trace of desire or nature perhaps, that remained beyond the grasp of these images and stood as 'their radical alternative, the irreducible difference that denies them'.[14] Only three years later, in his essay 'Clone Story' (1979), Baudrillard appears to have abandoned the body to its fate; rather jumping the gun about cloning (he seems to be writing the essay under the mistaken belief that a human had indeed been cloned), Baudrillard is sufficiently excited about the possibilities of genetics to assert that this marks nothing less than 'the end of the body'.[15]

A postmodern reading of these plays might suggest that their images of bodily fragility are symptomatic of the emergence of the posthuman body. Similar images have appeared in 'body art' since the 1960s and Amelia Jones, in a book on the subject, has argued that these images are all part of a process of breaking down the Cartesian legacy of modern Western society. Descartes's philosophical separation between mind and body, says Jones, is an attempt to negate the body and place an idealized rational self at the centre of the philosophical project. Jones's project is for the reclamation of the body – especially the female body, posited as 'other' by rationalism – rather than its transcendence, though her position and Baudrillard's overlap in their hostility to current conceptions of the body; what Baudrillard calls the end of the body may mean only the end of a certain epochal experience of the body, in which case his position aligns neatly with Jones's. Either way, in body art as in in-yer-face plays, the destruction of the body's physical boundaries may, in a sense, be a metaphor for the collapse of the boundary between human and animal, or between human and technology. By showing Carl's hands and feet being cut off in *Cleansed*, the argument might run, Kane is responding subliminally to a shift in the cultural imagination; the culmination of Tinker's experiments in the play are the transplantation of Graham's genitals onto his sister, Grace. This is an image of the almost limitless plasticity of the body, its permeability, interchangeability and the irrelevance of the 'natural' or 'organic' wholeness of the 'original' human form.

There are some interesting aspects to this argument, and certainly the postmodern perspective encourages an alertness to the ways that contemporary society is breaching the species gap. However, I am not inclined to accept this viewpoint. Indeed, I would go further and suggest that postmodernist analysis of contemporary society is so ludicrous, so obviously and dazzlingly preposterous, that it is hardly worth entertaining, even for a page or two. But for one thing: postmodernism is, I shall argue, not merely a misdescription of the world, which would be perhaps trivial, but is in fact fundamentally complicit with the new structures of exploitation that it celebrates and misdescribes as postmodernity. Postmodernism is, I would suggest, the ideological form of global capitalism.

the body and capitalism

There is nothing new in what the postmodernists claim. The transformation of the body through technology is as old as history, one might even say, as Marx seems to, that this *is* history. Specifically, however, the substitution of the body by machinery and the transformation of the body into a machine are inseparable from the modern history of industrial capitalism.

Between 1880 and 1920, industrial production in Europe and America underwent a major transformation, associated with the work of two men, Fred Taylor and Henry Ford, who gave their names to the twin processes of Taylorism and Fordism.

Taylor was the inventor of time-and-motion study and of performance-related pay. Armed with a stopwatch and a notebook, he would watch someone engaged in an activity, say, punching holes in an aluminium sheet, and time the various operations, eventually working out the most efficient method of achieving the task, dictating down to the last detail the worker's movements, dispensing with anything extraneous to the strict achievement of the task. All industrial operations were standardized, and this was a key development in the transformation of craft skills into industrial processes, as human operations were standardized as mechanical repetitions. Physical and mental processes were sharply separated to the point where the physical actions could be performed virtually without thought: by 'an intelligent gorilla', said Taylor, charmingly.[16] In that sense, Taylorism is Cartesianism in the workplace.

Henry Ford's great innovation was the production line, whereby the operations comprising an industrial task were separated out and divided among a line of workers. The conveyor belt would pass the object down the line at a fixed speed, and each individual worker's job was reduced to the repetition of one single operation all day. Ford only wanted people who 'will simply do what they are told to do, over and over again, from bell-time to bell-time'.[17] The bell, like the conveyor belt, is an example of technology operating the worker, rather than the other way round.

The physical effect of repeating the same movement every day of your life was soon evident, despite Ford's denial. Between them, Taylor and Ford invented an entire new class of industrial injury and left a generation of workers with unequally distended forearms, thighs and calves. The risks associated with performing tasks that actively do not require thought – inattention and carelessness – were acknowledged and dismissed.

Although Ford and Taylor are often regarded as extremist proponents, their methods continue to be applied. George Ritzer, in *The McDonaldization of Society*, has argued that Taylorist and Fordist methods have been revived by the fast-food industry, and from there once again applied to a host of new fields, including health and education. Call centres, one of the main growth areas in the 1990s, have frequently been likened to 'assembly lines' and to sweatshops. Furthermore, automatic call distributors and various computerized data-collecting technologies provide means of surveillance and monitoring that Fred Taylor only dreamed of. Each month, each week, each day, an employee's performance can be monitored down to the nearest second. Janette Menday's *Call Centre Management* coyly claims that this allows you simply to benchmark an employee's performance, and also help them map their own contribution to the company.[18] Meanwhile call centre technology also dominates, even operates, the worker; Kevin Hook, in *An Idea a Day for Call Centre Management* (1998), recommends that the technology be set to 'force' the next call through your employees' headsets and thereby save 'a few extra seconds' in which they might be tempted to dawdle or relax.[19]

Of course, burger bars and call centres are service-industry jobs and in the postwar period Europe and America saw a sharp decline in industrial production of the type that Ford and Taylor operated. This itself has had an effect on the body; the decline of heavily physical manual labour is in part responsible for the new problems with obesity in America and more recently in Europe. There are new repetitive injuries that can be produced by operating a computer all day, for example. But by and large, the muscular, labouring body no longer has a functional connection with labour in our society.

This is just one of the effects of a shift in the British industrial profile from production to the service sector. It has also been accompanied by, and in part facilitated by, the decline of trade unionism. It also fostered the Thatcherite agenda of encouraging people to see themselves as consumers first and producers second. Both of these tended to encourage individuals to experience themselves as individuals far more prominently than as members of a group with common interests.

This rapid dissociation between the body and work has left a kind of body-deficit; there is a store of cultural imagery based on the labouring body that is now without an obvious visual reference. But the functional shift of the body, simultaneous with the new consumerism of the 1980s, has seen a shift in attitude. Chris Shilling argues that thanks to contemporary developments in medical technology, 'the body is potentially no longer subject to the constraints and limitations that once characterised its existence'. As a result of this new-found malleability, we are able to engage in what Shilling calls 'body projects': 'the body is a project whose interiors and exteriors can be monitored, nurtured and maintained'.[20] And we do this through dieting, jogging, going to the gym, piercing, tattooing, having plastic surgery, and so on.

You can see evidence of this transition in one of the great best-sellers of the 1980s: *Jane Fonda's Workout Book*. Fonda's political convictions are still evident from the last chapter, which calls for action against environmental damage, corporate food, and the unhealthy workplace. But much of the rest of the book evinces a profound, almost autistic, individualism: she announces that 'the most satisfying way of life come[s] from affirming your own uniqueness', and claims that when she approaches her workout 'I have to push myself to my limit and beyond because I'm preparing for competition. But the competition is with myself.'[21] Before the beginner's workshop, in large bold print, she announces:

NO DISTRACTIONS
CENTER YOURSELF
THIS IS YOUR TIME [22]

The vision of the body implied by Fonda's book demonstrates the persistence of Taylorism in the conception of the body as something entirely separate from the mind that has to be monitored, disciplined, trained: when she became pregnant, she says, 'I began to realize my body needed to be listened to and strengthened, not ignored and weakened.'[23] The body has become a possession, another commodity that you should invest in, keep in good condition, and then show off to colleagues and neighbours.

Body projects are ambiguous. Depending on their size, position and design, tattoos can either be a fashionable adornment or a permanent mark that announces your exclusion from society. But there can be a sense of consumerist choice, even of commodity fetishism. In Featherstone's collection of essays, *Body Modification*, one person is quoted as explaining their own body modifications: 'I make a statement. I've chosen myself.'[24] The syntax curiously seems to suggest that this person could have meaningfully chosen someone else, as if there were a complete disjunction between self and the body, linked only by choice. In the most recent (at time of writing) series of the reality TV show *Big Brother* (Series 7, 2006), the various housemates share a repeated belief that 'being real' is good but 'being fake' is bad. Unexceptional, one might think. Strikingly, though, these sentiments frequently came from three of the four women in the house who have had breast implants and other forms of plastic surgery. The apparent contradiction can be resolved, however, by recognizing in it the new Cartesianism. Consumer choices are the only things that are real; the body is a disposable item that functions only as the object of one's choices.[25]

re-membering the body

I have tried to show that the overlap between body and technology under contemporary capitalism has given rise to a new Cartesianism, in which the mind/body separation is reified through a series of industrial processes and acts of consumption. Amelia Jones has argued that the war against Cartesianism is most interestingly waged on the cultural level in contemporary body art. However, in some ways, many contemporary body artists seem entirely complicit with the legacy of Taylorism and its consumerist transformations. The French performance artist, Orlan, has commissioned a series of plastic surgical procedures, performed on herself under local anaesthetic so that she can chat to the camera as her face is lifted away from muscle. These operations would be completed, she once said, by her being given a new name, to be chosen and announced by an advertising agency.[26] In *Four Scenes in a Harsh Life* (1993), Ron Athey made a series of prints from the blood produced by cuts made in the back of his stage partner, pegging them up on a line that he fed out across the audience; the visual image echoed the assembly line, and Athey referred to the sequence as the 'human printing press'.[27]

Australian performance artist Stelarc is the most extreme of all in his willingness to embrace the fate of the body under capitalism; imagine how delighted Taylor or Ford would have been by the robotic third arm that Stelarc constructed for himself, or indeed the notion of electronically operating a human being's muscles via the Internet in his pieces *Fractal Flesh* (1995) and *Ping Body* (1996); in one of his performances, Stelarc placed monitors and cameras inside his own body, in a curious parody of the time-and-motion study, opening his entire body for inspection.[28] Stelarc has a particular fondness for technocratic language which is perhaps intended to sound bracingly a-humanist, but often comes across as mainstream corporatese. In a manifesto statement from the late 1970s, his vision of the cybernetic future even sounds like an advertising slogan: 'Evolution by the individual, for the individual.'[29]

In the plays, however, rather than celebrate the dismemberment and hybridization of the human body, there is a contrary move to re-member the body as a whole. Howard Barker's *Victory* (1983), set during the restoration of the monarchy in the 1660s, begins with royalist troops disinterring the body of John Bradshaw, a signatory to Charles I's death warrant. His corpse is displayed, then scattered across London. Susan Bradshaw, his widow, travels the play reassembling her husband's scattered organs. A similar pattern of spectacular dismemberment and ultimate reassembly structures the playwriterly imagining of the contemporary body.

On the face of it, violations of the body figure as emblematic of violently aggressive relations between people. In *Mojo*, Ezra's body is cut in half and dumped in two dustbins; the image, though grotesquely Jacobean, is certainly one of barbarous violence, a savage breakdown of relations between former friends and colleagues. The successive amputations of Carl's limbs in *Cleansed* is too. Simon's act of blinding Clifford in *The Treatment* is an act of bloody revenge. In 1999, in Brother Wolf

Theatre's *Dead Meat*, a nurse dismembers an entire wardful of patients. But are they merely images of violence, realist statements about the way of the world? [30]

I want to argue that these images, taken as a group, suggest a rather more complex view. It is a commonplace among some writers – and, as we have seen, Aleks Sierz is among them – that in-yer-face theatre represents the turning away from socialist politics of a new generation of playwrights, who offer us immediacy in place of ideology. But I would suggest that these moments of violence offer a kind of socialist analysis, though one reconstructed and recast in the experience of capital, and one that operates at the level of feeling and metaphor, rather than explicit analysis.

As we have seen, a market society encourages a certain kind of individualism, an emphasis on ourselves as individual consumers rather than a class of producers. Also, because the market's mechanism is centrally that of competition, antagonism replaces solidarity as the basic mode of workplace relations. Everyone is in competition with everyone else, just as products on the shelves compete for our attention. The sharper the competition, the more the market can do its work; neo-liberal governments tend to promote individualism through policies like abolishing the closed shop and collective bargaining, and introducing league tables, competitive tendering, and performance-related pay. In a competitive environment, the most important consideration is always 'me'. If an altruistic view of the world involves a 'capacity to regard oneself as merely one individual among many', we might say that a market society tends to undermine our altruistic responses to one another.[31]

There is a theatrical motif that captures the bonds of connectedness that altruism evokes and it is not much older than the intensification of images of dismemberment: theatrical doubling. One actor playing two or more parts has always been a feature of the stage; and since the late 1970s one where a virtue has been made of necessity. In the premieres of Caryl Churchill's *Cloud Nine* and *Top Girls*, the doubling was part of the meaning. When, for example, Carole Hayman played Dull Gret in the first scene of *Top Girls* and then Angie in the later scenes, the first character seemed to hang ghostlike in the presence of the second, and the vision of hell conjured by Gret carried forward and underscored Angie's own journey into nightmare. In David Greig's *Victoria* (2000) and *The Cosmonaut's Last Message to the Woman He Once Loved in the Former Soviet Union* (1999), the doubling produces effects that heighten this still further as at moments in both plays we are uncertain about which character we are looking at. In doubling, the edges of the individual are not absolute. People spill into one another, and as such the effect is a kind of staging of the altruistic self.

This is why it is the other side of dismemberment. If doubling is the affirmation of our mutual dependence, dismemberment is the sign of its negation. We are completed by others, but when we are separated from one another, we are less than whole. It is, metaphorically, a dismemberment; the mutilation of the body is a sign of our severance from one another. On all of those stages, the body's agonies come accompanied by an implied vision of the whole body.

This is not a literally whole body, but a body freed from instrumentalization. In the 1920s, Siegfried Kracauer, an early associate of the Frankfurt School, wrote 'The Mass Ornament', an analysis of the Tiller Girls. Where some have seen these dancing troupes as pure frivolity and unworthy of serious attention, Kracauer argues that they are in fact a profoundly realist cultural form because they reflect very closely the contemporary relations of production under mass production. The choreography of the Tiller Girls can only be watched in terms of the mass of bodies (everyone kicking in unison) or individual body parts (the legs, the hands, the smiles). This responds precisely to the experience of capital which can mobilize people in large numbers (a production line may need fifty operators) or as body parts (arms to pull levers, feet to press treadles, and so on). The emergence of capital gave rise to a new kind of abstract thinking: rationalism, which was a great intellectual development, but, under capitalism, rationality 'does not encompass human beings'.[32] It aims both too broadly and too narrowly, and the body suffers directly from this failure. The whole body that Kracauer evokes will only be graspable under communism. The whole body that lurks beneath these fragmented bodily images is a utopian object, a placeholder for an experience yet to come.

Seventy years later, the images of the body are less cheery, less ornamental; its fragmentation is quite literal. The consumerist wave in our culture has further fragmented the social body, and the individual body has followed. In Ravenhill's *Shopping and Fucking*, Mark's need for other people is pathologized as a form of unhealthy addiction; financial transactions therefore become a kind of prophylactic against the dangers of 'emotional dependencies'.[33] Unsurprisingly, other people's bodies become things to fear; blood is an object of disgust to be wiped or washed away.[34]

The final speck of blood in the play perhaps belongs to Gary, the young rent boy whose sexual fantasy is to be raped by his father, an act he begs Robbie to carry out with a knife or a screwdriver. Gary's wish to be desired is also a wish to be killed, as if the thought of being needed or desired by someone else is so unimaginable that it cannot be thought as part of this life.

This is a further category of mutilation in these plays: mutilation as a sign of twisted altruism. In Sarah Kane's *Cleansed*, Tinker operates on Grace, surgically grafting her dead brother's genitals onto her. It is the nightmarish repetition of an earlier scene where, perhaps in Grace's imagination, brother and sister make love; this time their union is unambiguously physical. In David Greig's *San Diego* (2003), a young woman who has been committed to a psychiatric hospital begins to cut herself and eventually cuts off parts of herself to cook. In a final move, she feeds these parts of herself to her boyfriend in the hospital. On one level, the action is a parody of transubstantiation and echoes another character's curious religious awakening, but on another it is an act of love, which builds to Laura's passionate defence of their relationship: 'I feel like I've suddenly fallen into the arms of an old, old city. Rome. He's Rome and I'm a Roman.'[35] Here, acts of mutilation take on a perversely positive quality, an emblem of our connectedness to one another.

In several of these plays, violence figures as a perverse attempt at connection, a desperate and failed affirmation of the altruistic instinct. A cruel act of violence is often overlaid with an unexpected tenderness or affirmation; in *Blasted* the soldier rapes Ian, but cries for the memory of his girlfriend; in Anthony Neilson's *Penetrator*, Tadge's terrorization of the two friends seems at times to proceed from desire as much as aggression; in Simon Stephens's *Motortown* (2006), another ex-squaddie kidnaps, tortures and kills a young woman as a hideous response to a world apparently without values. In each case, the ghost of a better world, a better way of being with others, haunts the violence.

It is surely right to say that the explicit discussion of socialist politics that characterizes plays like Trevor Griffiths's *The Party* (1973) or David Hare's *Fanshen* (1975) is abandoned by these plays. But there remains a political affirmation of a world beyond capital, visible in the grimmest demonstrations of humanity's capacity for inhumanity. That these intimations are implicit rather than explicit is, no doubt, in part due to the decline of an explicit socialist discourse in British public life; but perhaps it also reminds us that thinking *beyond* capital is a project that cannot be fully thought *under* capital.

writing the body

It is, I hope, clear why I think images of extreme bodily mutilation intensified so dramatically in the 1990s. I would like to end by suggesting a reason why *plays* – rather than any other form of performance – may be a particularly appropriate medium for exploring the fate of the body. The actions of many body artists, their deliberate infliction of pain on their own bodies, makes a spectacle of the suffering body. But pain being a subjective experience, we can only flinch at, not share, the experience of an artist sewing his lips together. This situates these actions on a narcissistically individual level. Kane's stage direction of the body under attack – 'a vulture descends and begins to eat his body' in *Phaedra's Love* – is opening out to other bodies, not engaging in the circle of self-regarding individualism.[36] But there is a more fundamental analysis to be offered here. There is something in the way that the production of a play sets up the relationship between stage image, representation and audience that intensifies this bodily utopianism.

Kane always described her plays as unperformable in any medium except the theatre: *Cleansed* would be, in some ways, easier to do on screen, where the simplest digital effects could conjure Carl's mutilation.[37] On stage, this presents major production problems. The more real it is, the less convincing it is, since the audience will always be aware that no real mutilation can be taking place. Minor acts of violence can be 'really' committed on stage; one actor may slap another performer's face. But the acts of spectacular violence and dismemberment characteristic of in-yer-face theatre are, if not impossible, certainly illegal to perform on stage. At such moments we hold apart in our minds the play and the performance; in one the body is dismembered, in the other it remains whole. In other words, the mutilation will never be entirely identical with the bodies on stage. Stage violence presents both the body's mutilation and its persistent non-mutilation, and this is emphasized in performances of plays where the division is not merely prompted by illusion but by the relations of representation. This theatrical principle of non-identity creates a space and a distance in which the fate of the body can be understood and challenged.

Images of physical dismemberment are not a rejection of political engagement, nor, I suggest, are they necessarily an opportunity to involve the audience in purely instinctual, unreflective experiences. While the images themselves are shocking and immersive, they divide representation against itself, creating images that carry with them an unspoken implication – and open up an unnameable possibility of a better world of bodily integrity and freedom.

notes

1. M. Crimp, *Plays: 1* (London: Faber, 2000), p. 368.
2. S. Kane, *Complete Plays* (London: Methuen, 2001), p. 136.
3. M. Ravenhill, *The Cut and Product* (London: Methuen, 2006), p. 24.
4. A. Sierz, *In-Yer-Face Theatre: British Drama Today* (London: Faber, 2001) p. 4, p. 5.
5. Ibid., p. 206.
6. Ibid. p. 6.
7. D. Haraway, *Simians, Cyborgs, and Women: The Reinvention of Nature* (London: Free Association Books, 1991), p. 149.
8. J. Halberstam and I. Livingston (eds), *Posthuman Bodies* (Bloomington and Indianapolis, IN: Indiana University Press, 1995), p. 3.
9. J. Baudrillard, *The Ecstasy of Communication* (New York: Semiotext(e), 1988), p. 18, p. 27.
10. M. Foucault, *Language, Counter-Memory, Practice: Selected Essays and Interviews* (Ithaca, NY: Cornell University Press, 1977), p. 148.
11. M. Crimp, *Plays: 2* (London: Faber, 2005), pp. 228–9; pp. 234–9.
12. See C. Waldby, *The Visible Human Project: Informatic Bodies and Posthuman Medicine* (London: Routledge, 2000).
13. A. Kroker and M. Kroker (eds), *Body Invaders: Sexuality and the Postmodern Condition* (Basingstoke: Macmillan, 1988), p. 20.
14. J. Baudrillard, *Symbolic Exchange and Death*, trans. I. H. Grant (London: Sage, 1993), p. 114.
15. J. Baudrillard, *Simulacra and Simulations*, trans. S. F. Glaser (Ann Arbor, MI: University of Michigan Press, 1994), p. 97.
16. F. W. Taylor, *Scientific Management* (London: Harper and Row, 1964), p. 40.
17. H. L. Arnold and F. L. Faurote, *Ford Methods and the Ford Shops* (New York: Engineering Magazine Company, 1919), p. 42.
18. J. Menday, *Call Centre Management: A Practical Guide* (Surrey: Callcraft, 1996), pp. 60–61.
19. K. Hook, *An Idea a Day for Call Centre Managers* (Surrey: Callcraft, 1998), p. 163.
20. C. Shilling, *The Body and Social Theory* (London: Sage, 1993), p. 3; p. 5.
21. J. Fonda, *Jane Fonda's Workout Book* (London: Allen Lane, 1982), p. 16; p. 24.
22. Ibid., p. 74.
23. Ibid., p. 9.
24. M. Featherstone (ed.), *Body Modification* (London: Sage, 2000), p. 2.
25. Ariel Levy's recent book, *Female Chauvinist Pigs: Women and the Rise of Raunch Culture* is a useful reminder that the infinite plasticity of the body in practice resolves itself into familiar patriarchal patterns.

26. See J. Goodall, 'An Order of Pure Decision: Un-Natural Selection in the Work of Stelarc and Orlan', in *Body Modification*, pp. 149–70.
27. M. Wessendorf, 'Bodies in Pain: Towards a Masochistic Perception of Performance – The Work of Ron Athey and Bob Flanagan', 1995, http://www2.hawaii.edu/~wessendo/Bodies.htm. Accessed 19 July 2006.
28. Kroker, *Body Invaders*, p. 25.
29. T. Warr and A. Jones, *The Artist's Body* (London: Phaidon, 2000), p. 285.
30. I am deeply indebted to Aleks Sierz for pointing out this production to me.
31. T. Nagel, *The Possibility of Altruism* (Oxford: Clarendon, 1970), p. 3.
32. S. Kracauer, 'The Mass Ornament', trans. B. Correll and J. Zipes, in S. E. Bronner and D. M. Kellner (eds), *Critical Theory and Society: A Reader* (London: Routledge, 1989) p. 149.
33. M. Ravenhill, *Plays: 1* (London: Methuen, 2001), p. 17.
34. Ibid., p. 26; p. 27; p. 90.
35. D. Greig, *San Diego* (London: Faber, 2003), p. 87.
36. Kane, *Complete Plays*, p. 103.
37. Public Interview with Sarah Kane, Royal Holloway College, London, 3 November 1998. Cited in G. Saunders, *'Love Me or Kill Me': Sarah Kane and the Theatre of Extremes* (Manchester: Manchester University Press, 2002), p. 87.

11
rough theatre
david greig

I want to tell you about the first time I glimpsed Rough Theatre. In early March 2001 my mortgage was overdue, I was at the limits of my over-draft and I was a long way from delivering a play to anybody so I rang my agent, Mel Kenyon, and told her I needed a job: any job so long as it paid up front and quickly. 'Don't worry,' she said, 'I'll find you some-thing.' An hour or so later she called me back. 'Darling, how would you like to go to the West Bank and write a comedy about the intifada – in Arabic?'

In 2001 the West Bank was in the news because the second 'Al Aqsa' intifada had recently broken. My invitation had come because the producer at the Al Kasabah Theatre in Ramallah, George Ibrahim, had invited director Rufus Norris to make a show for his troupe of actors. Rufus wanted a writer to help him create the piece. The idea was that Rufus and I would experience life in Ramallah, and produce some work in response. We could cover any subject we liked – checkpoints, settle-ments, targeted assassination – whatever we wanted as long as it was a comedy. George wanted a comedy because, understandably, he felt that the people in Ramallah needed cheering up.

That summer Rufus and I went to Ramallah and made a play, *Mish Alla Ruman* (*Not About Pomegranates*). Working in a conflict zone raised a lot of questions for me but I felt that, given the complexity of the brief, the play succeeded well enough. It played to decent houses despite increasing practical upheaval in the region. *Mish Alla Ruman* was not an easy play to make but it wasn't Rough Theatre. The play that changed my theatrical thinking was not the play that I made in Palestine but a play that I saw in a garage in a village near Bethlehem.

While we were in Palestine, Rufus and I ran some writing workshops in Bethlehem for young writers under the auspices of the Royal Court's international programme. These workshops were collaborations with a small theatre company called INAD, based in the small Palestinian village of Beit Jala, near Bethlehem. The aim of the workshops was to encourage teenage Palestinians to write their own plays which might eventually be staged at the Royal Court. INAD was the Palestinian partner in this development process.

INAD is a young company, its founders Raeda Gezaleh and Marina Barham barely older than the workshop participants. They began INAD as a theatre-in-education company touring the West Bank performing plays for children on the back of a flatbed truck. In their short history they had organized workshops, new writing development and plays for adults: but their core work remained for and with children and it was with children in mind that they had eventually built their own studio theatre. The theatre was basically a converted lock-up garage on a steep terrace of houses high above a valley. On the other side of the valley was the Israeli settlement of Giloh. Three tanks were parked on the settlement edge with their guns pointed squarely over to Beit Jala. When the intifada broke out, INAD suddenly found its theatre on the front line. At night Palestinian fighters from Beit Jala would fire speculative rounds over to Giloh and the Israeli army opposite would respond with tank shells and sniper fire.

Shortly before our arrival the situation had worsened for INAD. In early 2001 the caretaker was shot by an Israeli sniper. Then the theatre came under attack during a workshop and the children had to be quickly evacuated. Finally, after the theatre itself suffered a direct hit from a tank shell, it was decided that it was no longer safe for performances and closed it down.

Raeda and Marina had worked for years to make these writers' workshops happen. Fifteen young people had gathered from all over the West Bank – from Jericho, Tulkarm, Nablus, Ramallah and Bethlehem. Most of the participants had never even seen a play before. How could they be expected to write for a form they had never experienced? So on the first night of the workshop Raeda and Marina invited us all to come and see a show. They put us all in a little minibus and we drove through Beit Jala, up to their little theatre on the hill.

We arrived just at dusk. A couple of kids were kicking a ball against a wall. I saw the three tanks squatting like malevolent toads on the hill opposite. I noticed that my palms were sweating. I felt very exposed. Raeda and Marina unlocked the theatre and led us inside. The floor was covered in rubble, bits of the roof had fallen down and the walls were pockmarked with bullet holes. There was no electricity so the company lit candles around the small stage. We all sat on two low children's benches and one of the INAD founding members stepped on to the low rostrum and performed a monologue. The piece was an adaptation of a short story by Ghassan Khanafani. As we sat and watched the play I felt my palms still sweating. I was afraid the theatre might be shot at. But I was also felt something else, something transformative in the moment of performance.

Now, I don't understand Arabic and so I can't tell you much about the quality of the writing: the actor was good but it was not his acting that struck me so forcefully. No, what hit me was the sense, viscerally present in the room, of theatre as an act of resistance. This simple act of our gathering together to watch a play suddenly seemed, in itself, resistant to the situation around us. The play contained all the nuance and complexity of its creation and performance, and yet it inhabited a room that had shell holes in it. The existence of a complex and nuanced piece of art in this brutal environment seemed to affirm the complexity and nuance of these young people's lives in the face of the brutal simplicities of power. The play fed the desire of the young people to question and reflect upon their situation, and it offered them a space in which to do it. The simple theatrical conjuring of a different world laid like a ghost image over a visible and threatening 'real' world somehow offered up the idea that – because the imagination made one thing possible – the imagination could make all things possible.

This moment was, I believe, a profoundly political moment but it did not happen because the play was 'political'. The show was not a consciousness-raising exercise, nor was it propaganda. On the contrary, it was a quiet, personal piece of introspection rendered even more so by the low-key performance style. And yet, despite the immanent threat of violence, this play had held the young Palestinians transfixed for its duration. During its short existence, this halting questing monologue lit by guttering candles had carved a liberated space out of the brutality of violent threat.

'Inad' is Arabic for 'stubborn'. As I emerged from the theatre I noticed that INAD's logo on the steel plate of the theatre door had been punctured by bullet holes. Yesterday I was at the Royal Court to watch a performance of my play *Outlying Islands* (2002) in the newly named Jerwood Theatre Upstairs, and I couldn't help but notice that the new Royal Court logo looks as if it has bullet holes in it as well. I also observed that, like the interior of INAD's shelled garage, the new Royal Court's interior design contains a great deal of 'distressed', or unfinished, features such as bare brickwork and exposed plaster. The semiotics of these design details indicate the spontaneity of performance and the integrity of process over finish. These design features seem to be an explicit statement of the theatre's political history and intent.

What I want to discuss in this chapter, then, is the difference between the politics of creating self-conscious theatre amongst real bullet holes and the creation of self-consciously political theatre amidst a 'bullet-hole' look. I want to explore whether this difference has anything to teach us about the creation of genuinely liberatory theatre spaces and I will finally make a very tentative proposal for a new model of political theatre which might offer the possibility of resistance in the new conditions of power in the early twenty-first century.

This spring I was in Lisbon to see a performance of my play, *The Cosmonaut's Last Message to the Woman he Once Loved in the Former Soviet Union*, performed by a company called Artistas Unidos. AU is led by George Silva De Melo. George, in his sixties now, recently abandoned a long and illustrious career in mainstream Portuguese theatre and, by sheer force of charisma, he has gathered around him a collective of young actors and directors. Together they have squatted an abandoned newspaper office in the centre of Lisbon and made it their base. They formed a company and raised some money. They had no money for the building and only a little grant to pay a few permanent staff. George immediately committed the company to producing a high turnover of contemporary work on shoestring budgets. He simply declared the building a theatre and began performances.

The building has something like forty different rooms, holes in the roof, and wallpaper peeling off the walls. Brickwork and plaster are exposed and the curiously shaped rooms retain the feel of a recently abandoned space. AU's policy is to decide which play to perform and then simply to occupy whichever room seems the best space in which to perform it. They rig up a few lights on stands, put some benches in, rehearse the play and perform. The repertoire is mostly contemporary European plays by Fosse, Pinter, Kane, Harrower, Koltes and so forth, but George was also working hard to develop and perform the work of young Portuguese writers.

In a few years George has built up a dedicated young audience for contemporary European work and nurtured a new generation of Portuguese writers, actors and directors. As I spent time with AU I felt that here was a theatre company whose work seemed urgent and committed and – that word again – transformative. Both the theatre and the company seemed to be a space of endless possibility. I wondered why I hadn't experienced the same sense of immanent possibility in British theatre spaces.

Now, imagine that AU were a British company that had found an old newspaper office in central London, a place full of possibility with exposed floors and wallpaper peeling and ghosts in every room. Would it be able to put on a show? It's unlikely. Health and safety rules simply wouldn't allow them to operate. If the company, inspired by a moment of energy or impulse, pursued its dream, it would have to make its space habitable, and for that it would need a lottery grant. Instead of getting £5,000 for a few computers and being told to get on with it in the build-ing as it was, the building itself would quickly become the project. The company would get a board of directors. It would seek and obtain core funding. Marketing and architecture experts would be paid high consul-tation fees to put together proposals in bids for millions of pounds to transform the old newspaper offices into a multipurpose community arts venue. And finally, when the newly refurbished building opened, it would have, as its interior design, the same distressed, unfinished look as the new Royal Court.

Now I love the Royal Court as an institution and I like its new design, but as a theatre-maker I have to ask myself whether an 'unfinished look' is the same as unfinished. I don't think it is. An unfinished space creates a sense that the work made in it is temporary and of the moment. An 'unfinished look' space creates the sense that everything wants to seem temporary and of the moment while in fact being embedded in a safe, solid and long-term structure. Unfinished is dangerous: it tells you that at any moment things could change. 'Unfinished look' is safe: it tells you that deep down everything is the same.

Some years ago I was asked to deliver a talk on Political Theatre at a conference David Edgar organized. I think I had been asked because my play, *Europe*, has been perceived as being political in the Brechtian tradi-tion. In that talk I proposed the idea that truly political theatre was theatre of any type that created a world in which change was possible. I wanted to get away from theatre that proposed dialectical solutions in the old left-wing tradition and offer a theatre that tore at the fabric of reality and opened up the multiple possibilities of the imagination. Put simply, I was saying that there is no 'political' theatre but that theatre is, by its own nature, political. This was my way of body-swerving David Edgar's attempt – as I saw it then – to co-opt me into a happy band of 1970s left-wing dinosaurs.

I accepted the invitation to speak at the Bristol Conference some time ago, but it was only on the train to Bristol that I finally read the conference programme and noticed that I had again been billed as speaking about 'political theatre'. I was very tempted to body- swerve the issue again. After all, everything people do is political. 'Political' seems such a meaningless term to append to theatre anyway. It's just not very helpful. Surely when we say 'political theatre' we really mean 'left-wing theatre', or ' theatre with a progressive agenda'. But as I sat on the train staring out at the industrial estates of Reading and Slough, I couldn't help reflecting that since the conference I had attended in Birmingham the landscape of politics had changed. Globalization, 9/11 and the War on Terror, climate change and peak oil all seem to have created new answers to the old political questions – how should we organize ourselves? What harm do we do each other with our actions? Is this how the world should be? Politics has changed, and after my experiences in Palestine, I had changed. I was no longer satisfied with letting my work simply exist and not questioning whether it was help- ing or hindering the powers shaping our lives.

The question I now ask myself is 'How can I, as a theatre-maker, explore, map and advance a progressive agenda?' While looking for answers in Palestine and Portugal I have begun to glimpse a connection between the unfinished 'rough' nature of these temporary spaces and political qualities of the work made in them. I also sense a link with a creative theme I have been developing on my own, which I call 'Rough Writing'.

I believe that truth sometimes arrives in art when the artist uncovers something which – if stated openly – might embarrass them. I think it is part of the artist's role to expose themselves so that we, the audience might see ourselves as we are and not as we feel we ought to be. The best art reveals – lays itself bare. To produce such work, an author needs to 'trick' his or her conscious mind into letting out the unsayable and unacceptable.

'Rough Writing' began as a selection of exercises that I used in work- shops to help me explore this unconscious hinterland. These exercises included drawing, playing with toys, using music, automatic writing and other techniques intended to bypass the writer's conscious mind and expose the images and stories underneath. The idea is to bring unconscious images or themes out into the light, and then to start to work on them creatively and with craft.

To help explain the qualities of these first, unconscious expressions, I use the word 'rough' – as in a 'rough draft' – something done quickly, a sketch. 'Rough' as in 'not smooth' – something with texture, a form whose joins and bolts are visible. Rough as in the 'rough boys' whom one was not encouraged to play with at school – something threatening and dangerous and even perhaps adolescent. 'Rough' as in 'rough approximation' – not exact or precise but near and useful. 'Rough' as in 'I'm feeling a little rough this morning' – emotionally fragile, discombobulated, dislocated from time and place, hung over. 'Rough' as in 'unfinished'.

Is it possible that by putting rough plays into rough theatre spaces like INAD's garage or AU's newspaper office one might produce a new resistant, liberatory and progressive – rough – theatre? Perhaps, but if Rough Theatre is intended as resistance, then perhaps I ought to examine that which it is intended to resist – the management of the imagination by power.

Let us take the example of power in the form of global capital. The institutions of global capital manage the imagination in the first instance through media institutions. Hollywood cinema, the television and newspapers of the great media empires like Fox and CNN. These forms create the narrative superstructure around which our imagination grows. In this way we learn to think along certain paths, to believe certain truths, all of which tend, in the end, to further the aims of capital and the continuance of economic growth. Once the superstructure is in place, our own individual creativity will tend to grow around it and assume its shape so that the stories we tell ourselves, the photographs we take and so forth, are put in the service of the same narratives and assumptions.

For example, every newspaper now has a travel supplement. Travel journalism promotes the narrative that a destination can transform you. We are told about new destinations. There is a destination to fit every purpose we might want. We are encouraged to dream of destinations. Our imagination begins to place us in cities to which easyJet has opened up a new route. We take photographs of ourselves at the destination. The destination becomes part of our self-description so that we can say 'Prague is my favourite city' just as easily as we might say 'Nirvana is my favourite band'.

But in the travel supplement there seems to be little room for stories about the transformative power of the journey. The narrative of the journey would lead us, of course, to walk and not to fly, to write a journal not to read a guidebook, not to spend but to beg, to take photos of others rather than ourselves – and so forth. The destination narrative is in the service of capital and the journey narrative tends to be resistant to it.

By intervening in the realm of the imaginary, power continually shapes our understanding of reality. I remember sitting in a hotel room in Bethlehem and watching, on CNN, an account of a young man being shot at a checkpoint through which I had passed earlier in the day. The CNN reporter said that Israeli security forces had shot dead a Palestinian gunman. When I spoke to my Palestinian friends they raised their eyebrows and sighed – 'A gunman? Really?' They did not believe that the man who had been shot had been armed. It occurred to me that all shooting I had seen in Palestine – from Giloh and from the settlements near Ramallah – had been frighteningly random. All the anecdotes from the people I was working with had told me that one did not have to be armed to be shot at by Israeli soldiers; it was enough simply to be in the wrong place at the wrong time. Now, this man may or may not have had a gun – I have not investigated the incident – but what interests me is that, despite actually being in the physical location of the story and having powerful evidence to the contrary, I had simply accepted the CNN version of the story. My imagination had been managed. I accepted that Israel has 'security forces' whereas Palestine has 'gunmen', not 'teenagers', not 'protestors', not even 'soldiers', but 'gunmen'. The same shooting story was reported quite differently on Palestinian television. On the Bethlehem local station the Palestinian was given a face and a name.

The management process does not come from a secret cabal dictating orders from above, nor is it particularly the work of politicians or government. It is the result of individual decisions in the context of a particular set of economic processes. It is not a totalitarian process either. Very few imaginations are totally colonized, just as very few are totally liberated. In most of our minds there is a constant back and forth – a dialogue between challenge and assumption like waves washing against a shoreline.

In 1999 I went to Lesotho to visit my brother who was working on a wildlife project there. This was my first visit to southern Africa. I soon noticed that for every town on the map which had a European name there was, right next to it, a mirror town or 'township' which would have an African name. This mirroring is noticeable because elsewhere in the world it would be odd to have two large cities right next to each other, but in South Africa Johannesburg is next to Soweto. The town would have paved roads, running water, swimming pools in the gardens and so forth. The township would have none of those things. The people from the township would provide service and labour for the people in the town. Because the people in the town were mostly white and the people in the township invariably black, the disparity of power pertaining to the inhabitants of the different places was peculiarly visible. This mirroring applied from the big cities right down to the smallest Transvaal dorp. I had gone to South Africa somewhat romantically looking for the rainbow nation, and so I was taken aback at the sheer visceral shock of how blatant were the disparities of power I saw. I felt very tense while I was there. People I spoke to were full of stories of violence. Almost every white person to whom I spoke carried a gun. They seemed to spend much of their lives in a state of fear. To my outsider's eye the disparity of wealth was so visible it was almost taunting. It seemed to me then that the fear of the whites came, in fact, from empathy. They could not suppress the awareness that, were they in the shoes of the blacks, they would feel very angry. No matter how hard they tried, they could not make the situation 'normal' and so they felt afraid.

When I came back I spoke to the Scottish playwright, John Clifford, about this, and he pointed out to me that Edinburgh and London and Bristol have their own mirror towns in the third world – we just don't know where they are. In South Africa the connections were visible. Here, global capital has managed our imaginations so that our wealth and their poverty seem 'normal'. However, our empathy with our mirror township dwellers is more effectively suppressed.

Imagine a household where a rich family lives with a hundred servants. Everything seems normal, everything seems eternal – but there is always a fear which has to be held down and repressed. There is always 'that which cannot be imagined': that 'they' – the servants – are the same as 'us' – the family. Or, alternatively, that 'they' – the family – are the same as 'us' – the servants. We must not imagine ourselves in the position of the other because if we do, the moral edifice upon which we have built our wealth will suddenly crumble. We cannot imagine ourselves in the position of the other, or our subjugation will feel intolerable. We must choose not to see that we only occupy our position through the operation of raw power and violence upon the lives and bodies of human beings. So we manage our imaginations in such a way that we simply do not have to think about these things. We construct an otherness for people that justifies their poverty or pain, their wealth or their power. But the fear is always there, a shadow in the background that we can never quite shake off.

I read recently of a war game conducted by the American military in which they modelled the invasion of Iraq. They spent millions and millions of dollars on this exercise. There were hundreds of thousands of troops involved. It was, so the *Guardian* said, the biggest war game since the Second World War. The Americans' strategy was to use over-whelming force but they needed an enemy to test their strategy against, so they asked a retired Marine general to play the part of Saddam Hussein. He realized that, if you want to fight Mike Tyson, you don't do it in a boxing ring. He decided to use a different battlefield.

The general filled the Persian Gulf with pleasure craft full of suicide bombers who launched themselves at the American ships and sank half the fleet. America was defeated. So the organizers of the war game said to the general, 'No, you can't do that. We have to go back and start again.' They made all the American soldiers alive again and landed them on the beaches. This time the general employed the resistance of the local civilians in his tactics. He won again and, again, he was told to stop using these tactics. The American troops were being slaughtered on the beaches and the generals on the other side were going around tapping them on the shoulder saying – 'Come on, get up, you're alive again.' Apparently at one stage they told him to switch off his air defence because they were going to bomb, and they needed to win. Eventually the general said he stopped giving orders because the oppo-sition were talking to his sub-commanders and telling them not to do this or that. The game could not be lost. American power could not be vincible, even in a game. American defeat was unimaginable.

And so we fight off the fear until one day the unimaginable erupts into the real. Imagine the household with its hundred servants and then, one bright spring day, the family wakes up to find the youngest son has been murdered in his bed with a kitchen knife.

It's quite interesting how some recent events have been described as unimaginable. I'm thinking here of the events of 9/11. It was difficult for some people to come to terms with the fact that, in some parts of the world, there were celebrations at these attacks. We read stories in the newspapers of people in Brazil naming their children 'Osama', of children dancing in the Gaza strip. Why might these people all over the world, who have little reason to connect with militant Islamic spiritu-ality, thrill to the spectacle of the 9/11 attacks? Is it possible that they experienced joy because, for a very few moments, it seemed possible that the very powerful people of the world were in fact very vulnerable and that, equally, the very vulnerable people of the world were, in fact, very powerful? Did they wish to celebrate because the unimaginable had suddenly erupted into the realm of the real?

Terror and violence are certainly one way in which the imaginable is disrupted by the unimaginable. A suicide bomb is a physical demonstra-tion that things are not 'as they are' but can be suddenly and horribly different. The problem with violence as a method of resistance, though, is that violence is, in itself, unimaginative. To commit violence, one must suppress empathy. One must not imagine what it is like to be 'the other'. The perpetrator of violence cannot empathize, at least not for long. It seems to me that violence in the service of resistance relies upon the same inhuman suppression of the imagination as violence in the service of power and is, therefore, not a fruitful way to seek to resist it.

So if not violence, then what? What tools are available to us if we want to intervene in the management of the imagination? Is it possible that art, the theatre in particular, could provide a way of cracking open the carapace of the imagined world and allowing us to glimpse, underneath, all the possibilities of its reality?

Let's examine one famous intervention: Sarah Kane's *Blasted*. Kane's debut emerged in the context of war in Europe, in particular the Balkan conflict of the early 1990s. Here was a war taking place in towns which resembled British towns, disrupting lives which resembled British lives. For the government and the media in Britain, at the time, this similarity was the elephant in the room. It was the unimaginable. Much mainstream media focused on the 'ancient ethnic rivalries' of different 'tribes'. We were asked to imagine the situation as hopeless, natural and absurd. This management strategy allowed NATO, the UK government and the European Union to do nothing in particular about the situation. It allowed a 'peacekeeping' mandate for UN troops with rules of engagement predicated on keeping apart 'ancient enemies'.

A by-product of this management strategy was that it allowed consumers of the media to avoid empathy with the victims or the perpetrators of this violence. We were not asked to put ourselves in their place. After all, if a normality so similar to our own could be suddenly and utterly overturned into a world of hell and bloodshed, then how solid was our 'normality'? If violence was not being perpetrated by 'ancient rivals' but in fact by ordinary men then what in fact is an ordinary man? If the *Sun* newspaper reports that the rape camps of Tuzla were operated by ordinary men, and populated with ordinary women, then what questions might we begin to pose regarding the *Sun*'s coverage of other aspects of male/female relations in our society? As far as the Bosnian conflict was concerned, the mainstream British media was open to sympathy, pity even, but not empathy.

This was the context in which Sarah Kane imagined *Blasted* into existence. It is interesting that she did not dissect the conflict journalistically, nor did she try to represent it accurately but instead she imagined it. She imagined, very rigorously and clearly, what it might be like to be in that world of hell and bloodshed. She imagined a British city, Leeds, and an ordinary British man and woman and finally – in the form of the famous blast – she allowed the eruption of the unimaginable into their lives. She took a hammer to the carapace of normality and exposed all the possibilities underneath.

It is interesting that the press furore at the time focused on Kane's imagination. Her sanity was questioned. She was vilified for imagining horrors that did not exist. She was attacked for trying to shock us. The coverage of *Blasted* seems to me to reflect the punishment that must be meted out to those who confront us with the unimaginable.

Theatre doesn't change the world. I have no illusions that a play of mine will lead to mass demonstrations or the overthrow of governments. However, I do believe that if the battlefield is the imagination, then the theatre is a very appropriate weapon in the armoury of resistance. Let's look at some of the reasons for this.

First of all, the theatre cannot be globally commodified. It is not possible to manufacture cheaper theatre in Shanghai and then ship it to London. The very form of theatre is about people coming together in a local physical space – one of the few remaining public spaces – and experiencing something together. It's true to say that global shows such as *Mamma Mia!* or *Les Misérables* can be franchised and performed in different cities, but this process seems remarkably heavy-footed capitalism to me. I doubt that it forms a model which will dominate or detract from the general experience of theatre as a local form. So, even before a word has been spoken on stage, the theatre has already offered a grain of resistance to the frictionless movement of capital. It cannot efface its humanity. It cannot erode its locality.

Second, theatre is an experimental playing out of possibilities in time. It builds upon the question 'what if?' There is a sense in which any play is an experiment whereby we establish a given set of possible conditions and then observe what happens if we put people into those conditions and set them loose in real time. Theatre reminds us constantly of the contingency, the changeability of things.

Third, theatre is accessible to everybody. Anybody can make theatre so long as they have ground on which to draw a circle and an imagination. As a story-telling method, theatre is what might be called 'an appropriate technology'. It requires no equipment to view it, no electricity to power it and it needs no computer power to operate it.

Finally, theatre is transcendent. It draws its transcendence from the inherent 'negative dialectic' of theatrical performance. Adorno's concept of negative dialectic rests on power of the contradiction. A contradiction disrupts rationality. It throws a spanner in the works. Adorno suggests that we could imagine 'normality' or 'reality' as a *trompe l'oeil* painted on a cloth and held in front of the real world. The contradiction pulls at the fabric of the cloth. Eventually, if the contradiction is strong enough, the fabric of 'reality' will tear and we will be able see, behind it, the real world with its its rifts and crevices, as indigent and distorted as it will appear one day in the messianic light.[1]

Theatre is built upon a contradiction. When one watches a play one must hold two worlds in one's head: the actor (real) and the character (imagined), the stage (real) and the world (imagined). The better the performance, the more profound the contradiction and the greater the chance that – in the enaction of the play – the fabric of 'reality' will tear and we can experience transcendence. This moment of transcendence is, for me, the political foundation of Rough Theatre. What we glimpse in that moment we cannot then be made to un-see. What we feel in that moment we cannot then be persuaded to un-feel. Theatre cannot change the world, but it can allow us a moment of liberated space in which to change ourselves.

So what might a Rough Theatre look like? In the coffee bar just now I drew up a list in the hope that you might be persuaded to add it to it in similar spirit and that together we might announce a manifesto together. So let's see – a Rough Theatre would be

Poetic rather than prosaic.
Irrational and intuitive.
It would be childish and infantile.
It would be transcendent and it would be about transcendence.
It would take place in rough spaces.
It would take over spaces and demand that they become theatres.
I think it would be cheap.
It would be written fast, rehearsed fast and performed fast.
It would contain music and song.
It would be enchanting.
I think it would be written for children.
I think it would be performed by amateurs and students.
I think it would be non-fiction as well as fiction.
It would be unfinished . . .

notes

1. T. Adorno, *Minima Moralia: Reflections from a Damaged Life* (London: Verso, 1974) p. 247.

bibliography

plays

Adshead, K., *The Bogus Woman* (London: Oberon, 2001)

Ali, T., H. Brenton and A. De La Tour, *Collateral Damage* (London: Oberon, 1999)

Angelis, A. de, *Playhouse Creatures* (London: Samuel French, 1994)

Arden, J., *Plays: 1* (London: Methuen, 1994)

Atkins, E., *Vita and Virginia* (London: Samuel French, 1995)

Bancil, Parv, *Crazy Horse* (London: Faber, 1997)

Black and Asian Plays Anthology (London: Aurora Metro, 2000)

Barker, H., *Collected Plays Volume One* (London: John Calder, 1990)

Blakeman, H., *Caravan* (London: Samuel French, 1998)

Block, S., *Not a Game for Boys* (London: Nick Hern, 1995)

Bond, E., *Plays: 1* (London: Methuen, 1977)

Bond, E., *Plays: 2* (London: Methuen, 1978)

Bond, E., *Plays: 4* (London: Methuen, 1992)

Brenton, H., *Plays: 2* (London: Methuen, 1990)

Brenton, H., *Berlin Bertie* (London: Nick Hern, 1995)

Brenton, H., and D. Hare, *Pravda* (London: Methuen, 1985)

Brewster, Y. (ed.), *Black Plays* (London: Methuen, 1987)

Brewster, Y. (ed.), *Black Plays 2* (London: Methuen, 1989)

Brewster, Y. (ed.), *Black Plays 3* (London: Methuen, 1995)

Bryden, B., *Willie Rough* (Edinburgh: Southside Publishers, 1972)

Buchanan, W., *Under Their Influence* (London: Aurora Metro, 2001)

Buffini, M., *Plays: 1* (London: Faber, 2006)

Butterworth, J., *Mojo* (London: Nick Hern, 1995, rev. ed. 1996)

Butterworth, J., *The Night Heron* (London: Nick Hern, 2002)

Castledine, A. (ed.), *Plays by Women: 9* (London: Methuen, 1991)

Castledine, A. (ed.), *Plays by Women: 10* (London: Methuen, 1994)

Churchill, C., *Plays: 1* (London: Methuen, 1985)

Churchill, C., *Plays: 2* (London: Methuen, 1990)

Churchill, C., *Top Girls* (London: Methuen, 1991)

Churchill, C., *Plays: 3* (London: Nick Hern, 1997)

Churchill, C., *Blue Heart* (London: Nick Hern, 1997)

Churchill, C., *This is a Chair* (London: Nick Hern, 1999)

Churchill, C., *Far Away* (London: Nick Hern, 2000)

Cleugh, Grae, *F****ing Games* (London: Methuen, 2001)

Coming on Strong: New Writing from the Royal Court Theatre (London: Faber, 1995)

Corthron, K., *Breath, Boom* (London: Methuen, 2000)

Crimp, M., *The Treatment* (London: Nick Hern, 1993)

Crimp, M., *Plays: 1* (London, Faber, 2000, repr. 2002)

Crimp, M., *Plays: 2* (London: Faber, 2005)

Daniels, S., *Plays: 1* (London: Methuen, 1991)

Davies, J. (ed.), *Lesbian Plays* (London: Methuen, 1987)

Dean, K., *Down Red Lane* (London: Faber, 1998)

Din, A. K., *East is East* (London: Nick Hern, 1997)

Edgar, D, *Plays: 3* (London: Methuen, 1991)

Edgar, D, *Pentecost* (London: Nick Hern, 1995)

Edgar, D., *Playing with Fire* (London: Nick Hern, 2005)

Edwardes, P. (ed.), *Frontline Intelligence 1: New Plays for the Nineties* (London: Methuen, 1993)

Edwardes, P. (ed.), *Frontline Intelligence 2: New Plays for the Nineties* (London: Methuen, 1993)

Edwardes, P. (ed.), *Frontline Intelligence 4: New Plays for the Nineties* (London: Methuen, 1994)

Edwardes, P. (ed.), *Frontline Intelligence 3: New Plays for the Nineties* (London: Methuen, 1995)

Eldridge, D., *Festen* (London: Methuen, 2004)

Eldridge, D., *Serving It Up & A Week with Tony* (London: Methuen, 1997)

Ellis, M. (ed.), *Black Plays* (London: Methuen, 1987)

Elyot, K., *My Night With Reg* (London: Nick Hern, 1997)

Ensler, E., *The Vagina Monologues* (London: Virago, 2001)

Evaristi, Marcella, *Mouthpieces* (Fife, Scotland: Crawford Centre for the Arts, 1981)

Evaristi, Marcella, *Commedia* (Edinburgh: Salamander, 1983)

Frayn, M., *Democracy* (London: Faber, 2004)

Gay Plays 5 (London: Methuen, 1994)

George, K. (ed.), *Six Plays by Black and Asian Women Writers* (London: Aurora Metro Press, 1993)

Gems, P, *The Snow Palace* (London: Oberon, 1998)

Gems, P., *Plays: 1* (London: Oberon, 2004)

Glover, S., *Shetland Saga* (London: Nick Hern, 2000)

green, d. t., *born bad* (London: Nick Hern, 2003)

green, d. t., *dirty butterfly* (London: Nick Hern, 2003)

green, d. t., *trade* (London: Nick Hern, 2005)

green, d. t., *stoning mary* (London: Nick Hern, 2005)

Greenhorn, S., *Passing Places*, in P. Howard (ed.), *Scotland Plays* (London: Nick Hern Books, 1998)

Greig, D., *One Way Street*, in P. Howard (ed.), *Scotland Plays* (London: Nick Hern Books, 1998)

Greig, D., *Victoria* (*London*: Methuen, 2000)

Greig, D., *Plays: 1* (London: Methuen, 2002)

Greig, D., *San Diego* (London: Faber, 2003)

Greer, B., 'Dancing on Blackwater', unpublished draft (Courtesy Nitro, 1994)

Greer, B, *Munda Negra*, in Y. Brewster, ed. *Black Plays 3* (London: Methuen, 1995)

Griffiths. T, *The Party* (London: Faber, 1974)

Griffiths. T, *Hope in the Year Two and Thatcher's Children* (London: Faber, 1994)

Griffiths. T., *Theatre Plays: 1981–2001* (Nottingham: Spokesman Books, 2006)

Grosso, N., *Peaches*, in *Coming on Strong: New Writing from the Royal Court Theatre* (London: Faber, 1995)

Grosso, N., *Kosher Harry* (London: Methuen, 2002)

Gupta, T., *The Waiting Room* (London: Faber, 2000)

Gupta, T., *Sanctuary* (London: Oberon, 2002)

Hanna, G. (ed.), *Monstrous Regiment* (London: Nick Hern, 1991)

Hannan, C., *The Evil Doers* (London: Nick Hern, 1990)

Hare, D., *The Asian Plays* (London: Faber and Faber, 1986)

Hare, D., *The Secret Rapture* (London: Faber, 1988)

Hare, D., *Racing Demon* (London: Faber, 1990)

Hare, D., *Murmuring Judges* (London: Faber, 1991)

Hare, D., *The Absence of War* (London: Faber, 1993)

Hare, D., *Amy's View* (London: Faber, 1997)

Hare, D., *Via Dolorosa & When Shall we Live* (London: Faber, 1998)

Hare, D., *The Permanent Way* (London: Faber, 2003)

Harrower, D., *Dark Earth* (London: Faber, 2002)

Harvey, J., *Beautiful Thing* (London: Methuen, 1996)

Harwood, K. (ed.), *First Run 1: New Plays by New Writers* (London: Nick Hern, 1989)

Harwood, K. (ed.), *First Run 2: New Plays by New Writers* (London: Nick Hern, 1990)

Holman, R., *Making Noise Quietly* (London: Nick Hern, 1999)

Holman, R., *Holes in the Skin* (London: Nick Hern, 2003)

Howard, P. (ed.), *Scotland Plays* (London: Nick Hern Books, 1998)

Jenkins, M., *More Lives Than One [Selected Work]*, (Cardigan: Parthian, 2004)

Johnson, C., *Shang-a-Lang* (London: Faber, 1998)

Kane, S., *Complete Plays* (London: Methuen, 2001)

Kay, J., *Chiaroscuro*, in J. Davies (ed.), *Lesbian Plays* (London: Methuen, 1987)

Kelly, D., *Debris* (London: Oberon, 2003)

Kureishi, H., *Sleep With Me* (London: Faber, 1999)

Kwei-Armah, K., *Elmina's Kitchen* (London: Methuen, 2003)

Kwei-Armah, K., *Fix-up* (London: Methuen, 2004)

Lavery, B., *Plays: 1* (London: Methuen, 1998)

Lavery, B., *Frozen* (London: Faber, 2002)

Letts, T., *Killer Joe* (London: Samuel French, 1999)

Lloyd, M. (ed.), *First Run 3: New Plays by New Writers* (London: Nick Hern, 1991)

Lucas, P., *The Dice House* (London: Oberon, 2004)

Luckham, Claire, *Plays: 1* (London: Oberon, 1999)

MacMillan, H., *The Sash (My Father Wore)* (Glasgow: Molendinar, 1974)

Marber, P., *Plays: 1* (London: Methuen, 2004)

Mason-John, V., *Brown Girl in the Ring* (London: Get a Grip Publishers, 1999)

McDonagh, M., *The Cripple of Inishmaan* (London: Methuen, 1997)

McDonagh, M., *Plays: 1* (London: Methuen, 1999)

McDonagh, M., *The Lieutenant of Inishmore* (London: Methuen, 2001)

McDonagh, M., *The Pillowman* (London: Faber, 2003)

McGrath, J., *Six Pack: Six of the Best from John McGrath* (Edinburgh: Polygon, 1995)

McIntyre, C., *My Heart's a Suitcase & Low Level Panic* (London: Nick Hern, 1998)

McLeod, J., *Raising Fires* (London: Bush Theatre, 1999)

McMillan, R., The *Bevellers* (Edinburgh: Southside Publishers, 1974)

McPherson, C., *The Weir* (London: Nick Hern, 2001)

Mitchell, Gary, *Tearing the Loom and In a little World of Our Own* (London: Nick Hern Books, 1998)

Mitchell, Gary, *Trust* (London: Nick Hern Books, 1999)

Mitchell, Gary, *The Force of Change* (London: Nick Hern, 2000)

Mitchell, Gary, *As the Beast Sleeps* (London: Nick Hern Books, 2001)

Mitchell, Gary, *Loyal Women* (London: Nick Hern, 2003)

The Methuen Book of Modern Drama (London: Methuen, 2001)

Munro, Rona, *Bold Girls*, in M. Lloyd (ed.), *First Run 3: New Plays by New Writers* (London: Nick Hern, 1991)

Nagy, P., *Plays: 1* (London: Methuen, 1998)

Nagy, P, *Never Land* (London: Methuen, 1998)

Neilson, A., *The Censor* (London: Methuen, 1997)

Neilson, A., *Plays: 1* (London: Methuen, 1998)

Norfolk, M., *Wrong Place* (London: Oberon Books, 2003)

Osborne, J., *Look Back in Anger* (London: Faber, 1978)

Penhall, J., *Blue/Orange* (London: Methuen, 2000)

Penhall, J., *Plays* (London: Methuen, 2005)

Pinnock, W., *Leave Taking*, in K. Harwood (ed.), *First Run 1: New Plays by New Writers* (London: Nick Hern, 1989)

Pinnock, W., *Talking in Tongues*, in Y. Brewster (ed.), *Plays: 3* (London: Methuen, 1995)

Pinnock, W., *Mules* (London: Faber, 1996)

Pinnock, W., *One Under* (London: Faber, 2005)

Pinter, H., *Plays: 4* (London: Faber, 1993)

Pinter, H., *Plays: 2* (London: Faber, 1996)

Pinter, H., *Plays: 1* (London: Faber, 1996)

Pinter, H., *Plays: 3* (London: Faber, 1997)

Prichard, R., *Fair Game: A Free Adaptation of Games in the Backyard by Edna Mazya* (London: Faber, 1997)

Prichard, R., *Essex Girls*, in *Coming on Strong: New Writing from the Royal Court Theatre* (London: Faber, 1995)

Prichard, R., *Yard Gal* (London: Faber, 1998)

Ravenhill, M., *Mother Clap's Molly House* (London: Methuen, 2001)

Ravenhill, M., *Plays: 1* (London: Methuen, 2001)

Ravenhill, M., *Shopping and Fucking*, D. Rebellato, ed. (London: Methuen Student Edition, 2005)

Ravenhill, M., *The Cut and Product* (London: Methuen, 2006)

Ridley, P., *Plays: 1* (London: Methuen, 1997)

Roche, B., *The Wexford Trilogy* (London: Nick Hern, 2000)

Rudet, J., *Basin*, in M. Ellis (ed.), *Black Plays* (London: Methuen, 1987)

Samuels, D., *Kindertransport* (London: Nick Hern, 1995)

Setren, P. (ed.), *The Best of the Fest: New Plays Celebrating 10 Years of London New Play Festival* (London: Aurora Metro, 1998)

Stephens, S., *Plays: 1* (London: Methuen, 2005)

Stoppard, T., *The Invention of Love* (London: Faber, 1997)

Stoppard, T., *Plays: 5* (London: Faber, 1999)

Thomas, E., in B. Mitchell (ed.), *Three Plays* (Bridgend: Seren, 1994)

Thomas, E., *[Selected] Work '95–'98* (Cardigan: Parthian, 2002)

Upton, J., *Bruises & The Shorewatchers' House* (London: Methuen, 1996)

Upton, J., *Confidence* (London: Methuen, 1998)

Upton, J., *Sliding with Suzanne* (London: Methuen, 2001)

Upton, J., 'Introduction', in *Plays: 1* (London: Methuen, 2002), pp. vii–viii

Upton, J., *Plays: 1* (London: Methuen, 2002)

Wallace, N., *In the Heart of America, and Other Plays* (New York: Theatre Communications Group, 2001)

Walker, C., *Been So Long* (London: Faber, 1998)

Welsh, Irvine, *You'll Have Had Your Hole* (London: Methuen, 1998)

Welsh, Irvine, *4 Play* (London: Vintage, 2001)

Wertenbaker, T., *The Break of Day* (London: Faber, 1995)

Wertenbaker, T., *Plays: 1* (London: Methuen, 1996)

Wesker, A., *Plays: 1* (London: Methuen, 2001

Wesker, A., *Plays: 2* (London: Methuen, 2001)

Williams, R. , *The Gift* (London: Methuen, 2000)

Williams, R., *Sing Yer Heart Out for the Lads* (London: Methuen, 2002)

Williams, R., *Clubland* (London: Methuen, 2003)

Williams, R., *Fallout* (London: Methuen, 2003)

Williams, R., *Sweet Little Thing* (London: Methuen, 2005)

Woods, S., *Soap* (London: Oberon, 2005)

Zajdlic, R., *Infidelities*, in M. Lloyd (ed.), *First Run 3: New Plays by New Writers* (London: Nick Hern, 1991)

Zindika, *Leonora's Dance*, in K. George (ed.), *Six Plays by Black and Asian Women Writers* (London: Aurora Metro Press, 1993)

books and journals

Adorno, T., *Minima Moralia: Reflections from a Damaged Life* (London: Verso, 1974)

Anderson, L. M., *Mammies No More: The Changing Image of Black Women on Stage and Screen* (New York: Rowman and Littlefield, 1997)

Ansorge, P., *From Liverpool to Los Angeles: On Writing for Theatre, Film and Television* (London: Faber, 1997)

Ansorge, P., 'Really a Golden Age?' in D. Edgar (ed.), *State of Play. Issue 1: Playwrights on Playwriting* (London: Faber, 1999), pp. 37–47

Arnold, H. L. and Faurote, F. L. *Ford Methods and the Ford Shops* (New York: Engineering Magazine Company, 1919)

Artaud, A., 'The Theatre and the Plague' and 'Letters on Cruelty', in *The Theatre and Its Double*, trans. M. C. Richards (New York: Grove Press, 1958)

Aston, E., *Feminist Theatre Voices* (Loughborough: Loughborough Theatre Texts, 1997)

Aston, E., *Caryl Churchill* (Tavistock: Northcote House, 2001)

Aston, E., *Feminist Views on the English Stage: Women Playwrights, 1999–2000* (Cambridge: Cambridge University Press, 2003)

Aston, E. and J. Reinelt (eds), *The Cambridge Companion to Modern British Women Playwrights* (Cambridge: Cambridge University Press, 2000)

Barthes, R., *Mythologies*, trans. A. Lavers (London: Jonathan Cape, 1972)

Bassett, Kate. 'Dancing on Blackwater Review', *Theatre Record*, vol. 14, no. 20 (1994), 1193

Bataille, G., 'The Practice of Joy Before Death', in *Visions of Excess: Selected Writings, 1927–1939*, trans. A. Stoekl with C. R. Lovitt and D. M. Leslie, Jr (Minneapolis, MN: University of Minnesota Press, 1985), pp. 235–9

Batley, E. and D. Bradby (eds), *Morality and Justice: The Challenge of European Theatre* (Amsterdam: Rodopi, 2001)

Baudrillard, J., *The Ecstasy of Communication* (New York: Semiotext(e), 1988)

Baudrillard, J., *Symbolic Exchange and Death*, trans. I. H. Grant (London: Sage, 1993)

Baudrillard, J., *Simulacra and Simulations*, trans. S. F. Glaser, S.F (Ann Arbor: University of Michigan Press, 1994)

Bignell, J., and S. Lacey (eds), *Popular Television Drama: Critical Perspectives* (Manchester: Manchester University Press, 2005)

Billington, M., 'What Price the Arts?' in N. Buchan and T. Summer (eds), *Glasnost in Britain? Against Censorship and in Defence of the Word* (London: Macmillan, 1989), pp. 162–70

Billington, M., *The Life and Work of Harold Pinter* (London: Faber, 1996)

Bhabha, H. K., *The Location of Culture* (London: Routledge, 1994)

Bhui, K. (ed.), *Racism & Mental Health: Prejudice and Suffering* (London: Jessica Kingsley, 2002)

Bignell, J., and S. Lacey (eds), *Popular Television Drama: Critical Perspectives* (Manchester: Manchester University Press, 2005)

Blackman, Lisa, *Hearing Voices: Embodiment and Experience* (London: Free Association Press, 2001)

Blandford, S., 'BBC Drama at the Margins: The Contrasting Fortunes of Northern Irish, Scottish and Welsh Television Drama in the 1990s', in J. Bignell and S. Lacey (eds), *Popular Television Drama: Critical Perspectives* (Manchester: Manchester University Press, 2005), pp. 166–82

Blair, T, *New Britain, My Vision of a Young Country* (London: Fourth Estate, 1996)

Bond, E., Letter to Graham Saunders, 29 June 2000

Borthwick, S. and R. Moy, *Popular Music Genres* (Edinburgh: Edinburgh University Press, 2004)

Bracewell, M., *When Surface Was Depth: Death by Cappuccino and Other Reflections on Music and Culture in the 1990s* (Cambridge, MA: De Capo, 2002)

Bronner, S. E. and D. M. Kellner (eds), *Critical Theory and Society: A Reader* (London: Routledge, 1989)

Brooks, A. et al., *Sensation: Young British Artists from the Saatchi Collection.* (London: Thames and Hudson, 1997)

Bruce, S., 'Turf War and Peace: Loyalist Paramilitaries Since 1994', *Terrorism and Political Violence*, vol. 16, no. 3 (2004), 501–21

Buchan, N. and T. Summer (eds), *Glasnost in Britain? Against Censorship and in Defence of the Word* (London: Macmillan, 1989)

Bull, J., *Stage Right: Crisis and Recovery in British Contemporary Mainstream Theatre* (Basingstoke: Macmillan, 1994)

Bull, J., 'A Review of In-Yer-Face Theatre: British Drama Today', *Contemporary Theatre Review*, vol. 13, no. 1 (2003), 123–5

Burke, A. W. and J. Bierer (eds), *Transcultural Psychiatry* and *Racism & Mental Illness. The International Journal of Social Psychiatry*, vol. 30, nos 1 & 2 (1984)

Carpenter, H., *The Angry Young Men: A Literary Comedy of the 1950s* (London: Penguin, 2003)

Case, S. E., 'The Power of Sex: English Plays by Women, 1958–1988', *New Theatre Quarterly*, vol. 12, no. 27 (1991), 238–45

Castells, M., *The Power of Identity* (Oxford: Blackwell, 1997)

Castells, M., *The Rise of the Network Society* (Oxford: Blackwell, 1997)

Chambers, C., *Inside the Royal Shakespeare Company: Creativity and the Institution* (London: Routledge, 2004)

Christopher, J., 'Dancing on Blackwater Review,' *Theatre Record*, vol. 14, no. 20 (1994)

Clark, M. S., 'Against Pessimism', in M. M. Delgado and C. Svich (eds), *Theatre in Crisis? Performance Manifestos for a New Century* (Manchester: Manchester University Press, 2002), pp. 82–8

Collin, M., *Altered State: The Story of Ecstasy Culture and Acid House* (London: Serpent's Tail, 1997)

Cooke, L., *British Television Drama* (London: BFI Publishing, 2003)

Coulter, C. (ed.), *Contemporary Northern Irish Society – An Introduction* (London: Pluto Press, 1999)

Craig, C., 'Scotland Ten Years On: The Changes that Took Place While RipMacWinkle Slept', *Radical Scotland* (1989), 8–10

Craig, N., *I An Actor*, rev. edn (London: Methuen 2001)

Critchley, S., *Very Little . . . Almost Nothing: Death, Philosophy, Literature* (London: Routledge, 1997)

Croft, S., *She Also Wrote Plays: An International Guide to Women Playwrights from the 10th to the 20th Century* (London: Faber, 2001)

Dahl, M. K., ' "Postcolonial British Theatre": Black Voices at the Center', in J. E. Gainor (ed.), *Imperialism and Theatre: Essays on World Theatre, Drama and Performance* (London: Routledge, 1995), pp. 38–55

Dancing on Blackwater programme

Deeney, J., 'Workshop to Mainstream: Women's Playwriting in the Contemporary British Theatre', in M. B. Gale and V. Gardner (eds), *Women, Theatre and Performance: New Histories, New Historiographies* (Manchester University Press: Manchester, 2000), pp. 142–62

Deleuze, G., 'On the Difference between the *Ethics* and a Morality', *Spinoza: Practical Philosophy*, trans. R. Hurley (San Francisco, CA: City Lights, 1988)

Deleuze, G., *Negotiations*, trans. M. Joughin (New York: Columbia University Press, 1995)

Delgado, M. M. and C. Svich (eds), *Theatre in Crisis? Performance Manifestos for a New Century* (Manchester: Manchester University Press, 2002)

Dolan, J., *The Feminist Spectator as Critic* (Ann Arbor: University of Michigan Press, 1988)

Dromgoole, D., *The Full Room: An A–Z of Contemporary Playwriting* (London: Methuen, 2000, repr. 2002)

Du Bois, W. E. B., *The Souls of Black Folk*, in H. L. Gates Jr and T. H. Oliver (eds), *A Norton Critical Edition* (London: W. W. Norton and Company, 1999)

Edgar, D., 'Provocative Acts: British Playwriting in the Post-War Era and Beyond', in D. Edgar (ed.), *State of Play, Issue One: Playwrights on Playwriting* (London: Faber, 1999), pp. 1–34

Edgar, D., *State of Play. Issue 1: Playwrights on Playwriting* (London: Faber, 1999)

Edgar, D., 'Unsteady States: Theories of Contemporary New Writing', *Contemporary Theatre Review*, vol. 15, no. 3 (2005), 297–308

Eldridge, D., 'In-Yer-Face and After', *Studies in Theatre and Performance*, vol. 23, no. 1 (2003), 55–8

Esslin, M., *The Theatre of the Absurd*, rev. edn (London: Methuen, 2001)

Evaristo, B., 'Black Women in Theatre', in K. George (ed.), *Six Plays by Black and Asian Women Writers* (Aurora Metro Press: London, 1993), pp. 5–7

Faludi, S., *Backlash: The Undeclared War Against Women* (London: Vintage, 1992)

Fanon, F., *Black Skin, White Masks*, trans. C. L. Markmann (London: Pluto Press, 1986)

Featherstone, M. (ed.), *Body Modification* (London: Sage, 2000)

Feay, Suzi, '*Leonora's Dance* Review', *Theatre Record*, vol. 12, no. 3 (1993)

Feldman, A., *Formations of Violence: The Narrative of the Body and Political Terror in Northern Ireland* (Chicago: The University of Chicago Press, 1991)

Finlayson, Alan, 'Discourse and Contemporary Loyalist Identity', in P. Shirlow and M. McGovern (eds), *Who are 'The People'?: Unionism, Protestantism and Loyalism in Northern Ireland* (London: Pluto Press, 1997), pp. 72–94

Fonda, J. *Jane Fonda's Workout Book* (London: Allen Lane, 1982)

Foucault, M. *Language, Counter-Memory, Practice: Selected Essays and Interviews.* (Ithaca, NY: Cornell University Press, 1977)

Gainor, J. E. (ed.), *Imperialism and Theatre: Essays on World Theatre, Drama and Performance* (London: Routledge, 1995)

Gale, M. B., *West End Women: Women and the London Stage 1918–1962* (London: Routledge, 1996)

Gale, M. B. and V. Gardner (eds), *Women, Theatre and Performance: New Histories, New Historiographies* (Manchester: Manchester University Press, 2000)

Goddard, L., 'West Indies *vs.* England in Winsome Pinnock's Migration Narratives', *Contemporary Theatre Review*, vol. 14, no. 4 (November 2004), 23–33

Goddard, L., *Staging Black Feminisms: Identity, Politics, Performance* (Basingstoke: Palgrave, 2007)

Godiwala, D. (ed.), *Alternatives Within the Mainstream: British Black and Asian Theatres* (Newcastle: Cambridge Scholars Press, 2006)

Goodall, J., 'An Order of Pure Decision: Un-Natural Selection in the Work of Stelarc and Orlan', in M. Featherstone (ed.), *Body Modification* (London: Sage, 2000), pp. 149–70

Goodman, L., 'Who's Looking at Who(m)?: Re-viewing Medusa', *Modern Drama*, vol. 39, no. 1 (1996), 190–210

Goodman, L., *Mythic Women/Real Women: Plays and Performance Pieces by Women* (London: Faber, 2000)

Gordon, L. (ed.), *Pinter at 70. A Casebook* (London. Routledge, 2001)

Gottlieb, V., 'Lukewarm Britannia', in V. Gottlieb and C. Chambers (eds), *Theatre in a Cool Climate* (Oxford: Amber Lane, 1999), pp. 201–12

Gottlieb, V., and C. Chambers (eds), *Theatre in a Cool Climate* (Oxford: Amber Lane, 1999)

Gottlieb, V., 'Theatre Today – the "New Realism"', *Contemporary Theatre Review*, vol. 13, no. 1 (2003), 6–14

Graham, B. (ed.), *Modern Europe: Place, Culture and Identity* (London: Arnold, 1998)

Griffin, G., *Contemporary Black and Asian Women Playwrights in Britain* (Cambridge: Cambridge University Press, 2003)

Gussow, M., *Conversations with Pinter* (London: Nick Hern, 1994)

Halberstam, J. and I. Livingston (eds.), *Posthuman Bodies* (Bloomington and Indianapolis, IN: Indiana University Press, 1995)

Haraway, D. J., *Simians, Cyborgs, and Women: The Reinvention of Nature* (London: Free Association Books, 1991)

Hare, D., 'A Defence of the New', in *Platform Papers 9* (London: Royal National Theatre, 1997), pp. 5–17

Harvie, C., 'Scottish Journey', *Cencrastus* (1989), 4–9

Harvie, J., *Staging the UK* (Manchester: Manchester University Press, 2005)

Heidegger, M., *The Question of Being*, trans. W. Kluback and J. T. Wilde (New York: Twayne, 1958)

Hensman, S., 'Presentation of Self as Performance: The Birth of Queenie aka Valerie Mason-John', in N. Rapi and M. Chowdhry (eds), *Acts of Passion: Sexuality, Gender and Performance* (London: The Haworth Press, 1998), pp. 209–19

Hemming, S., '*Leonora's Dance* Review', *Theatre Record*, vol. 12, no. 3 (1993)

Hook, K. *An Idea a Day for Call Centre Managers* (Surrey: Callcraft, 1998)

Howell, E. and M. Bayes (eds), *Women and Mental Health* (New York: Basic Books, 1981)

Humphreys, E., *The Taliesin Tradition* (London: Black Raven, 1983)

Innes, C, *Avant Garde Theatre 1892–1992* (London: Routledge, 1993)

Innes, C., *Modern British Drama: The Twentieth Century* (Cambridge: Cambridge University Press, 2002)

Jancovich, B., '*Leonora's Dance* Review', *Theatre Record*, vol. 12, no. 3 (1993)

Jenkins, M., 'Virtual Reality Wales', *New Welsh Review*, no. 30 (1995), 74–7

Johnston, J., *The Lord Chamberlain's Blue Pencil* (London: Hodder & Stoughton, 1990)

Jones, A., *Body Art: Performing the Subject* (Minnesota: University of Minnesota Press, 1998)

Jünger, E., *Über die Linie* (Frankfurt am Main: Vittorio Klostermann, 1958)

Kelly, A, *Irvine Welsh* (Manchester: Manchester University Press, 2005)

Kershaw, B. (ed.), *The Cambridge History of British Theatre: Vol. 3 – Since 1895* (Cambridge: Cambridge University Press, 2004)

Klein, N., *No Logo* (New York: Picador, 2000)

Klimenko, S., 'Playing for Readers: Anxiety about the Written Word in Modern British Theatre', *Anglo Files: Journal of English Teaching*, vol. 126 (2002), 27–34

Kracauer, S., 'The Mass Ornament', trans. B. Correll and J. Zipes, in S. E. Bronner and D. M. Kellner (eds), *Critical Theory and Society: A Reader* (London: Routledge, 1989), pp. 145–54

Kroker, A. and Kroker, M. (eds), *Body Invaders: Sexuality and the Postmodern Condition* (Basingstoke: Macmillan, 1988)

Leonora's Dance programme

Kustow, M., theatre@risk, rev. edn (London: Methuen, 2001)

Lesser, W., *A Director Calls* (Berkeley, CA: University of California Press, 1997; London: Faber, 1997)

Letwin, S. R., *The Anatomy of Thatcherism* (London: Fontana, 1992)

Levy, A., *Female Chauvinist Pigs: Women and the Rise of Raunch Culture* (Simon & Schuster: London, 2005)

Lewis, H. B., 'Madness in Women', in E. Howell and M. Bayes (eds), *Women and Mental Health* (New York: Basic Books, 1981), pp. 207–27

Llewellyn-Jones, Margaret, *Contemporary Irish Drama and Cultural Identity* (Bristol: Intellect, 2002)

London, J., 'Dancing with the Dead Man: Notes on a Theatre for the Future of Europe', in M. N. Delgado and C. Svich (eds), *Theatre in Crisis? Performance Manifestos for a New Century* (Manchester: Manchester University Press, 2002), pp. 103–7

Luckhurst, M. (ed.), *On Acting* (London: Faber, 2001)

Luckhurst, M. (ed.), 'An Embarrassment of Riches: Women Dramatists in 1990s Britain', in B. Reitz and M. Berninger (eds), *British Drama of the 1990s* (Heidelberg: Universitätsverlag Carl Winter, 2002), pp. 65–77

Luckhurst, M. (ed.), 'Contemporary English Theatre: Why Realism?' in *(Dis)Continuities: Trends and Traditions in Contemporary Theatre and Drama in English*, eds M. Rubik and E. Mettinger-Schartmann (Trier: Wissenschaftlicher Verlag, 2002), pp. 73–83

Luckhurst, M. (ed.), 'Infamy and Dying Young: Sarah Kane, 1971–1999', in M. Luckhurst and J. Moody (eds), *Theatre and Celebrity in Britain 1660–2000* (London: Palgrave, 2005), pp. 107–26

Luckhurst, M. (ed.), *Dramaturgy: A Revolution in Theatre* (Cambridge: Cambridge University Press, 2006)

Luckhurst, M. (ed.), *A Companion to Modern British and Irish Drama: 1880–2005* (Oxford: Blackwell, 2006)

Luckhurst, M. (ed.), 'Torture in the Plays of Harold Pinter', in *A Companion to Modern British and Irish Drama: 1880–2005*, ed. M. Luckhurst (Oxford: Blackwell, 2006), pp. 353–70

Luckhurst, M., and J. Moody (eds), *Theatre and Celebrity in Britain 1660–2000* (London: Palgrave, 2005)

Lyotard, J., *The Postmodern Condition: A Report on Knowledge* (Manchester: Manchester University Press, 1984)

Mama, A., *Beyond the Masks: Race, Gender and Subjectivity* (London: Routledge, 1995)

Marcus, L. and P. Nicholls (eds), *The Cambridge History of Twentieth-Century English Literature* (Cambridge: Cambridge University Press, 2004)

Marmion, Patrick, 'Busting Loose', *What's On*, 10 February 1993, pp. 10–11

Martin, Mick, '*Dancing on Blackwater* Review', *Theatre Record*, vol. 14, no. 20 (1994), 1506

McAuley, J. W., 'Fantasy Politics? Restructuring Unionism after the Good Friday Agreement', *Éire-Ireland*, 39: 1 & 2 (2004), 195

McAuley, J., '"Flying the One-Winged Bird": Ulster Unionism and the Peace Process', in P. Shirlow and M. McGovern (eds), *Who are 'The People'?: Unionism, Protestantism and Loyalism in Northern Ireland* (London: Pluto Press, 1997), pp. 158–75

McDonald, H. and J. Cusack, *UDA – Inside the Heart of Loyalist Terror* (Dublin: Penguin Ireland, 2004)

McGrath, J., *A Good Night Out: Popular Theatre: Audience, Class and Form* (London: Methuen 1981)

McGrath, J., *The Bone Won't Break: On Theatre and Hope in Hard Times* (London: Methuen, 1990)

McKay, S., *Northern Protestants: An Unsettled People* (Belfast: The Blackstaff Press, 2000)

McRobbie, A., *In the Culture Society: Art, Fashion and the Popular* (London: Routledge, 1999)

Menday, J., *Call Centre Management: A Practical Guide* (Surrey: Callcraft, 1996)

Meyer-Dinkgräfe, D. (ed.), *The Professions in Contemporary Drama* (Bristol: Intellect Books, 2003)

Michaels, Melissa, '*Dancing on Blackwater* Review', *Theatre Record*, vol. 14, no. 20 (1994), 1193

Milne, D., 'Pinter's Sexual Politics', in P. Raby (ed.), *The Cambridge Companion to Harold Pinter* (Cambridge: Cambridge University Press, 2001), pp. 195–211

Mohr, H. U. and K. Mächler (eds), *Extending the Code – New Forms of Dramatic and Theatrical Expression* (Trier: Wissenschaftlicher Verlag, 2004)

Müller, K. P., 'Political Plays in England in the 1990s', in B. Reitz and M. Berninger (eds), *British Drama of the 1990s* (Heidelberg: Universitätsverlag Carl Winter, 2002), pp. 15–36

Nagel, T., *The Possibility of Altruism* (Oxford: Clarendon, 1970)

Napier-Bell, S., *Black Vinyl, White Powder* (London: Ebury, 2002)

Neaman, E. Y., *A Dubious Past: Ernst Jünger and the Politics of Literature after Nazism* (Berkeley, CA: University of California Press, 1999)

Nietzsche, F., *Thus Spoke Zarathustra: A Book for All and None*, in *The Portable Nietzsche*, ed. and trans. W. Kaufmann (London: Penguin, 1954), pp. 103–439

Nietzsche, F., *Ecce Homo*, in *On the Genealogy of Morals and Ecce Homo*, trans. Walter Kaufmann (New York: Vintage, 1967)

Nietzsche, F., *The Will to Power*, W. Kaufmann and R. J. Hollingdale, eds (New York: Vintage, 1968)

Nietzsche, F., *The Gay Science*, trans. Walter Kaufmann (New York: Vintage, 1974)

Nightingale, B., '*Leonora's Dance* Review', *Theatre Record*, vol. 12, no. 3 (1993)

Obel, K., 'The Story of V-Day and the College Initiative', in E. Ensler, *The Vagina Monologues* (London: Virago, 2001), pp. 129–71

Owen, R., 'Powerful Simplification: Theatre in Wales in the 1990s and Beyond', in B. Kershaw (ed.), *The Cambridge History of British Theatre vol. 4* (Cambridge: Cambridge University Press, 2004), pp. 485–97

Parkinson, A., *Ulster Loyalism and the British Media* (Dublin: Four Courts Press, 1998)

Parrish, S., 'The Power of Tradition', *The Glass Ceiling* (London: pamphlet, n.d.)

Patrice, P., 'Ravenhill and Durringer, or the *Entente Cordiale Misunderstood*', trans. D. Bradby, *Contemporary Theatre Review*, vol. 14, no. 2 (2004), 4–16

Pattie, D., 'The Decentring of *Docherty*: The Scotsman in Modern Scottish Drama', *International Journal of Scottish Theatre*, vol. 1, no. 2 (2000)

Peacock, D. K., *Thatcher's Theatre: British Theatre and Drama in the Eighties* (London: Greenwood Press, 1994)

Pilger, J., *The New Rulers of the World* (London: Verso, 2002)

Pinnock, W., 'Breaking Down the Door', in C. Chambers and V. Gottlieb (eds), *Theatre in a Cool Climate* (Oxford: Amber Lane, 1999), pp. 27–38

Portillo, M., *Clear Blue Water: A Compendium of Speeches and Interviews Given by the Rt. Hon. Michael Portillo* (London: Conservative Way Forward, 1994)

Pountain, D. and D. Robins, *Cool Rules: Anatomy of an Attitude* (London: Reaktion Books, 2000)

Quigley, A., 'Pinter, Politics and Postmodernism', in P. Raby (ed.), *The Cambridge Companion to Harold Pinter* (Cambridge: Cambridge University Press, 2001), pp. 7–27

Rabey, D., *English Drama Since 1940* (Edinburgh: Longman, 2003)

Raby, P. (ed.), *The Cambridge Companion to Harold Pinter* (Cambridge: Cambridge University Press, 2001)

Rack, P., *Race, Culture and Mental Disorder* (London: Tavistock Publications, 1982)

Rapi, N. and M. Chowdhry (eds), *Acts of Passion: Sexuality, Gender and Performance* (London: The Haworth Press, 1998)

Ravenhill, M., 'A Tear in the Fabric: The James Bulger Murder and New Theatre Writing in the "Nineties"', *New Theatre Quarterly*, vol. 20, no. 4 (2004), 305–14

Rebellato, D., *1956 And All That: The Making of Modern British Drama* (London and New York: Routledge, 1999)

Rebellato, D., 'New Theatre Writing: Simon Stephens', *Contemporary Theatre Review*, vol. 4, no. 1 (2005), 174–8

Reinelt, J., '"Politics, Playwriting, Postmodernism": An Interview with David Edgar', *Contemporary Theatre Review*, vol. 14, no. 4 (2004), 42–53

Reitz, B. and M. Berninger (eds), *British Drama of the 1990s* (Heidelberg: Universitätsverlag Carl Winter, 2002)

Ritzer, G. *The McDonaldization of Society: An Investigation into the Changing Character of Contemporary Social Life*, rev. edn (Thousand Oaks: Pine Forge, CA, 1996)

Roberts, P., *The Royal Court and the Modern Stage* (Cambridge: Cambridge University Press, 1999)

Ross, N., 'Leaving the Twentieth Century: New Writing on the Welsh Language Mainstage 1979–1995', in A. M. Taylor (ed.), *Staging Wales: Welsh Theatre 1979–1997* (Cardiff: University of Wales, 1997), pp. 18–32

Rubik, M. and E. Mettinger-Schartmann (eds), *(Dis)Continuities: Trends and Traditions in Contemporary Theatre and Drama in English* (Trier: Wissenschaftlicher Verlag, 2002)

Rushdie, S., *Shame* (London: Jonathan Cape, 1983)

Russell Taylor, J., *Anger and After: A Guide to the New British Drama*, 2nd edn (London: Eyre Methuen, 1969)

Sakellaridou, E., 'New Faces for British Political Theatre', *Studies in Theatre & Performance*, vol. 20, no. 1 (1990), 43–51

Saunders, Graham, *'Love Me or Kill Me': Sarah Kane and the Theatre of Extremes* (Manchester: Manchester University Press, 2002)

Saunders, Graham, 'The Apocalyptic Theatre of Sarah Kane', in B. Reitz and M. Berninger (eds), *British Drama of the 1990s* (Heidelberg: Universitätsverlag Carl Winter, 2002), pp. 123–36

Savill, C., 'Wales is Dead!', *Planet* (February/March 1991), pp. 86–91

Sergeant, J., *Maggie: Her Fatal Legacy* (Basingstoke: Macmillan, 2005)

Scullion, A., 'Self and Nation: Issues of Identity in Modern Scottish Drama', *New Theatre Quarterly*, vol. 17, no. 4 (2001), 373–90

Shepherd, S., 'Theatre and Politics', in L. Marcus and P. Nicholls (eds), *The Cambridge History of Twentieth-Century English Literature* (Cambridge: Cambridge University Press, 2004), pp. 635–52

Shields, T., 'Theatricality & Madness: Minding The Mind-doctors', in D. Meyer-Dinkgräfe (ed.), *The Professions in Contemporary Drama* (Bristol: Intellect Books, 2003), pp. 37–45

Shilling, C., *The Body and Social Theory* (London: Sage, 1993)

Shirlow, P. and M. McGovern (eds), *Who are 'The People'?: Unionism, Protestantism and Loyalism in Northern Ireland* (London: Pluto Press, 1997)

Sierz, A., *'Leonora's Dance* Review', *Theatre Record*, vol. 13, no. 4 (1993)

Sierz, A., 'Cool Britannia? "In-Yer-Face" Writing in the British Theatre Today', *New Theatre Quarterly*, vol. 14, no. 4 (1998), 324–33

Sierz, A., *In-Yer-Face Theatre: British Drama Today* (London: Faber, 2000, repr. 2001)

Sierz, A., ' "The Element That Most Outrages": Morality, Censorship and Sarah Kane's *Blasted*', in E. Batley and D. Bradby (eds), *Morality and Justice: The Challenge of European Theatre* (Amsterdam: Rodopi, 2001), pp. 225–39

Sierz, A., 'Raising Kane', *What's On*, 28 March 2001

Sierz, A., 'In-Yer-Face Theatre: New British Drama Today', *Anglo Files: Journal of English Teaching*, no. 126 (2002), 8–14

Sierz, A., 'Still "In-Yer-Face"?: Towards a Critique and a Summation', *New Theatre Quarterly*, 69 (2002), 17–24

Sierz, A., ' "In Yer Face" Bristol', *New Theatre Quarterly*, vol. 19, no. 1 (2003)

Sierz, A., ' "Me and My Mates": The State of English Playwriting', *New Theatre Quarterly*, vol. 20, no. 1 (2004), 79–83

Sierz, A., ' "To Recommend a Cure": Beyond Social Realism and In-Yer-Face Theatre', in H. U. Mohr and K. Mächler (eds), *Extending the Code – New Forms of Dramatic and Theatrical Expression* (Trier: Wissenschaftlicher Verlag , 2004), pp. 45–62

Sierz, A., 'Beyond Timidity?: The State of British New Writing', *Performing Arts Journal*, vol. 27, no. 3 (2005), pp. 55–61

Sierz, A., 'Sarah Kane: A Última Entrevista', *Artistas Unidos*, no. 14 (2005), 66–7

Skeggs, B., 'The Making of Class and Gender through Visualizing the Moral Subject Formation', *Sociology*, vol. 39, no. 5 (2005), 965–82

Smartt, D., *Connecting Medium* (Leeds: Peepal Tree Press, 2001)

Stephens, S., *Motortown* (London: Methuen, 2006)

Stephenson, H. and N. Langridge, *Rage and Reason: Women Playwrights on Playwriting* (London: Methuen 1997)

Szondi, P., *Theory of the Modern Drama* (Cambridge: Polity, 1987)

Taylor, A. M., 'Introduction', in A. M. Taylor (ed.), *Staging Wales: Welsh Theatre 1979–1997* (Cardiff: University of Wales, 1997), pp. 1–7

Taylor, A. M., 'Welsh Theatre and the World', in A. M. Taylor (ed.), *Staging Wales: Welsh Theatre 1979–1997* (Cardiff: University of Wales, 1997), pp. 111–19

Taylor, A. M. (ed.), *Staging Wales: Welsh Theatre 1979–1997* (Cardiff: University of Wales, 1997)

Taylor, F. W. *Scientific Management* (London: Harper and Row, 1964)

Thomas, E., 'Wales and a Theatre of Invention', in N. Wallace (ed.), *Thoughts and Fragments about Theatres and Nations* (Glasgow: Guardian Publications, 1991), pp. 15–16

Tizard, B. and A. Phoenix, *Black, White or Mixed Race?: Race and Racism in the Lives of Young People of Mixed Parentage*, rev. edn (London: Routledge, 2002)

Tomlin, L., 'English Theatre in the 1990s and Beyond', in B. Kershaw (ed.), *The Cambridge History of British Theatre: Vol. 3 – Since 1895* (Cambridge: Cambridge University Press, 2004), pp. 498–512

Upton, J., 'Afterword', in P. Edwardes (ed.), *Frontline Intelligence 3: New Plays for the Nineties* (London: Methuen, 1995), p. 261

Urban, K., 'Towards a Theory of Cruel Britannia: Coolness, Cruelty, and the 'Nineties', *New Theatre Quarterly*, vol. 20, no. 4 (2004), 354–72

Urban, K., ' "An Ethics of Catastrophe": The Theatre of Sarah Kane', *Performing Arts Journal*, no. 69 (2001), 36–46

Ussher, J. *Women's Madness: Misogyny or Mental Illness?* (London: Harvester Wheatsheaf, 1991)

Waldby, C. *The Visible Human Project: Informatic Bodies and Posthuman Medicine* (London: Routledge, 2000)

Wallace, N. (ed.), *Thoughts and Fragments about Theatres and Nations* (Glasgow: Guardian Publications, 1991)

Walter, N., *The New Feminism* (London: Virago, 1999)

Walton, J. K., *The British Seaside: Holidays and Resorts in the Twentieth Century* (Manchester: Manchester University Press, 2000)

Warr, T. and A. Jones, *The Artist's Body* (London: Phaidon, 2000)

Whelehan, I., *Overloaded: Popular Culture and the Future of Feminism* (London: Women's Press, 2000)

Williams, G. A., *When Was Wales?* (London: Black Raven, 1985)

Wilson, A., *Mixed Race Children: A Study of Identity* (London: Allen and Unwin, 1987)

Woddis, C., *Theatre Record,* vol. 19 (1999), 432–33

Wolf, N., *The Beauty Myth* (London: Vintage, 1990)

Young, H., *One of Us: A Biography of Margaret Thatcher* (London: Pan, 1990)

newspaper sources

Bassett, K., 'Theatre: Seasick but Ship-Shape', *Independent*, 20 April 2003

Billington, M., 'Closed World of Loyalist Hard Men', *Guardian*, 5 March 1998

Billington, M., 'Trust', *Guardian,* 18 March 1999

Billington, M., 'Closing Time', *Guardian*, 11 September 2002

Blair, T., 'Britain Can Remake It', *The Guardian*, 22 July 1997

Cavendish, D., 'Whatever Happened to Anger?', *Daily Telegraph*, 11 January 2006

Edgar, D., 'New State of Play', *Guardian*, 1 March 1993

Edgar, D., 'Secret Lives', *Guardian*, 19 April 2003

Elliott, L., 'Blair Urges "Quantum Leap" on Aid to Africa as Debate about Finance Rages', *Guardian*, 28 January 2005

Fay, L., 'Perfectly Beastly', *The Sunday Times,* 10 February 2002

Flett, K., 'We're Old, Grumpy and Proud', *Observer Review*, 13 November 2005

Gross, J., 'The Emperor of Ice Cream', *New Criterion*, June 1998

Hare, D., 'Enter Stage Left', *Guardian*, 30 October 2004

Heaney, M., 'Paying Dues to the Union', *The Sunday Times*, 17 February 2002

Hewison, R., 'Rebirth of a Nation', *The Times*, 19 May 1996

Kingston, J., 'Loyalist's Loyalty Ends at Home', *The Times*, 17 March 1999

Lloyd, J., 'Cool Britannia Warms Up', *New Statesman*, 13 March 1998

Marmion, P., 'Busting Loose', *What's On*, 10 February 1993

Maxwell, D., 'Why so Grumpy Ladies? Your Tour's a Hot Ticket', *The Times*, 8 April 2006

McGrath, J., 'No Politics Please, We're British', *Guardian*, 5 October 1984

Mitchell, G., 'Balancing Act', *Guardian*, 5 April, 2003

Nightingale, B., 'Ten With the Playwright Stuff', *The Times*, 1 May 1996

Nightingale, B., 'Playing Belfast and Furious', *The Times*, 12 April 2003

Observer, Review of *Blasted*, 5 February 1995

Pinter, H., 'Nobel Prize Acceptance Speech', *Guardian*, 8 December 2005

Romney, J., 'The Acid House-Bleak House', *Guardian*, 1 January 1999

Shuttleworth, I., 'The Horrifying Minutiae of Life in Ulster', *The Financial Times*, 18 March 1999

Sierz, A., 'Outrage Theatres gave Young Writers Freedom – No Ideologies, No Rules, No Taste', *Daily Telegraph*, 17 February 2001

Smith, A., 'Play For Today', *Observer Magazine*, 31 October 1999

Spencer, C., 'A Grown Up Portrait of Immaturity', *Daily Telegraph*, 5 September 2001

Spencer, C., 'Memorable Trip to the Other Side of the Troubled Divide', *Daily Telegraph*, 25 September 2001

websites

http://www.bbc.co.uk/radio4/science/allinthemind_20031118.shtml

'The Big Interview: Jenny Eclair', http://www.officiallondontheatre.co.uk/news/biginterview/display/cm/contentId/73860

Bloomberg, R., interview with Jenny Eclair, http://www.thebloomsbury.
com/extras/jennyeclair.php

Coleman, S., 'The Vagina Monologues Goes Global', http://www.worldpress.
org/Americas/606.cfm

Ensler, E., 'Beyond the Vagina Monologues', http://www.hopedance.org/
archive/issue30/articles/ensler.htm

Gonda, A., 'In-Yer Face?' http://www.writernet.co.uk/php2/news.php?id=324

Owen, R., 'The Play of History: The Performance of Identity in Welsh
Historiography and Theater', The North American Journal of Welsh Studies, vol.
1, no. 2 (2001), http://spruce.flint.umich.edu/~ellisjs/VolOne.html

Pattie, D., 'The Decentring of Docherty: The Scotsman in Modern Scottish
Drama', http:// www.artsqmuc.ac.uk/ijost/Volume1_no2

Rampton, J., 'Comedy Gig of the Week – Jenny Eclair, Independent, 20 October
2001, http://www.findarticles.com/p.articles/mi_qn4158/is_20011020/
ai_n14436418

Ravenhill, M., 'Reputations: Edward Bond', Theatre Voice webcast,
www.theatrevoice.com

Sphinx Theatre Company website http://www.sphinxtheatre.co.uk/index.cfm

Wessendorf, M., 'Bodies in Pain: Towards a Masochistic Perception of
Performance – The Work of Ron Athey and Bob Flanagan', 1995, http://
www2.hawaii.edu/~wessendo/Bodies.htm

'The World According to . . . Jenny Eclair', interview, Independent, 19 January
2005, http://www.findarticles.com/p/articles/mi_qu4158/ is_20050119
/ai_n9692315

videos

Abba's All Time Greatest Hits, ITV1, 2005

index